Pauline Hermeneutics:
Exploring the "Power of the Gospel"

LWF STUDIES 2016/3

THE
LUTHERAN
WORLD
FEDERATION

Pauline Hermeneutics:
Exploring the "Power of the Gospel"

Edited by
Eve-Marie Becker and Kenneth Mtata

LWF Studies 2016/3

Bibliographic information published by the German National Library
The *Deutsche Nationalbibliothek* lists this publication in the *Deutsche Nationalbiblio-grafie;* detailed bibliographic data are available on the internet at dnd.dnd.de

© 2017 The Lutheran World Federation
Printed in Germany

This book was printed on FSC-certified paper

Cover: LWF Communications
Editorial assistance: Department for Theology and Public Witness
Typesetting and inside layout: LWF Communications/Department for Theology and Public Witness
Design: LWF Communications/EVA
Printing and Binding: druckhaus köthen GmbH & Co. KG

Published by Evangelische Verlangsanstalt GmbH, Leipzig, Germany, under the auspices of The Lutheran World Federation
150, rte de Ferney, PO Box 2100
CH-1211 Geneva 2, Switzerland

ISBN 978-3-374-04842-7
www.eva-leipzig.de

CONTENTS

Acknowledgements..7

Preface...9
    Martin Junge

Introduction...11
    Eve-Marie Becker and Kenneth Mtata

The "Gospel" as the Hermeneutic of Emancipation in Paul's Letters:
Contemporary Implications...13
    Kenneth Mtata

EXPLORING PAUL AND PAULINE HERMENEUTICS

How and Why Paul Deals with Traditions..27
    Eve-Marie Becker

Principles of Paul's Hermeneutics...37
    Oda Wischmeyer

Slave and Free: Hermeneutical Reflections on Paul's Use of the Slave–Master
Metaphor..47
    Magnus Zetterholm

READING PAULINE TEXTS AND CONTEXTS

Paul on Charismata (1 Corinthians 12–14): The Principles of Diversity and
Community Edification...63
    Rospita Deliana Siahaan

Creation and Reconciliation in 2 Corinthians 5: Impulses from Paul and
Luther..73
    Roger Marcel Wanke

Towards an Intersectional Hermeneutics: Constructing Meaning with and not
of Galatians 3–4..85
    Marianne Bjelland Kartzow

Paul on Citizenship: Pauline hermeneutics in Philippians 1:27 and 3:20 99
Lubomir Batka

APPLYING PAUL'S THEOLOGY AND HERMENEUTICS TO CHURCH AND SOCIETY

The Paradox of Reading Paul in the Context of the Lutheran Churches in
Africa...113
Faustin Mahali

The Pauline Letters and (Homo)Sexuality: Examining Hermeneutical
Arguments Used in the Estonian Discussion 127
Urmas Nõmmik

Called and Cold Saints: Some Thoughts on Holiness in the Hebrew Bible and
in Paul.. 143
Mercedes L. García Bachmann

A New Life in Christ: Pauline Ethics and its Lutheran Reception.................. 155
Bernd Oberdorfer

Christians Engaging in Culture and Society
and Hoping for the World to Come 167
Hans-Peter Grosshans

List of Contributors 181

ACKNOWLEDGEMENTS

The fourth and final international hermeneutics conference was made possible through the generous sponsorship of Aarhus University (School of Culture and Society), Aarhus Universitets Forskningsfonden (AUFF), Aarhus Stift and the Evangelical Lutheran Church of Bavaria (ELCB). Last but not least, we would like to thank the dedicated and gracious local organizer and host of this conference, Dr Eve-Marie Becker, whose untiring efforts ensured the successful and effective running of the conference.

PREFACE

Martin Junge

Among the many biblical writings that influenced Martin Luther and the sixteenth-century Reformation only very few were as influential as the Pauline writings. The Reformation breakthrough is based on these writings (Rom 1:17) and Luther's interpretation of the Pauline letters has had a huge influence on modern biblical interpretation, notwithstanding its recent reevaluation.

Instead being a source for Christian consensus building, Paul's letters have given rise to intensive discussions regarding many of today's ethical questions. Some of the questions raised pertain to the role of women in the church, or the right engagement of Christians and the church in relationship to the secular government.

It was a deliberate decision to conclude the Lutheran World Federation's hermeneutics program with the study of the Pauline epistles. The study of the Gospel of John, the Psalms and the Gospel of Matthew gave the working group enough time to establish a clear interpretive structure so as adequately to deal with some of those issues addressed in the letters that have given rise to serious debate and difference within and among churches.

This last publication in the LWF hermeneutics series, like the three previous ones, focuses on the rigorous study of the biblical text in light of Luther's writings in response to various contemporary questions. It is my hope that it will give the reader a glimpse into how theological considerations can inform and be informed by biblical interpretation in ways that speak to contemporary questions, without denying the biblical text the authority to speak on its own terms. It is this dynamic of the biblical text, theological tradition and contextual location of the reader that is highlighted here.

I wish to express my gratitude to staff and representatives of the LWF member churches who have led and supported this very important process.

For a communion of churches such as the LWF, the ability jointly to read the Scriptures, to dialogue, together to reflect on what we have read and to be accountable to one another in view of the hermeneutical keys that inform all of this is essential. The hermeneutics program has meaningfully contributed to this process.

The essays included in this volume were first presented at the international conference on hermeneutics held in Aarhus, Denmark, in 2015, co-organized, cosponsored and cohosted by the Lutheran World Federation and Aarhus University. This event would not have been possible without the generous financial contributions received from Aarhus University, Aarhus Universitets Forskningsfonden (AUFF), Aarhus Stift and the Evangelical Lutheran Church of Bavaria (ELCB).

I commend this book to teachers at theological institutions and faculties, pastors and all those who wish to deepen their understanding of the Pauline letters in light of the Lutheran tradition and in response to the various contextual challenges.

INTRODUCTION

Eve-Marie Becker and Kenneth Mtata

In times when highly ambiguous global power plays gain traction in politics, the economy, sports and the military, it is not surprising that Lutheran theologians reflect on the power of the gospel. The expression of the *euaggélion* as a *dynamis theou*—coined and used by Paul in his letter to the Romans—reflects how the apostle understood the value and meaning of the early gospel message in and as his individual apostolic ministry through which he wanted to disseminate the gospel globally.

Generations of Christians have been inspired by Paul's apostolic ambition and his personal dynamic efforts. Martin Luther might be one of the most impressive, if not congenial, exponents of gospel interpretation in early modern times. It is not only in 2017—the 500th Anniversary of the Reformation—that Christians around the globe remember and reinterpret Paul's apostolic activity as well as Luther's adaptation of it. Lutheran theologians from around the world thus share the privilege to join both of those inspiring traditions of gospel hermeneutics: Paul's tradition as much as Luther's.

In a series of international conferences (2011–2015) that endeavored to reevaluate the principles of scriptural interpretation, scholars from all over the world met in Nairobi, Eisenach and Chicago to reflect on the contemporary interpretation of various biblical texts: the Gospel of John, the Psalms and the Gospel of Matthew. The fourth and last of these international LWF conferences took place at Aarhus University, 24–29 September 2015.

In light of the topic, "The Power of the Gospel: Developing Pauline Hermeneutics," international scholars returned to the literary and theological origins of gospel interpretation that we find in Paul and his letters. By bringing together exegetical, hermeneutical and theological expertise from all parts of the world, the 2015 conference did not only reconsider the Pauline tradition of gospel interpretation from a Lutheran perspective and in view of current scholarly debates in New Testament studies. It also aimed at developing Pauline hermeneutics in the sense that the power of the gospel can be explored as a crucial paradigm by which we might express what Christian identity in the twenty-first century is about. The "Power of the Gospel" might open up ways for ingeniously revisiting ways in which Pauline hermeneutics can inspire global discourses about Christian life in its various societal, political and cultural settings.

The essays in this publication were first presented at the international conference in Aarhus. We would like to thank all contributors for their valuable articles and the most collegial way of working with us on the publication of this volume. All contributors seek to reflect on the paradigms of Paul's hermeneutics and Pauline hermeneutics by revealing the methodological criteria, theological principles, historical contexts and current meanings of how Paul himself acted as a hermeneut of the gospel message and Scripture, and of how later readers, such as Luther and contemporary exegetes and theologians, might approach and further develop the never ending hermeneutical task of reading and interpreting Paul and his thinking in his letter writing. The contributions included in this book will not bring the endeavor of developing Pauline hermeneutics to an end, but constitute milestones on the long road that lies ahead of us.[1]

---

[1] See *"In the Beginning was the Word." The Bible in the Life of the Lutheran Communion. A Study Document on Lutheran Hermeneutics,* at www.lutheranworld.org/content/beginning-was-word-bible-life-lutheran-communion

The "Gospel" as the Hermeneutic of Emancipation in Paul's Letters: Contemporary Implications

Kenneth Mtata

> For I am not ashamed of the gospel; it is the power of God for salvation to everyone
> who has faith, to the Jew first and also to the Greek (Rom 1:16).

Introduction

One evening, during evening prayers with my wife and children, we read a part of the story of the Old Testament where Moses is said to have become angry and to have hit the rock twice (Num 20:11). Our son, who was ten years old at the time, remarked, "but this is wrong that the leader should be angry like that." I wondered where he had learnt that such rage could be negatively assessed, even if it is manifested by an eminent biblical figure such as Moses.

In contemporary biblical hermeneutics, we are taught to begin our interpretation with this recognition that the "modern interpreter, no less than the text, stands in a given historical context and tradition."[1] My son had been socialized to organize biblical data in certain value categories through his interaction with his parents, school and other sources of knowledge. His interpretation and indeed everyone's interpretation is shaped by certain pre-understandings that provide frameworks that en-

---

[1] Anthony C. Thiselton, *Thiselton on Hermeneutics: The Collected Works and New Essays of Anthony Thiselton* (Burlington: Ashgate, 2006), 441.

able us to order not only biblical but also social data. To a certain extent, I was happy to realize that such interpretive frameworks can be so strong that they can give such a young person a sense of authority to reject the actions of a highly regarded biblical figure such as Moses in ways that do not necessarily undermine the value of sacred texts for the faith community. On the other hand, I was anxious to realize that such pre-understanding could deny the text to speak on its own terms.

When we encounter "texts," whether they are "written texts" (such as the biblical text or newspaper texts) or they are "social texts" (such as the numerous migrants coming to Europe), or whether we are engaging with the image world of social media, we already come with assumptions that make interpretation possible. In liberation theology and liberation hermeneutics, two elements determine whether one approaches the text as holding possibilities for liberation or oppression. If the reader assumes that the texts being read simply reflect ideologies and self-interests, the reader will approach it with suspicion, in case they are coopted into its oppressing ideology. This was called the hermeneutic of suspicion. The masters of this hermeneutics of suspicion such as Marx, Freud and Nietzsche helped us to recognize that it was not only the text but also we, ourselves, who bring such self-interests to the reading process, whether we are aware of it or not. While the historical critical tradition assumes that one needs to rid oneself of this self-interest, Rudolf Bultmann helped readers to appreciate this self-interest—what was important was to become aware of such self-interest.

On the other hand, if the reader approaches the text with the assumption that the author had wished for the harmonious coexistence of all people, or had wanted to enhance spiritual growth or simply to increase the knowledge of their audience, then we are working with a hermeneutic of trust. Such hermeneutics of trust tends to inform many devotional readings of Scripture. If we assume this reading attitude, then the jarring contradictions and the discomfort encountered in the texts are either explained or simply ignored.

What happens if one takes the hermeneutics of suspicion and the hermeneutics of trust as complimentary attitudes toward reading the Bible? As Lutherans, we believe that human beings are at the same time righteous and sinners, *simul iustus et peccator*. Hence, when reading and interpreting texts, we need both to trust ourselves that we are looking for that which is edifying and to believe that the Scriptures provide such. At the same time, we must also be aware of our conscious and unconscious inclination to dominate. It is possible to draw on both resources—the hermeneutic of suspicion and the hermeneutic of trust. A suspicious or, rather, a critical approach enables us comfortably to engage with a certain level of openness to words of Scriptures without feeling any sense of disrespect. On the other hand, a hermeneutic of trust enables us to draw positive conclusions from the reading process to enable community building, albeit based on tentative conclusions.

Maybe in approaching texts, especially biblical texts, we should seek to draw on what Habermas has identified as the emancipatory cognitive interests, where we are suspicious of the ideological baggage of the text, while drawing on the same texts resources to critique ideologies in our life-worlds. It is said that Habermas "wrote *Knowledge and Human Interests* to show that critical theory cannot be dismissed as mere ideology." Rather, he wanted to "defend a critical moral standpoint as a form of reason. His strategy was to identify a will to freedom or to be free or unnecessary constraint as embedded in the very structures of everyday life [...]."[2] It is this emancipatory dimension that has informed the hermeneutics program of the Lutheran World Federation since 2011.

BACKGROUND OF THE HERMENEUTICS PROGRAM

This publication is the last in the LWF's hermeneutics series. When the program was initially introduced to the Council of the LWF, one member of the Council questioned why the LWF needed to explore Lutheran hermeneutics since there are many interpretations of the Lutheran traditions. She was afraid that the LWF wanted to homogenize the diverse Lutheran traditions and impose one totalizing version on the whole Lutheran communion. Was such a project essential? Was it necessary to reflect on how we read texts in relationship to certain theological tradition in the hope to contribute to addressing pressing sociopolitical and economic concerns?

The reasons given for embarking on the hermeneutics process were, first, that Christians who belong to the same Lutheran tradition that is grounded in the Scriptures need to explore this background in light of the 500th Anniversary of the Reformation. If the Scriptures and new ways of engaging with them were a core aspect of the Reformation, it made sense that this power of the Word of God be rediscovered in the church's contemporary contexts. If the many past renewals were stimulated by the rediscovery of and recommitment to the sacred writings, it was necessary that Lutheran teaching theologians come together in an ecumenically open space to develop common tools for engaging biblical texts in order

---

[2] Steven Seidman, *Contested Knowledge: Social Theory Today* (Chichester: Wiley Blackwell, 2013/2017), 123.

to stimulate such internal renewal of the churches, as well as equipping them for their mission in the world.

The second reason was to find ways of addressing the tensions regarding different interpretations of certain biblical texts in light of certain contemporary ethical questions. The idea was not to solve these challenges, but to create a civilized space within which the LWF member churches could engage in meaningful dialogue on issues that tend to be emotive and divisive. It was hoped that through such a process, the member churches would test themselves to see if they are in the faith (2 Cor 13:5) or, rather, for each to test their own work "rather than their neighbor's work" and hence to avoid pride (Gal 6:4). The aim was to find ways of engaging with the Scriptures in ways that are academically robust, contextually relevant but also attentive to the shared theological tradition. The aim was to rediscover the "power of the gospel" as Paul puts it in Romans 1:16-17 or his empowering hermeneutic of "gospel" or "good news."

Why Pauline letters last in the LWF hermeneutics series?

Only very few or perhaps even no other biblical writings had as much influence on Martin Luther and the sixteenth-century Reformation as the Pauline writings. Although Luther "returned to a rigorous Augustinian view of the human condition," his own thought process was greatly shaped by "his readings of St. Paul, particularly Romans and Galatians."[3] It was on the basis of these writings that Luther made his Reformation breakthrough. In reading Romans 1:17, he discovered the doctrine of justification and the power of the gospel that influenced his overall interpretation of the Pauline writings. Appold observed that "Luther's teachings on justification emphasize 'the Word'." By this he means primarily the Word of God as encountered in Scripture. It is "the Word" that teaches us that we are saved through grace by faith in Christ (that message is also called *euaggélion*, or "the gospel," and contrasted with "the Law," by which we are accused and our shortcomings revealed)."[4]

Martin Luther's interpretation of Paul has had a huge influence on modern biblical interpretation, notwithstanding the recent reevaluation.

Paul's writings have not always provided the same renewing impetus they had on Luther since some of his writings have raised intense debate

---

[3] Kenneth G. Appold, *The Reformation: A Brief History* (Chichester: Wiley-Blackwell, 2011), 73.
[4] Ibid., 74.

regarding many contemporary ethical questions, especially those related to the role of women in the church and sexual ethics. Luther sometimes provides some helpful resources in these matters while, at other times, he complicates issues since he was addressing the contemporary questions of his time.

Within the LWF hermeneutics study program, the study of the Pauline writings was deliberately taken on last. By concluding with Paul's letters, after having studied the Gospel of John, the Psalms and the Gospel of Matthew, a clear interpretive structure had been put into place to allow for dealing with the more controversial issues in Paul.

As the last publication in the LWF hermeneutics series, this publication maintains the focus of the previous series, with a commitment to rigorous study of the biblical text in light of Luther's writings and in response to various contemporary questions. Like in the previous studies, this study also seeks to give readers a glimpse of how theological considerations might inform and be informed by biblical interpretation in ways that speak to contemporary questions, without denying the biblical text the authority to speak on its own terms. It is this dynamic of the gospel that this study seeks to draw from Paul, and hence the focus on the notion of "the gospel" as a hermeneutical key for reading Paul's letters.

THE CENTRALITY OF THE GOSPEL FOR PAUL

Paul's identity and the identity of those he invites to the new life is guided by what he calls the good news or gospel (εὐαγγέλιον) (1 Cor 9:12). This gospel has such a dominant presence in Paul's letters that understanding it can help us to understand Paul. The gospel is, as it were, almost a hermeneutical key to Paul's letters. Paul's scriptures were the Old Testament and from these he could make a connection to what he understood as the good news or gospel. As Hays has observed, Paul does not "wrest the Scripture from Israel" nor does he "subordinate Scripture to his own belated conceptions" but rather, his "urgent hermeneutical project is to bring Scripture and gospel into a mutually interpretive relation in which the righteousness of God is truly discovered."[5]

DIVINE ORIGIN OF THE GOSPEL

Paul understands himself has having been "set apart for the gospel" (Rom 1:1), which he also calls "my gospel" (Rom 2:16; 16:25), even though his un-

---

[5] Craig A. Evans and James A. Sanders (eds), *Paul and the Scriptures of Israel* (Sheffield: Sheffield Press, 1993), 62.

derlying understanding is that it is God who is actually speaking through him: "For I want you to know, brothers and sisters, that the gospel that was proclaimed by me is not of human origin [...] I received it through a revelation of Jesus Christ" (Gal 1:11-12). Paul is therefore a mouthpiece for the "gospel of God" (Rom 1:1), which is also sanctioned by the council of elders (Gal 2:2) who gave him the "right hand of fellowship, agreeing that we should go to the Gentiles and they to the circumcised" (Gal 2:9).

THE GOSPEL AND ACCOUNTABILITY

By ascribing the gospel to divine origin but the authority to the Jerusalem elders for preaching it to the Gentiles, Paul wants to affirm both the divine revelation and the communal authority of Jesus Christ's message that he proclaims. This approach highlights the value of accountability to the community as well as to God. Above all though, he seeks to highlight that the final accountability regarding the gospel lies with God: "but just as we have been approved by God to be entrusted with the message of the gospel, even so we speak, not to please mortals, but to please God who tests our hearts" (1 Thess 2:4). This empowers all those who will receive this gospel because they will see themselves as being addressed by God and not "human word but as what it really is, God's word [...]" (1 Thess 2:13).

THE GOSPEL AS IDENTITY MARKER

Through the gospel, God utters words of judgment to those who do not receive God's invitation (Rom 10:16), words of promise to those who will receive it, and words of warning to those who distort the gospel. The understanding is that there are other forces at work that prevent people from comprehending the gift that God has given us through the gospel (2 Cor 4:3). As they are blinded, they cannot see "the light of the gospel of the glory of Christ, who is the image of God" (2 Cor 4:4). The gospel is distorted within the community of faith when it reverts back to those systems that oppressed them before they came to know the truth such as demanding circumcision for Gentiles in order to participate fully in Christian life (Gal 1:8-9).

THE HOLY SPIRIT AND THE GOSPEL

While unbelief is a result of the blinding veil, belief is also the result of a powerful effect that comes not by "word only, but also in power and in the

Holy Spirit and with full conviction" (1 Thess 1:5). This is the case because "faith comes from what is heard, and what is heard comes through the word of Christ" (Rom 10:17). In the joy of the Spirit as well as by suffering persecution they become imitators of Paul and indeed Jesus who called them (1 Thess 1:6; 1 Thess 2:2; Phil 1:7).

THE NATURE OF THE GOSPEL

What is that gospel that Paul talks about? Paul nowhere defines this gospel but we find hints here and there in the apophatic or negative descriptions in his discussions. For example, in the Galatian controversy, Paul says that his opponents are "not acting consistently with the truth of the gospel" (Gal 2:14). He therefore challenged Cephas before them all saying "If you, though a Jew, live like a Gentile and not like a Jew, how can you compel the Gentiles to live like Jews?" (Gal 2:14). He suggests that the gospel does not require Gentile converts to adopt Jewish cultural practices in order to become true Christians.

The gospel is also presented as God's overall promise that both Jews and Gentiles will be rendered justified before God through faith in Jesus as God "declared the gospel beforehand to Abraham" (Gal 3:8). Since God has made such a promise, Paul feels compelled to make it known to all too (1 Cor 9:16).

One dimension of the gospel is its reconciliatory character. This is the reconciliation between human beings and God and between human beings themselves. So he urges the two women, Euodia and Syntyche, "to be of the same mind in the Lord," because they have more important things to share in the ministry than that which separates them (Phil 4:2-3). This reconciliatory approach is borne out of a sense of compassion that comes from the gospel and Paul's compassion for the people (1 Thess 2:8). The message about Christ that informs Paul's preaching and informs any basis for reconciliation between people and God is that of the cross of Christ (1 Cor 1:17).

ROMANS 1:16-17 AS A HERMENEUTIC OF EMANCIPATION

What stands out in Paul's interpretation of the Scriptures is his interest to express the liberating power of God's communication in the gospel. Under normal circumstances the message of the cross that constitutes the gospel should be a source of shame: "For the message about the cross is foolishness to those who are perishing, but to us who are being saved it is the power of God" (1 Cor 1:18). It is this message of the cross that forms what Meira Z. Kensky has called the "crux of the letter's message":

> For I am not ashamed of the gospel; it is the power of God for salvation to everyone who has faith, to the Jew first and also to the Greek. For in it the justice of God is revealed through faith for faith; as it is written, "The one who is just will live by faith" (Rom 1:16-17).[6]

Kensky suggests that the overall theme of Romans 1:18–3:21 is that humankind, Jews and Gentiles, stand in a state of condemnation before God, and yet that condemnation has been overturned by Christ's death and resurrection "which form the necessary conditions of the potentiality of man's [sic] salvation." According to this understanding, verses 16–17 assert the "salvific power and the function of the gospel" which is followed by the two chapters in which Paul explains exactly why human beings need this salvation as demonstrated by the human condition "before the advent of Christ."[7] In the following I seek to highlight the contemporary implications of two emancipatory hermeneutic elements.

FREED FROM SHAME

The first element is that which addresses the underlying shame that affects human beings. This use of the language of shame draws on the narrative of Adam and Eve, who experienced shame and nakedness in the presence of God. Jesus as the new Adam is then presented by Paul as God's way of identifying with human shame—God's statement of identification with human shame and nakedness. Hengel has pointed to this shame of the crucified Christ as a feature that "distinguishes the new message from the mythologies of other peoples."[8]

The sense of shame has been perfectly captured by Melito of Sardis, the second-century Christian authority,

> He who hung the earth (in its place) is fixed there, he who made all things fast is made fast upon a tree, the Master has been insulted, God has been murdered. O strange murder, strange crime! The Master has been treated unseemly fashion,

---

[6] Meira Z. Kensky, *Trying Man, Trying God: The Divine Courtroom in Early Jewish and Christian Literature*, WUNT II (Tübingen: Mohr Siebeck, 2010), 185.

[7] Ibid., 185.

[8] Martin Hengel, *The Cross of the Son of God* (London: SCM Press, 1986), 93.

his body naked, and not even deemed worthy of a covering, that (his nakedness) might not be seen. Therefore, the lights (of heaven) turned away, and the day darkened, that it might hide him who is stripped upon a cross."[9]

Reading Paul in this way points to the first hermeneutical principle of emancipation that addresses human shame. The three main representatives of the hermeneutics of suspicion, Marx, Freud and Nietzsche, are said to have contributed to hermeneutics by probing

behind what they conceived as an illusory self-consciousness to a deeper-lying, more unpleasant or "shameful" one [...]. A characteristic of hermeneutics through-out its history has otherwise been the absence of such suspicion and instead a reverent attitude to the tradition mediated—a tradition which should be restored to its authentic meaning, and not stripped of its false deities by the interpreter tearing away the veil of illusion from the embarrassingly naked secret.[10]

On the cross, Jesus, bears human shame and nakedness and enables human beings to face without deception their fears and shame with boldness. This Jesus on the cross, according to Schütz, is the gospel preached by Paul in three ways: (a) "the fixed object of preaching"; (b) the "act of preaching"; and (c) "something rather more elusive, an on-going entity 'in' which one can 'be' or 'stand.'" This gospel is a "pregnant" notion, which "exhibits its significance as an 'effective force'" and offers new language to address the human condition without seeking to avoid difficulties but confronting them. Jesus opens up possibilities for accessing the goods that God discloses "from faith to faith," where ἀποκαλύπτεται does not only refer to that which the preached gospel expounds when it teaches about righteousness, but that through this revelation, "righteousness becomes a possibility" and even a reality through faith.[11]

At the 1965 LWF Assembly in Helsinki there was serious disagreement on whether to appropriate Romans 1:16–17 in terms of theological justifica-tion or socioeconomic justice. This concern remains pressing for us as we reflect on hermeneutics since the world is confronted by both concerns.

In many parts of the world the shame experienced by citizens can only be appropriately addressed by helping them attain justice because they have been sinned against. In others, many feel ashamed and inadequate

---

[9] *Homily on the Passion,* 96.
[10] Mats Alvesson, Kaj Skoldberg, *Reflexive Methodology: New Vistas for Qualitative Research* (London: SAGE, 2009), 130.
[11] Howard Schutz, *Paul and the Anatomy of Apostolic Authority,* SNTSMS 26 (Cambridge: Cambridge University Press, 1975), 43.

because they cannot meet the demands made on them by society. This includes young children who experience cyberbullying leading in some cases to suicide. Many also feel inadequate and hence ashamed because they cannot keep up appearances. For instance, even children feel under pressure to have certain electronic gadgets and wear certain brands of clothes in order to fit in with their peers.

An emancipatory hermeneutic according to Paul's understanding of the gospel of the cross addresses this sense of inadequacy and shame by disclosing the ideological baggage in the social texts that confront people today. It is such a text from Paul that can be drawn on as a resource to critique ideologies of our contemporary life-worlds. It is from this perspective that Paul could be a resource of liberation, even for those who initially cannot identify with the call of the gospel. In this sense, the results of hermeneutics can become resources to enable people today to read their social text with healthy suspicion while, at the same time, being drawn to something constructive in the gospel.

EMANCIPATED IDENTITIES

The second element of hermeneutic of emancipation draws on Paul's reformulating different identities, especially of Jews and Gentiles, who constituted the major populations of his "globalizing" world. They were ethnically separated by different standards of attaining righteousness, and hence challenged by coexistence, even in the Christian communities. Paul does not obliterate their differences but seeks to find ways in which they can still authentically be themselves, without losing a broader identity attained in Jesus.

Paul's solution could greatly enhance our hermeneutical efforts in today's situation, where the quest for identities is likely to become a source of conflict, especially in view of the increasing movement of people due to economic and political unrest. There is no way Europe will remain the same in light of recent migration patterns. The first problem that confronts Europe is the unwillingness accurately to describe the challenges the generosity of accepting people of different cultural backgrounds will bring to the historically Christian world. What can distort accurate conversation is the fact that we are operating in a context in which politically correct but intolerant language has developed, which does not accept that people from different cultural backgrounds may have problems of coexistence, not because the other group is racist or right wing. The same is also true for discussions regarding human sexuality; the discussions have become so politically and emotionally charged that there is no space for critical engagement on how these identities relate with other identities. In his approach, Paul refuses to submit to the simplistic merging of different identities by naming real differences while, at the same time, offering a common identity in Jesus.

The second reality that Paul tackles through his hermeneutic of emancipation is to provide a new language to address the changing globalization process of his day. He does this not only by confronting the differences between Jews and Gentiles as citizens of the new emerging world, but also by addressing different conflicting parties based on dietary regulations, the observation of certain festivals and other such identity markers. By proposing the gospel as an identity marker, Paul offers one narrative that privileges no group, so that identities are not established on the grounds of obliterating one group.

For our contemporary context, such a view could be emancipating in that it recognizes the reality of the globalizing effect of totalizing narratives that shape the pre-understandings of reading both written and social texts. Due to the effect of the internet and the dominance of the electronic media, all of us are forced to read the world using the same lens; in many cases subconsciously. It is natural for us to say we "google" something when we are surfing the internet. So dominant are the totalizing frameworks of reading the world that only such exercises as were undertaken throughout the LWF hermeneutics process enable us to engage as well as to empower our faith communities to do the same.

Such an emancipatory reading of Paul gives rise to many interesting questions:

- How do we appropriate our own religious tradition like Paul and find innovative ways of rereading it for the renewal of the church and society?

- How do we deal with many shame provoking experiences, including being ashamed of the gospel in a secularized society?

- If Paul was able to engage with the religious and societal ideas of his day and even provided thought leadership in some matters, what does it mean for our own work?

- If globalization as a general concept for describing the increased contact of peoples of different origins is shaping up as it did in Paul's time, what implications does it have for our ability to be "multilingual" in our engagement with the world, without losing our own Lutheran and Christian identities?

- If our contemporary world sometimes experiences different forms of intolerance, how do we use our hermeneutical competencies to contribute to meaningful and truthful dialogue?

- If the power of the gospel lies in the invitation of God to both the Jew and the Gentile through faith, what does it mean in the contemporary context of plurality?

- How does our hearing of Paul in his situation enable us to hear those who are separate and different from us without necessarily losing focus of those matters that affect all of humanity?

- If the gospel provided a bridge in a society of different identities (Jewish and Gentile), how can we appropriate its power again today to build bridges of reconciliation among different and conflicting relationships?

CONCLUSION

I gave the background of this hermeneutics program and some of its key motivations. I showed the assumptions we bring to the reading and making sense of written texts and social texts. I suggested that both the hermeneutics of suspicion and trust are helpful in acquiring both the critical and constructive engagement with texts. I went on to draw on Paul's use of the concept of the gospel as a hermeneutic of emancipation that we can draw on for engaging the Bible and many other texts in ways that faithfully address differences instead of covering them up. I leave many questions unanswered because I never sought to provide answers, but to find the best way of asking questions.

Exploring Paul and Pauline Hermeneutics

How and Why Paul Deals with Traditions

Eve-Marie Becker

Paul and the gospel "tradition"

Paul, the apostle, does not claim to be the founder of Christianity but maintains that he mediates, facilitates and transmits the gospel as *euaggélion*.
At the same time, he develops crucial elements of early Christ believing,
thinking and communicating by, for instance, shaping moral discourse and
transforming the Jesus story "into a metaphorical complex."[1] As an epistolary activist, Paul might be called the founder of early Christian literacy.

The Corinthian correspondence impressively documents how the apostle
as a missionary, founder and leader of communities, moral teacher, letter
writer and theologian constantly reacts to gospel interpretation at a time when
Christian discourse was nascent and "Christianity" was in the making. We
will take 1 Corinthians 15 as a point of departure for exploring how, within
the framework of various early Christian discourses and approaches, Paul
applies and transforms traditions that had so far only been passed on to him.

1 Corinthians 15:1–11 and 11:23–25

In 1 Corinthians 15, Paul takes an explicit stand on his mediating role as
apostle. 1 Corinthians 15 is a central, if not the most important Pauline
text, not only with regard to the topic of my essay: it shows us how Paul is
literally "forced" to deal with traditions and how he addresses this task and

---

[1] Wayne A. Meeks, *The Origins of Christian Morality: The First Two Centuries* (New
Haven/London: Yale University Press, 1993), 86.

appears to be the argumentative "climax" of the whole letter.[2] Especially in verses 1–11, the issue of pre-Pauline tradition is addressed. What does this passage reveal to us?

a) In 1 Corinthians 15:8–11 the apostle concedes that he is the last witness of the Easter epiphanies. Paul makes a confession here, but clearly intends to transform the obvious deficiency of his apostleship into a strength. In Paul's words,

> Last of all, as to one untimely born, he [Christ] appeared also to me. For I am the least of the apostles, unfit to be called an apostle, because I persecuted the church of God. But by the grace of God I am what I am, and his grace toward me has not been in vain [...] (vv. 8–10a).

In what follows, Paul defends his apostleship, which his opponents in Corinth constantly treat with hostility. Thus, Paul claims in a competitive and self-confident manner: "[...] I worked harder than any of them [= the apostles]" (v. 10b). It is not only in this Pauline passage that personal confessions and competitive claims go hand in hand. Paul constantly wishes to reinforce the power of his apostolic ministry.

b) As Paul portrays himself as the last of the apostles and as a mediator: even though he has founded the Corinthian congregation by preaching the gospel (v. 1), and thus in his later letter writing only needs to remind his addressees "of the good news that I proclaimed to you" (v. 1), he himself has only proclaimed (*paredóka*) to the Corinthians orally "what I in turn had received" (v. 3a: *parelabon*). Paul acknowledges that he is aware of his role as mediator: he is among the last of the first generation Christians and thus confronted with the stigma of being the "least."

c) Between his reminder about the beginnings of the gospel proclamation in Corinth (vv. 1–3a) and confessing that he is the "last" or even "least" apostle (vv. 8–11), Paul refers to the *paradosis* of the gospel's content:

> what I in turn had received: that Christ died for our sins in accordance with the scriptures, and that he was buried, and that he was raised on the third day in accordance with the scriptures, and that he appeared to Cephas, then to the twelve (vv. 3b–5).

---

[2] Wolfgang Schrage, *Der erste Brief an die Korinther*, vol. 4, Kor 15,1–16, 24 (Neukirchen-Vluyn: Neukirchener Verlag, 2001), 72.

Whether at this point Paul accurately quotes the early Christian message (kerygma) as a formula, or rephrases or formulates ad hoc what the kerygma, which he had earlier preached in Corinth, actually is about, continues to be a matter of debate in Pauline studies. The question to be examined is whether Paul deals with a specific pre-Pauline tradition here and, if so, what that looks like.[3] On the basis of linguistics (tradition terminology), word order, structure and motifs in vv. 3–5, Catholic (e.g., J. A. Fitzmyer; D. Zeller) and Protestant (e.g., C. Wolff; W. Schrage; already: J. Weiß) exegetes tend to see a tradition and, in particular, a *paradosis* (even though not necessarily the oldest version of the Easter kerygma viz. earliest Christian creeds, cf.: 1 Thess 4:14; Rom 4:25; 8:34; 14:9; 2 Cor 5:14f.),[4] at least behind v. 3b–5a, which Paul himself might have received in his earlier career. At the time, he was travelling around the Syro-Palestinian area. Scholars assume that Paul probably came into contact with this formula/kerygma as a tradition in the context of Jewish-Hellenistic communities located around Damascus,[5] in Jerusalem or Antioch.[6] It is a matter of scholarly debate how to define the so-called *Sitz im Leben* of this *paradosis* as, for instance, a creed, a homology, or a catechetic summary.[7]

d) Let us go one step further and ask, What does Paul do with this tradition which, as far as we can see, at this point has only been mediated in his oral proclamation and letters? In chapter 15, Paul uses the *paradosis* within the argumentative frame of discussing the reality or facticity of the resurrection. In 1 Corinthians 15:12 we read about the actual matter of controversy in Corinth. The question, "[...] how can some of you say there is no resurrection of the dead?" (v. 12b), reflects one of the most urgent challenges that Paul has to deal with: the *anastasis nekrón* might turn out to become the litmus test in Corinthian affairs.[8]

---

[3] Cf. the discussion in, Christian Wolff, *Der erste Brief des Paulus an die Korinther*, ThHK 7 (Leipzig: Evangelische Verlagsanstalt, 1996), 355–61.

[4] Cf. Schrage, op. cit. (note 2), 18f.

[5] Cf. Dieter Zeller, *Der erste Brief an die Korinther*, KEK 5 (Göttingen: Vandenhoeck & Ruprecht, 2010), 462. Cf. Johannes Weiß, *Der erste Korintherbrief*, KEK 5 (Göttingen: Vandenhoeck & Ruprecht, 1977, 2nd reprint), 47: "[...] a piece of early Christian *paradosis*"; Joseph A. Fitzmyer, *First Corinthians: A New Translation with Introduction and Commentary*, AncB 32 (New Haven/London: Yale University Press, 2008), 541.

[6] Cf. Wolff, op. cit. (note 3), 359.

[7] Cf. Schrage, op. cit. (note 2), 18.

[8] Cf. Oda Wischmeyer, "1. Korinther 15. Der Traktat des Paulus über die Auferstehung der Toten in der Wahrnehmung unterschiedlicher Textzugänge," in Eve-

Paul refutes those who doubt the reality of the resurrection by imagining, if "Christ has not been raised, then our proclamation has been in vain and your faith has been in vain" (v. 14).

As a result, Paul broadens his argument by moving toward using the *paradosis*. The resurrection of Christ is now as much a matter of belief or disbelief as the Corinthians' belief and his own apostolic preaching: Paul creates no less than a direct interdependence between (Christ's) resurrection, belief and kerygma. In conclusion, Paul must insist on sharing, mediating and furthermore passing on that particular gospel tradition. In communitarian discourses, the facticity of resurrection directly relates to the proper mediation of the gospel *paradosis* and its apostolic carrier.

e) Once more, we have to go a step further. Paul does not only use the gospel tradition in order to authorize himself; nor does he reveal its legitimizing function for proving the truth of Christ's resurrection. Something more is going on here. It is striking that Paul quotes the tradition in 1 Corinthians 15 with the same intention as he cites the Lord's Supper *paradosis* in 1 Corinthians 11:23–25. Here, he says: "For I received (*parelabon*) from the Lord what I also handed (*paredóka*) on to you [...]" (v. 23). There are only minor differences behind the structure of 1 Corinthians 15:3 and 11:23: the sequence of *parelabon-paredóka* is turned around; in 1 Corinthians 11:23 Paul also identifies the source of this *paradosis* as "from the Lord" (*apo tou kuriou*)—a phrase which in terms of textual criticism is philologically debatable.[9]

But why does Paul, in his letter writing, more or less balance 1 Corinthians 11:23–25, a tradition that dates back to a historical scene in Jesus' life just before the passion, and 15:3–5, a post-Easter kerygmatic tradition? Clearly, he intends to authorize his apostolic ministry. Even though or rather because he is the "last" and possibly "least" of all the apostles he needs to prove that he has had access to the kerygmatic as much as to the ritual origins of the belief in Christ. As a result, those Corinthians who might wish to count themselves among the "party of Peter" (1 Cor 1:12) and thus claim a more privileged admission to Jesus, are unmasked as pure pretenders.

Marie Becker (ed.), *Eadem, Von Ben Sira zu Paulus. Gesammelte Aufsätze zu Texten, Theologie und Hermeneutik des Frühjudentums und des Neuen Testaments*, WUNT 173 (Tübingen: Mohr Siebeck, 2004), 243–76, here 259.
[9] Codex D as well as the Latin tradition and Ambrosiaster read: *para kuriou*; F, G, 365 and (probably) D read: *apo (tou) theou*.

But what is the theological consequence of Paul's standardization of the different Jesus traditions? Within the framework of Paul's letter writing in 1 Corinthians 11-15, why are both traditions—although initially quite different (historical event/Jesus tradition, 1 Cor 11; post-Easter kerygma, 1 Cor 15)—described in a similar manner? Within the basic structure of Paul's letters both become part of an early Christian complex of traditions that Paul has to mediate. For him, both traditions have equal status. By combining and standardizing different traditions in his epistolary argumentation, Paul prepares for a merging of a post-Easter formula and a Jesus tradition: he thus combines kerygma and history.[10]

PAUL'S USE OF THE JESUS TRADITIONS

It is debatable whether in 1 Corinthians 11 and 15 Paul is forced to approach both traditions on equal terms because he himself only joined the group of Jesus' followers post-Easter, or whether he takes his specific type of apostleship as an opportunity to combine kerygma and history. The question that remains is to what extent Paul can convincingly claim initially to be familiar with the so-called Jesus traditions? And to what extent is he willing to engage in the process of further transmitting and distributing the proclamation and teaching of (the historical) Jesus?

The fact that besides 1 Corinthians 11:23-25 there are only two further instances where Paul explicitly refers to Jesus traditions or *logoi kuriou* has remained a riddle in New Testament studies. How do we best make sense of this? Not accidentally, since both instances are again to be found in 1 Corinthians (7:10f. and 9:14).[11] It seems that, especially in his first letters to the Corinthian community, Paul is continuously under pressure to prove his apostolic authority with regard to its genuine roots in the "inner circle" of Easter witnesses and/or followers of Jesus. In 50 CE, Peter might have become a determined competitor of Paul in Achaia.

Regarding Paul's use of Jesus *logia* we have to distinguish more precisely between three types of references to the Jesus traditions: (i) explicit references to the "words of the Lord"; (ii) formulistic claims of Jesuanic authority (cf. 1 Cor 14:37); or (iii) analogies to the synoptic Jesus traditions (1 Thess 2:12; 5:2, 15; Gal 5:21; 1 Cor 13:2; Rom 12:14, 17, 20; 14:14, 17)—the

---

[10] On this, cf. Eve-Marie Becker, "Patterns of Early Christian Thinking and Writing of History: Paul–Mark–Acts," in Kurt A. Raaflaub (ed.) *Thinking, Recording, and Writing History in the Ancient World* (Malden: Wiley-Blackwell, 2014), 276-96.
[11] Cf. e.g., Jens Schröter, "Jesus Christus als Zentrum des Denkens," in Friedrich W. Horn (ed.), *Paulus Handbuch* (Tübingen: Mohr Siebeck, 2013), 279-85, here 280-82.

latter occurs frequently in 1 Corinthians (1 Cor 4:20; 6:9f.; 15:24, 50).[12] In my view, the third group of more vague allusions to the Jesus traditions can even be expanded further: in 2 Corinthians 3, for instance, Paul's interpretation of Christ as the one unveiling the faces of all believers cannot only be seen as a contrastive analysis of the story of Moses in Exodus 34 but, rather, as a fundamental critique of how Peter might have claimed an exclusive and thus more authoritative witnessing of Jesus' transfiguration (cf. Mk 9:2ff.).[13]

However, even if we further develop the reconstruction of unspecific material of the Jesus traditions in the Pauline letters, we have to recognize how little attention Paul in general pays to Jesus and the transmission of the Jesus traditions. The most obvious reason for him must relate to his understanding of his apostolic ministry and the task of letter writing: he sees himself to be "called to be an apostle" (Rom 1:1) in order "to bring about the obedience of faith for the sake of his name" (Rom 1:5). This explains why, especially in his early career (cf. Gal 1–2), Paul hesitated to transmit the bulk of the Jesus traditions for their own sake and the way in which he approached the literary task of letter writing, which he started around fifteen years later, and how his approach varies from Christian literary activity fifteen to twenty years later. Contrary to how between 70 and 90 CE the later gospel writers considered it to be their literary task to inform contemporary and later readers about the "beginning" (*arché*: Mk 1:1) or the "truth" (*asphaleia*: Lk 1:4) as much as the content of the gospel story as proclaimed by Jesus, Paul, a first-generation literary activist, is particularly in charge of the *hupakoé pisteós* (cf. also 16:26). This expression that is unique in the "entirety of ancient literature, [...] was most likely coined by Paul."[14] As Robert Jewett argues, "Paul speaks here of the special sort of obedience produced by the gospel," which reflects both Jewish Christian and Gentile Christian concerns in Rome, since "obedience to the gospel leads to walking by the spirit and to the fulfillment of the law's demands to love and care for the neighbor."[15] In Paul's view, all transmission of

---

[12] Cf. Schröter, ibid., 283.

[13] Cf. Eve-Marie Becker, "2 Corinthians 3:14, 18 as Pauline Allusions to a Narrative Jesus-Tradition," in Craig A. Evans and H. Daniel Zacharias (eds), *"What Does the Scripture Say?": Studies in the Function of Scripture in Early Judaism and Christianity,* LNTS 470 (London/New York: T&T Clark International, 2012), 121–33.

[14] Rorbert Jewett, *Romans: A Commentary,* Hermeneia (Minneapolis: Fortress Press, 2007), 110.

[15] Ibid. Jewett rejects an objective, a subjective or an epexegetic understanding of the genitive *pisteós* as "adnominal" interpretations and instead sees the genitive in its limiting function of "the substantive on which it depends"; he reads the syntagm as "obedience produced by the gospel."

traditions has finally to be subordinated to the purpose of enforcing the *hupakoé pisteós.*

OTHER TYPES OF "TRADITIONS"

So far we have explored to what extent Pauline thinking and writing depends to a surprisingly small extent on post-Easter formulas and Jesus traditions. Paul refers only rarely to this latter group of traditions, which could illuminate Jesus' life and mission. In contrast, Paul is primarily concerned with communitarian life and apostolic missionary duties—the pragmatism and style of his letter writing has thus to be adjusted to the communitarian queries. At the same time, the apostle regularly indicates (especially in 1 Corinthians) that, whenever needed, he can well meet the standards of remembering, delivering and applying Jesus' sayings to current debates. We could therefore argue that, for Paul, the hermeneutical criterion for delivering the Jesus traditions as well as the post-Easter formulas was their relevance for contemporary communitarian needs.

There might be another reason why Paul does not pay complete attention to the pure transmission of the Jesus traditions (as the representatives of the Jerusalem community, Peter, James and John, the *stuloi*, did). Paul is inspired and influenced by other traditions, which are part of his religious and intellectual profile. In particular, we have to think of complexes of traditions such as the Septuagint, various Hellenistic-Jewish beliefs and traditions as much as common Hellenistic rhetorical and argumentative tools. When looking critically at how Paul approaches these sets of traditions we will find only little consistency:

a) Scholars tend to argue that Paul—influenced by diaspora Jewish thinking (cf. Acts 22:3) as much as Palestinian pharisaic education (cf. Phil 3:5; Acts 23:6)—was closely affiliated to the language of the Psalms.[16] It is obvious that he was familiar with different techniques of contemporary Jewish scriptural interpretation (as was practiced by the Pharisees; cf. later rabbinic texts).[17] Jörg Frey identifies especially the "Seven Middot Hillels" (e.g., Rom 5:9ff.; 11:2, 24; Rom 4:1-12), Midrash-like

---

[16] Cf. Jörg Frey, "Die religiöse Prägung: Weisheit, Apokalyptik, Schriftauslegung," in Horn, op. cit. (note 11), 59-66, here 62.
[17] This grouping is frequently described as a "Torah-based movement for sanctification": Roland Deines, "Pharisees," in John J. Collins and Daniel C. Harlow, *The Eerdmans Dictionary of Early Judaism* (Grand Rapids/Cambridge: Eerdmans, 2010), 1061-63, here 1062.

argumentations (Gal 3:6–14), typological interpretation (1 Cor 10:1–13; Rom 5:12-14) and allegory (cf. Gal 4:21–31) as techniques of scriptural interpretation practiced by Paul.[18] We can distinguish between "explicit" and "implicit" ways in which Paul refers to the LXX.[19] However, in neither is Paul concerned with scriptural interpretation as such. His task does not entail commentating Scripture(s).

Paul basically approaches Scripture in order to reveal its meaning and evidence for proclaiming and interpreting the gospel message (e.g., 1 Cor 9:10; 10:11).[20] His usage of Scripture is therefore selective. The basic hermeneutical criteria are: (i) relevance for contemporary communitarian discourse; (ii) legitimizing evidence for the gospel proclamation (cf. 1 Cor 15:3–5) and its messenger; and (iii) the exploration of Scripture's manifold immanent hermeneutical potential. Paul does not only refer to Scripture in order to affirm the gospel message (affirmation), but also in terms of revealing its critical potential for disclosing pre-Christian and Christ-believing existence *coram Deo* (critique, e.g., 1 Cor 10:12–13).

b) Paul's letter writing is influenced by the apocalyptic (e.g., *parousia*, resurrection, new creation) and sapiential (e.g., Christ as incarnation of God: 2 Cor 3:17f.) traditions, possibly communicated to him by his pharisaic education.[21] Besides, Paul can also communicate in prophetic images (Gal 1) or as a person who prepares himself (in a mystical sense?) for conformity with Christ (Phil 1–3). Why does Paul shift between different traditions and merge them? Is he willing to hand down and possibly evaluate the rich and manifold heritage of Jewish thinking and writing? To what extent does he actually intend to transform apocalyptic motifs into anthropological or existential thinking (R. Bultmann)?[22] It seems to me that Paul once more aligns his approach to traditional sources with his strategy of literary communication: in his epistolary teaching, exhortation, consolation, proclamation and various hermeneutical tasks he has to be inventive, flexible, critical,

---

[18] Cf. Frey, op. cit. (note 16), 63f.; see James L. Kugel, "Early Jewish Biblical Interpretation," in *The Eerdmans Dictionary of Early Judaism*, ibid., 121–41.

[19] Cf. Florian Wilk, "Schriftbezüge im Werk des Paulus," in Horn, op. cit. (note 11), 479–90, here 482–87.

[20] Cf. ibid., 490.

[21] Cf. Frey, op. cit. (note 16), 64–66.

[22] Cf. Rudolf Bultmann, *Geschichte und Eschatologie* (Tübingen: Mohr Siebeck, 1979), 46–53.

surprising. As a result of this mixture of motifs, traditions and argumentative claims the Pauline letters appear "weighty and strong" in the ears of his audience(s) (2 Cor 10:10).

c) Paul's literary strategy of selectively merging certain types of traditions can already be found in 1 Thessalonians. Already here, Paul begins "using rhetorical and philosophical traditions, in the process modifying them to suit his immediate purpose" (cf. 1 Thess 1:5).[23] As soon as he leaves the Syro-Palestinian area and moves to Asia Minor, Macedonia and further west, he is increasingly confronted with Hellenistic-Roman moral discourse. In light of the popular ethical debates, Paul could only communicate his message properly if he could demonstrate his ability to master relevant rhetorical and philosophical traditions. In this light, Acts 17:16ff. constitutes a proper, although much later, Lukan attempt to connect the Pauline heritage of arguing to the more general philosophical discourses of his time.

Brief conclusion

The investigation of how and why Paul uses various types of traditions has revealed how selective and connective the apostle is as a letter writer. Whenever needed, he refers to post-Easter formulas as much as the Jesus traditions within the context of his letter writing and authorial perspective. He quotes the Scripture viz. Septuagint in order to shape argumentative evidence of the truth of the gospel message and to express fundamental critique of (Christian) faith and life; he shows his familiarity with prophetic as well as sapiential and apocalyptic traditions in order to demonstrate the plurality of (religious) motifs by which intellectual discourse can develop beyond the simple game of raising and answering controversial questions (cf. *peri de* structure in 1 Corinthians). Furthermore, he uses general Hellenistic rhetorical and philosophical traditions in order to address those readers who are at this stage of affiliation to the *ekklésiai* only tentatively sympathizing with observing early Christian missionary activities and the communitarian life.

Paul's selective and connective way of dealing with traditions can only partly be explained by the circumstances under which his letters were written. In many ways, Paul develops a literary strategy: the apostle does not commit himself to one particular stream of tradition but, rather, frees

---

[23] Abaham J. Malherbe, *The Letters to the Thessalonians: A New Translation with Introduction and Commentary*, AncB 32B (New York: Doubleday, 2000), 111.

up space for innovatively shaping the individual profile of his, the Pauline, ministry. It is only at first sight then, that not to be part of the inner circle of the Jerusalem community (*stuloi*) causes authoritative problems. In Paul's view, his status as a late- or newcomer allows for self-styled apostolic activities that he, nevertheless, has to trace back to his commissioning by God and the previous agreements on missionary politics reached with the "pillars" in Jerusalem (Gal 1–2).

Paul's argumentative technique is no less than the literary part of his missionary strategy: "I have become all things to all people, that I might by all means save some. I do it all for the sake of the gospel" (1 Cor 9:22f.). As Paul does not "run aimlessly," nor "box as though beating the air" (1 Cor 9:26), his approach to and use of traditions is always intentional. Paul's selective and connective use of different sets of traditions might result from his apostolic ambition as much as his hermeneutical pragmatism.

We might today criticize Paul for not being more comprehensive, explicit, precise and distinctive when using and transforming traditional materials. As a result, Paul's place in intellectual life in the first century CE is hard to define. However, Paul tried hard to transform the stigma of being the "least" into the attribute of being unique and running first (1 Cor 9:24). In order to do so he accessed and arranged traditions in a highly selective and specifically connective manner.

Principles of Paul's Hermeneutics

Oda Wischmeyer

Paul's hermeneutics can be studied from a number of different perspectives. At the beginning of my essay, I shall refer to two important aspects that I have selected out of a multitude of approaches, most of which are familiar and therefore do not need to be touched upon here in detail.

Asking Paul himself

Let us first ask Paul himself. Imagine the following scenario: One evening, after work, you leave your home in Ephesus to attend a meeting of a newly established religious group, whose members the Roman authorities have recently called *Christianoí*. You will listen to a lecture delivered by one of their religious leaders, Paūlos, who used to give courses on the doctrines and way of life of this new community. The lectures take place in the *stoá* of Tyránnos. After the lecture you have the opportunity to ask Paul, "What is your doctrine on *hermeneīa*"?[1] Paul will probably answer, "Well, we have the gift of *hermeneīa* in our assemblies. Many members of the congregation can speak in tongues, and the community appreciates this spiritual gift. But, I argue, glossolalia should be interpreted in the service, since otherwise people will not understand what the spirit reveals in tongues. Therefore, *hermeneīa*, interpretation, is a special gift of the Spirit and an indispensable part of our services." Since this answer does not satisfy you, you will explain that your question does not refer to interpreting glossolalia but to understanding God's ways of communicating with human beings in general. Since you are Lutheran, you expect some plausible comment on reading and understanding Scripture. But you will surely be amazed by Paul's second answer:

---

[1] *Hermeneīa* only 1 Cor 12:10; 14:26.

> [I see. What you refer to is the *euaggélion*], the gospel of God which he promised beforehand through his prophets in the holy scriptures, the gospel concerning his Son, who was descended from David according to the flesh and was declared to be Son of God with power according to the spirit of holiness by resurrection from the dead, Jesus Christ our Lord, through whom we have received grace and apostleship to bring about the obedience of faith among all the Gentiles for the sake of his name, 6 including yourselves who are called to belong to Jesus Christ (Rom 1–6).

The opening phrase of Romans helps us immediately to understand that this teacher, philosopher or prophet, who knows who he is and what his self-description as *apóstolos Jesoū Christoū* actually implies, does not speak about the interpretation (*hermeneīa*) of the sacred book of the Jews, which he only touches on briefly as "Holy Scriptures," but about himself and his proclaiming of the gospel. He introduces himself as God's interpreter, adding however the strange term *euaggélion* for God's message that will need further explanation.

Probing scholarship

Now let us take a second step and ask ourselves as theologians and biblical scholars: what is it that we are investigating? What are we looking for when we discuss Paul's principles of hermeneutics within the framework of contemporary scholarship and today's church and life. Leaving aside the whole field of recent cultural hermeneutics, when we deal with hermeneutics in the classical sense of understanding written texts, we always face a twofold mission: the more or less practical exercise of reading, translating, explaining and interpreting and often also preaching the texts in question on the one hand, and the problem of understanding the conditions under which this understanding and interpretation developed on the other. This applies in particular to the Christian Bible, the most important collection of seminal texts for the Western world and beyond, which has had its own interpreters since Origen of Alexandria. The practical work of interpreting the Bible takes place in the fields of Old and New Testament philology and exegesis—biblical studies in academia—while the issue of understanding belongs not only to theology but also to philosophy. To ponder on understanding as such has, first and foremost, been a classical topic of philosophy since Plato and Aristotle. In light of the fact, however, that the Christian faith affirms that the Bible reveals God's message for humankind, fundamental hermeneutics has also been a major topic in Old and New Testament theology and systematic and practical theology since the times of the Church Fathers, in particular since Augustine's *De doctrina christiana*, the most important work of ancient Christian biblical hermeneutics.[2] In other words: our quest for hermeneutics cannot be understood without this long, learned and controversial history of biblical hermeneutics.

In the general quest to comprehend the Bible, the next question relates to the correct interpretation of earliest oral preaching and subsequent written texts that aim at encapsulating God's message for the world. The lasting importance of biblical hermeneutics can be interpreted in contradictory ways. On the one hand, as a result of the multitude of different interpretations, there has, for centuries, been the constant reproach that the Bible has been misunderstood or simply cannot be fully understood. From this perspective, words and texts that were originally meant to give advice and to clarify issues turn out to be the source of misunderstandings, quarrels, fights and separation or, even worse, give rise to enmity.

There is a another, positive perspective however, one that underlines the importance of interpretation: understanding and application depend on time, on context and, what is sometimes underestimated, on the individual or the interpreter, and are thereby necessarily manifold and often divergent. Interpretation and application in particular are related to their historical place and cultural environments. People who devote their lives to the interpretation of holy texts will always examine in which ways the texts speak to their time and to their conditions of life and what significance they have for themselves and for the persons they serve in the church, academia and in society.

Thus we learn how general hermeneutics are intertwined with the practical task of interpreting texts that promise to introduce us to God's communication with human beings. Therefore, we should start our investigation of Paul's hermeneutics by stating that the constant need for renewed interpretation and application as well as the controversy over different interpretations are a result of the normative status of the Tanach, the Septuagint and later the Christian Bible. This includes Paul's letters which, since Irenaeus, have turned out to be the most controversial among those texts that we know as the New Testament.

THE JEWISH FOUNDATION OF PAUL'S
HERMENEUTICAL CONCEPT

So far, we have gained an insight into the twofold dimension of biblical hermeneutics: its theoretical and practical task. When we want to deal with Paul's hermeneutics more in detail, we are confronted with the same scenario, that is

---

[2] See Oda Wischmeyer (ed.), *Handbuch der Bibelhermeneutiken* (Berlin/Boston: de Gruyter, 2016).

to say, with practical and theoretical issues. Investigating Paul's hermeneutics leads us in different directions. First, the practical task of interpreting his letters, beginning with his terminology and mindset, delineating rules of Paul's way of communicating with the communities through letters and explaining his way of preaching and teaching. In the context of Paul's impact on Lutheran hermeneutics it is important to map Paul's theoretical or theological concepts of reading Scripture and his new way of understanding *en Christō*. Since our interest lies in Paul's general concept of understanding God and God's way of communicating with humankind *en Christō*, our overarching question concerns not only his interpretation of Scripture, but his understanding of God's communication with humankind. In other words: we do not limit ourselves to asking how Paul uses and interprets Scripture, which he knows and refers to in the form of the Septuagint canon, what kind of authority he claims for his interpretation, and to which extent he understands Scripture as God's revelation and as given by the Spirit but, primarily, at what point he leaves Scripture behind and dares to argue beyond Scripture.

Scripture and Spirit are the references and sources of Paul's hermeneutics. In which way do they fit together? First and foremost Paul's concept of theological hermeneutics—that is of revelation, understanding and interpretation—is based on the Jewish concept of Scripture that is part of the Jewish theology of the Second Temple period and, more precisely, the result of Israel's encounter with Hellenism and the anti-Hellenistic Maccabean revolt. The Qumran scrolls on the one hand and Philo's commentaries on the other are the most significant witnesses to the eminent status of Scripture in early Judaism. Paul's personal experience with Scripture is that of a devout young Jewish student, a Pharisee, who studied the Torah, probably in Jerusalem. This means that Paul, although he originated from Hellenistic Tarsus, was brought up in a very particular way of thinking, far removed and deeply separated from the predominant culture of his time. His intellect was trained in reading "holy Scripture," a specific concept of "sacred books" that is unparalleled in the manifold world of ancient pagan or Greco-Roman religion. Ancient religion in general does not work by sacred books, but by sacrifice and rites and worship, performed by priests and citizens, not by scholars. In other words: Paul's commitment to interpret Scripture, which means the Septuagint, is by no means self-evident. James L. Kugel points to the fact that,

> None of these elements was absent from Second Temple Judaism, but along with them, and ultimately displacing them, was the oddest sort of act: reading words written centuries earlier and acting as if they had the highest significance for people in the present age.[3]

---

[3] James L. Kugel, "Early Jewish Biblical Interpretation," in John J. Collins and Daniel Harlow (eds), *The Eerdmans Dictionary of Early Judaism* (Grand Rapids/

The only parallel in the ancient world, and not a very close one, is Homer. It is with Homer that young boys were taught to read and write. Homer's texts needed a considerable ethical explanation in order to avoid interpreting the narrations of the Homeric Gods in ways that no longer fitted the moral and philosophical standards of the Hellenistic-Roman age. Homer's anthropomorphisms were interpreted in ways similar to those that Philo of Alexandria and other Jewish exegetes applied to those texts of the Jewish Scripture that failed to meet the standards of early Jewish ethics. But, Homer is the cultural, not the religious, basis of Hellenism. Greco-Roman polis-religion recognizes and worships the Homeric or Olympic pantheon without reading Homer as the holy document of its manifold and diverse polytheistic religion. Therefore, when Paul argues by quoting or interpreting Scripture, he argues to a large extent outside the Greco-Roman religious and cultural world. Hence, Paul's concept of scriptural hermeneutics is by no means universal or self-explanatory and a necessary part of every religion and therefore expected by his addressees. Rather, it is a very particular concept that depends on the religion and culture of ancient Judaism. In other words, we are right to portray Paul as a person who understands hermeneutics as the interpretation of the holy text of the Septuagint and interprets and applies Scripture according to certain methodological rules that had been developed by Jewish scholars since Hellenistic times. This is what he does often in Romans, 1 and 2 Corinthians and Galatians but, unexpectedly enough, not in 1 Thessalonians, Philippians or Philemon.

To sum up: it is crucial that whenever we think of hermeneutics in terms of explaining Scripture in order to recognize God's nature and essence, God's covenant and commandments, we think and argue within the basic Jewish paradigm of hermeneutics. Only once we recognize that the rootedness of Paul's hermeneutics in ancient Judaism has remained a part of our present hermeneutical theology and our practical work in biblical studies, can we try to go one step further and look for the other element of his hermeneutics, the Spirit. Here we meet Paul's actual contribution to the issue of understanding and interpreting God's revelation. And this brings us back to the evening in Ephesus in the *stoá* of *Tyránnos* and the hermeneutical key concept of *euaggélion*.

2 CORINTHIANS 3: THE SPIRIT

In some sense we continue to act as the inheritors of the Jewish concept of scriptural hermeneutics and walk in Paul's footsteps. True as this may

---

Cambridge: Eerdmans, 2012), 121–41, here 122. Cf. also E. Ulrich, "The Jewish Scriptures: Texts, Versions, Canons," in ibid., 97–119.

be, it is only half the truth. Actually, Paul goes far beyond the theological and religious concepts of Jewish Scripture and its hermeneutics. His own hermeneutics is based on the Spirit as the eschatological mediator and interpreter of God's salvific history with humankind. The Spirit is not against Scripture as Romans 1 demonstrates. But, as I have already mentioned, in some of Paul's letters there is no reference to Scripture. That means that reference to Scripture is no longer indispensable, since Paul and the Christ confessing communities have received the Spirit (1 Thess 1:5; Gal 3:2–5).

We can examine his fundamentally individual approach to the whole issue of understanding God and God's covenant in light of the Spirit in Paul's second letter to the community of Corinth. Therefore, instead of reviewing all Pauline texts that deal with Scripture in one way or the other, I shall focus on one basic text: 2 Corinthians 3:1–4:18. In 2 Corinthians 3, Paul interprets God's communication with humankind in a way that ultimately constitutes a new paradigm of theological hermeneutics and of Scripture based on Jesus Christ, the Spirit and on the *euaggélion* proclaimed by Paul himself.

Although and because Paul is concerned with defending himself and his apostleship in 2 Corinthians 1–7,[4] chapter 3 turns out to be something like Paul's hermeneutical compendium or manifest. Paul develops his personal concept of hermeneutics by interpreting Exodus 34, the second version of the basic narrative of Moses receiving the Ten Commandments at Mount Sinai inscribed on two tablets of stone. Paul does so in a fresh and unexpected, but also complicated and sophisticated way of interpretation while, at the same time, significantly modifying the text in Exodus. His interpretation is a bold comparison between the narrative of the people of Israel and Moses, the Corinthian community and his own person. By choosing this narrative episode, Paul unexpectedly connects one of the summits of Israelite covenantal theology to his own mission, referring back to Moses, but primarily stating the superiority of the Corinthian community and of his own ministry over that of Moses. The subject matter is God's revelation. Paul emphasizes that although Moses spoke to God and heard God's voice and returned with the tablets, it was not only he himself and the people of Israel who were forbidden to see God's glory,[5] but what was worse: "the people of Israel could not gaze at Moses' face because of the glory of his face, a glory now set aside" (2 Cor 3:7).

To prove this, Paul changes the Exodus text in two points: first, he maintains that the Israelites could not look at Moses' face, while, according to the Septuagint, Moses talked to the Israelites while his face showed the

---

[4] 2 Cor 1:12–14 works as the *propositio generalis* (general theme) of the whole letter.
[5] As it is already narrated in Exodus 33:18–23.

brightness of God's splendor and the Israelites were able to see his face (Ex 34:35). Second, Paul interprets Exodus 34:34 (when Moses went to the Lord, he removed the veil from his face) as follows: When a person turns to the Lord, the veil is removed.[6]

These corrections aim at downgrading Moses' revelation and Israel's encounter with the Lord for the sake of emphasizing Paul's *euaggélion* and the status of the Corinthian community. Paul's strategy is to outdo Moses' revelation without revoking the fundamental continuity between Moses' and his own revelation, while affirming the significant superiority of his ministry. But Paul also has a second, different strategy. In 2 Corinthians 3, he outlines the basic discontinuity between Moses and himself, and the Israelites and the Corinthian community. In order to emphasize the fundamental discontinuity he works with a series of antitheses: ink vs Spirit (3:3); tablets of stone vs tablets of human hearts (3:3); old covenant vs new covenant (3:6, 14); letter vs Spirit (3:6);[7] death vs life (3:7, 8); condemnation vs justification (3:9); splendor that fades away vs splendor that is permanent (3:11, 13); and the veil that remains vs a veil that is removed (3:13–16). But discontinuity, even the ultimate division between life and death, is not Paul's last word. Instead of announcing the end of the old covenant he opens up the perspective of hope and a future of freedom and glory:

> but when one turns to the Lord, the veil is removed. Now the Lord is the Spirit, and where the Spirit of the Lord is, there is freedom. And all of us, with unveiled faces, seeing the glory of the Lord as though reflected in a mirror, are being transformed into the same image from one degree of glory to another; for this comes from the Lord, the Spirit (2 Cor 3:16–18).

Paul alludes to the veil covering Moses' face according to Exodus 34, arguing that the reading of Moses, the study of Scripture now (*ho nūn kairós*), under the presence of the Spirit, can be done in freedom. The concise phrase of "old covenant" "may be Paul's own formulation"[8] that came to him in connection with the semantic and metaphorical field of old and new and with the early Christian terminology of "new covenant" for the Last Supper. Although he points to the Pentateuch, the phrase does not mean "Old Testament" in the sense of the later bipartite canon of the ancient church. Paul always thinks in terms of revelation, not codification; in other words, in terms of God's communication with humankind, not of a holy book or Scripture.

---

[6] Luther translates, When Israel turns to the Lord [...].

[7] See Romans 7:6.

[8] Margaret E. Thrall, *The Second Epistle to the Corinthians*, vol. 1, 2 Corinthians 1–7, ICC (London/New York: T&T Clark, 1994, 2004), 266.

THE CASE OF AUTHORITY: CHRIST, THE SPIRIT, THE GOSPEL AND THE APOSTLE

In some ways we have now returned to Ephesus. For Paul, it is the Spirit and the gifts of the Spirit that constitute present reality. As he argues in Romans 1, God spoke through the prophets in the past, foreshadowing the gospel (*proepēggeílato*, Rom 1:2). Today, God speaks through the gospel that is preached by Paul (*euaggélion*). The gospel is about Jesus Christ, God's son and the Lord of the communities. In Romans 1:3f., Paul tries to map a Christology that combines Jesus' life and death with his pneumatic status *post resurrectionem* (after resurrection). Paul's authority derives from his message and from the interpretation of the era in which he lived. The gospel, that is his preaching, proclaims and at the same time fits the era of the Spirit that began with Jesus' resurrection. Paul's message is the right expression of the new time: the time *post resurrectionem* Christi.

PAULINE HERMENEUTICS BETWEEN SCRIPTURE, FREEDOM AND SPIRIT

Paul's hermeneutics is based on the Scripture as the source of God's words for Israel. Paul does not question the authority of Scripture; he is convinced that God's will is communicated by Scripture and is not subject to change. But Paul does not think in the categories of "the older is better or even best" or of the metaphysical concept of constant eternity, but in terms of salvific history: then and now, old and new, promise and fulfillment and, most important of all, the time to come. He lives in the period of fulfillment that is characterized by the coming of Jesus Christ and points ahead to the future:

> But when the time had fully come, God sent forth his son, born of woman, born under the law, to redeem those who were under the law, so that we might receive adoption as sons (Gal 4:4).

And,

> For he [God] says, "At an acceptable time I have listened to you, and on a day of salvation I have helped you" (Isa 49:8 LXX). See, now is the acceptable time; see, now is the day of salvation! (2 Cor 6:2).

And once more in the words of 2 Corinthians 3:16–18:

> [B]ut when one turns to the Lord, the veil is removed. Now the Lord is the Spirit, and where the Spirit of the Lord is, there is freedom. And all of us, with unveiled faces, seeing the glory of the Lord as though reflected in a mirror, are being transformed into the same image from one degree of glory to another; for this comes from the Lord, the Spirit.

Thus Paul is entirely free to interpret God's will and revelation due to the *kairós*, according to the gospel of Jesus Christ. In other words, in the "modern" way, the way that is appropriate for his time. He lives under the conditions of the presence and the action of the Spirit. He may quote Scripture, he may alter Scripture's sense in light of the gospel, he may put aside Scripture, or he may state that his concept of love fulfills the law[9] or that Christ is the end of the law.[10] So, the following sentence, addressed to the Corinthians, expressed in laconic brevity, applies not only to the apostles but also to Paul's hermeneutics: all things are yours (1 Cor 3:21).

CONCLUSION

First, according to Paul, the principal dimension of Christian hermeneutics is the message of the gospel, not the interpretation of Scripture. Whether or not or to what extent this hermeneutical principle includes the New Testament texts is a theological issue in its own right. But, we should always bear in mind that Paul did not know about what later on turned out to become the "New Testament." His letters are not "the gospel" (*euaggélion*), but a means of communication with his communities during his absence.

Second, we live in constant dialogue with two religions defined as religions based on a holy book or as "religions of the book." Accordingly, the interpretation both of the Tanach and the Qur'an is a crucial concern of Jewish and Muslim theologians. In order to participate in this exercise, Christian theology often interprets the Christian religion in the same way, for example by interpreting the Abraham narrative. This begs the question if and how, especially our Lutheran theological hermeneutics of Scripture, meets or misses Paul who emphasizes the Spirit as the ultimate way of God's communication with humankind and states: the Lord is the Spirit.

---

[9] Romans 13:10.
[10] Romans 10:4.

SLAVE AND FREE: HERMENEUTICAL REFLECTIONS ON PAUL'S USE OF THE SLAVE–MASTER METAPHOR

Magnus Zetterholm

INTRODUCTION

During the course of history, slavery, which has existed in virtually every culture, has created an enormous amount of suffering. Men, women and children have been killed, mutilated and sexually abused, families have been shattered and numerous people have been denied their right to live as free human beings. It is scandalous that slavery still affects a large number of people. According to the Global Slavery Index,[1] almost 36 million people today are estimated to live in slavery, if defined as "all of the practices that trap people in modern servitude, including human trafficking, forced labour, and slavery." Thus, even though slavery today is outlawed in every country,[2] the practice of holding slaves or people in slave-like conditions persists.

One reason for this is that all major world religions have traditions or texts that could and have been understood to legitimize slavery, and slavery is hence deeply integrated in human culture. The Qur'an contains detailed regulations on slavery and the rise of so-called Islamic State (IS) has drawn renewed attention to the issue of institutionalized slavery in parts of contemporary radical Muslim tradition. The Hebrew Bible and Jewish traditions, such as the Talmud, also regulate and thus legitimize

---

[1] www.globalslaveryindex.org.
[2] Mauretania was the last country to abolish slavery in 1981. Slavery was, however, criminalized only in 2007.

slavery. The Hindu caste system can be compared to slavery or slave-like practices and, according to the Global Slavery Index, only in India over 14 million people are in forced slavery, including intergenerational bonded labor, trafficking for sexual exploitation and forced marriage.

In the Christian tradition, the issue of slavery probably gained most attention in connection with the North American debates on slavery during the nineteenth century. In the fierce discussions between those who wanted to preserve institutionalized slavery and the abolitionists, both sides used biblical texts in defense of their respective view, a fact that is hermeneutically most interesting. The Bible can, of course, provide us with numerous texts on slavery.

If we concentrate on the New Testament only, we can easily conclude that the master–slave relation is an important theme in many of Jesus' parables.[3] Moreover, there is really no text in the gospels that problematizes or questions the institution of slavery. Slavery is simply taken as a normal social institution, and as such it provides a natural setting for describing the relation between God and humans. The same is true for Paul: Paul uses the words "slave" and "slavery" in ways that reveal that the institution as such is taken for granted and never really questioned.

PAUL AS A SERVANT OF CHRIST

Paul's use of the term slave can roughly be divided into five categories—some positive, some negative and some more or less neutral. First, Paul applies the term to himself in a positive way. In Romans 1:1 he presents himself as "a servant of Jesus Christ" according to the New Revised Standard Version (NRSV). The word for "servant" is, of course, the Greek word δοῦλος, which can indeed be translated as "servant," but then one has to remember that most "servants" in the Roman Empire were also "slaves," or former slaves.[4] Thus, there is no reason for not translating Romans 1:1 as "Paul, a slave of Jesus Christ." In 1 Corinthians 9:19, Paul claims that even though he is free with respect to all, he has made himself "a slave [ἐδούλωσα] to all." In Philippians 1:1, he includes Timothy in the introductory greeting:

---

[3] See e.g., Jennifer A. Glancy, "Slaves and Slavery in the Matthean Parables," in *Journal of Biblical Literature* 119 (2000), 67–90.

[4] For an overview of slavery in antiquity, see Anthony C. Thiselton, *The First Epistle to the Corinthians: A Commentary on the Greek Text* (Grand Rapids: Eerdmans, 2000), 562–65. See also S. R. Llewelyn and R. A. Kearsley (eds), *New Documents Illustrating Early Christianity: A Review of the Greek Inscriptions and Papyri Published in 1980-81: Volume 6* (North Ryde: Macquarie University, 1992), 48–81.

"Paul and Timothy, servants of Christ Jesus [δοῦλοι Χριστοῦ Ἰησοῦ], To all the saints in Christ Jesus who are in Philippi." In 2 Corinthians 4:5 Paul states that he and Timothy proclaim Jesus Christ and themselves as the Corinthians' slaves "for Jesus' sake."

It is possible, perhaps even likely, that Paul's claim to be Jesus' slave or servant reflects one of the most important master narratives in Jewish tradition—the Exodus motif. The story of how God, through Moses, delivers the people of Israel from slavery and brings them to Sinai, where they receive the Torah, soon became the model for God's salvation of God's people. As Christine Hayes points out, it is important to notice that God's physical redemption of the Israelites "is a redemption *for a purpose*, a purpose that becomes clear at Sinai. For at Sinai, the Israelites will become Yahweh's people, bound by a covenant."[5] This means that freedom from the oppressors in Egypt is not unconditional, but means freedom to serve the God of Israel in a new way. Since God is the creator of humans, who are created in God's image (Gen 1:26–27), God is the only rightful owner of the human being.[6] This relationship can be expressed by the slave/servant-master metaphor as in Leviticus 25:55: "For to me the people of Israel are servants; they are my servants whom I brought out from the land of Egypt: I am the Lord your God."

The word in the Hebrew Bible, here translated as "servant," is עבד, which has broader meaning than the Greek δοῦλος. עבד can indeed mean "slave," (e.g., Gen 9:25–27) but is also used to denote persons who technically are free, although subjects under a king or ruler (e.g., Gen 40:20). Thus, vassal kings, officials and soldiers and officers can be labeled עבד. The word עבד, meaning "worshipper," is derived from the same root. This broader meaning is probably reflected in the Greek translation of the Hebrew Bible, the LXX, which does not use the word δοῦλος in Leviticus 25:55 but two other nouns, οἰκέτης, which can mean "slave," but also "household," and παῖς, which can be translated as "slave," but also "child." Accordingly, it is possible to translate the Greek version of Leviticus 25:55 as follows: "For the sons [οἱ υἱοί] of Israel are for me my household, they are my children, whom I brought out from Egypt."

To summarize: Paul's presentation of himself as a δοῦλος Χριστοῦ Ἰησοῦ, probably builds on the Exodus motif, which emphasizes liberation from slavery in order for the people of Israel to enter into a new relationship with the God of Israel. This idea of freedom is far from the Enlightenment ideals

---

[5] Christine E. Hayes, *Introduction to the Bible* (New Haven: Yale University Press, 2012), 118.

[6] Goran Larsson, *Bound for Freedom: The Book of Exodus in Jewish and Christian Traditions* (Peabody: Hendrickson, 1999), 15.

of freedom and equality for all. In Paul's mind, liberation from slavery for the Jewish people means entering into the service of another master, and the purpose of redemption from slavery means acknowledging the fundamental call of Israel—to be "a light for the nations [εἰς φῶς ἐθνῶν]" (Isa 42:6, 51:4). Since Paul is convinced that he is living in the messianic age, to subordinate to God's messianic instrument, Jesus Christ, is perfectly logical, since Christ must reign "until he has put all his enemies under his feet ... when the Son himself will also be subjected to the one who put all things in subjection under him, so that God may be all in all" (1 Cor 15:25, 28). In addition, when presenting himself as a slave, Paul had, of course, another powerful role model—Jesus himself—who according to Paul "did not regard equality with God as something to be exploited, but emptied himself, taking the form of a slave [μορφὴν δούλου λαβών]" (Phil 2:6-7). As Jesus was God's slave, Paul is now the slave of Christ.

Slaves under sin

The idea that the Israelites are not really free but under the dominion of one or the other power—God or the Pharaoh—is hermeneutically transformed in a passage from Romans (6:17-22). In this case, however, the context is quite different. When Paul applies the term "servant of Christ" to himself, he draws on the notion of the relationship between the people of Israel and God. God liberated the Israelites from slavery so that they could serve God instead. In the passage from Romans, it is not the Jewish people who stand in the center, but the nations. It should be emphasized that Paul's intended audience of Romans are members of the nations, i.e., non-Jewish followers of Jesus. This is clear from the opening of the letter. "Through whom [Jesus Christ]," writes Paul "we have received grace and apostleship to bring about the obedience of faith among all the Gentiles for the sake of his name, including yourselves who are called to belong to Jesus Christ" (Rom 1:5-6).

In Romans 1:18-32 Paul defines the problem of the nations: God's wrath is revealed from heaven (in the present tense) against all ungodliness (ἀσέβεια) and unrighteousness (ἀδικία). As a result, God has surrendered (παρέδωκεν) the people in question to various sinful behaviors such as idolatry and prohibited sexual relations. It is commonly pointed out that here Paul picks up on Jewish stereotypes of the heathen world.[7] Paul's argument in 1:18-23 seems, for instance, to echo Wisdom 13:1-2:

---

[7] E.g., Wis 11-15; SibOr 3:8-45, see Joseph A. Fitzmyer, *Romans: A New Translation with Introduction and Commentary* (New York: Doubleday, 1993), 27; Ernst Käsemann, *Commentary on Romans* (Grand Rapids: Eerdmans, 1980), 45-46.

> For all people who were ignorant of God were foolish by nature; and they were unable from the good things that are seen to know the one who exists, nor did they recognize the artisan while paying heed to his works; but they supposed that either fire or wind or swift air, or the circle of the stars, or turbulent water, or the luminaries of heaven were the gods that rule the world.

From Paul's perspective, there was no hope of salvation for the nations before the Christ event. But through Christ, non-Jews, who were formerly slaves under sin, have been freed so they too can serve the God of Israel (Rom 6:17–22):

> Do you not know that if you present yourselves to anyone as obedient slaves [δούλους], you are slaves [δοῦλοι] of the one whom you obey, either of sin, which leads to death, or of obedience, which leads to righteousness? But thanks be to God that you, having once been slaves [δοῦλοι] of sin, have become obedient from the heart to the form of teaching to which you were entrusted, and that you, having been set free from sin, have become slaves [ἐδουλώθητε] of righteousness. I am speaking in human terms because of your natural limitations. For just as you once presented your members as slaves [δοῦλα] to impurity and to greater and greater iniquity, so now present your members as slaves [δοῦλα] to righteousness for sanctification. When you were slaves [δοῦλοι] of sin, you were free in regard to righteousness. So what advantage did you then get from the things of which you now are ashamed? The end of those things is death. But now that you have been freed from sin and enslaved [δουλωθέντες] to God, the advantage you get is sanctification. The end is eternal life.

Here, Paul uses the master–slave metaphor in basically the same way as when he applied the metaphor to himself. As the Jewish people were delivered from slavery in Egypt, the nations have now the possibility to obey a new master. This is how Paul fulfills his call to be a light of the nations.

So far, Paul's use of the slave-master metaphor has been positive, although the metaphoric use, of course, presumes the social institution of slavery. Paul's point seems to be that no human is truly free, but being God's slave or servant represents the existential perfection of humanity. As for the Jewish people, God achieved this at Sinai after having brought the Israelites out of Egypt. In Christ, this process reaches its culmination when also the nations are brought into a covenantal relationship with the God of Israel, the God of the whole cosmos. From this point of view, to be in slavery under a human master, such as the Pharaoh, represents a perversion, a diversion from the divinely instituted order.

However, even the slave–master metaphor seems inadequate in order properly to describe the relationship between God and humans. In some texts, Paul seems to admit that being a slave is not entirely a good thing. There is actually something better.

MORE THAN SLAVES

In Galatians, Paul's problem is to explain to the non-Jewish audience that they should not convert to Judaism. Contrary to most Pauline scholarship, I do not believe that Paul argues this because he finds something wrong with Judaism or the Torah. In my view, Paul remained entirely Jewish all his life and I believe he expressed his loyalty to God by observing the Torah. From Paul's point of view, Jesus-oriented Judaism is the culmination or the fulfillment of true Judaism.[8] Since God, through Jesus, has provided a way also for the nations to enter into a covenantal relationship with the God of Israel, Paul needs to find a theological way for bringing the nations into such a relationship. While some Jews within the early Jesus movement believed that non-Jews should convert to Judaism,[9] Paul's vision is different.

For Paul it seems vital that Jews remain Jews while non-Jews remain non-Jews. The reason for this is probably his belief that God is the God of the whole universe. Thus, humanity must be saved as Jews and non-Jews, otherwise God would only be the God of the Jews.[10] Since non-Jews should not become Jews, they are, accordingly, not to observe the Torah. Paul's problem, however, is that many non-Jews seem to have been encouraged to do precisely that. Our sources reveal that many non-Jews were attracted to Judaism and had adopted a semi-Jewish life style.[11]

In Galatians 4:1–7, Paul elevates the status of non-Jews in Christ to the status of children (sons). In the preceding section, which we will return to, Paul has explained that non-Jews in Christ are "Abraham's offspring" and thus heirs to the promise of Abraham. He continues:

> My point is this: heirs, as long as they are minors, are no better than slaves [δούλου], though they are the owners of all the property; but they remain under

---

[8] See e.g., Pamela Eisenbaum, *Paul Was Not a Christian: The Original Message of a Misunderstood Apostle* (New York: HarperOne, 2009); Mark D. Nanos and Magnus Zetterholm (eds), *Paul Within Judaism: Restoring the First-Century Context to the Apostle* (Minneapolis: Fortress, 2015); Magnus Zetterholm, *Approaches to Paul: A Student's Guide to Recent Scholarship* (Minneapolis: Fortress, 2009).

[9] Acts 15.

[10] Mark D. Nanos, *The Mystery of Romans: The Jewish Context of Paul's Letter* (Minneapolis: Fortress, 1996), 179–87.

[11] Michele Murray, *Playing a Jewish Game: Gentile Christian Judaizing in the First and Second Centuries CE* (Waterloo: Wilfred Laurier University Press, 2004), 11–21.

guardians and trustees until the date set by the father. So with us; while we were minors, we were enslaved [δεδουλωμένοι] to the elemental spirits of the world [τὰ στοιχεῖα τοῦ κόσμου]. But when the fullness of time had come, God sent his Son, born of a woman, born under the law, in order to redeem those who were under the law, so that we might receive adoption as children [τὴν υἱοθεσίαν ἀπολάβωμεν]. And because you are children [υἱοί], God has sent the Spirit of his Son into our hearts, crying, "Abba! Father!" So you are no longer a slave but a child, and if a child then also an heir, through God [ὥστε οὐκέτι εἶ δοῦλος ἀλλὰ υἱός· εἰ δὲ υἱός, καὶ κληρονόμος διὰ θεοῦ].

This text contains several difficulties. What does Paul mean by τὰ στοιχεῖα τοῦ κόσμου, here translated as "the elemental spirits of the world"? Furthermore, is Paul actually saying that the people of Israel have only in Christ been adopted as children? This would be quite surprising, since the child-parent relation is commonly used for describing the sometimes complicated, relation between God and Israel, or between the individual and God, in the Hebrew Bible.[12] This, however, does not need to concern us here, but what is important to realize is that Paul's focus in Galatians is to prevent non-Jews from becoming Jews and/or observing the Torah. Paul's rhetorical strategy is to convince the Galatians that they have already achieved the highest status possible, without becoming Jews. As Christ-believing non-Jews, they are, in fact, like Jews in the eyes of God. From being without any hope of salvation, through Christ, they have become children of God.

The same kind of status elevation is seen in Paul's letter to Philemon. The slave Onesimus, who seems to have run away from his master, becomes a follower of Jesus and is referred to as "brother" by Paul. He is no longer a slave "but more than a slave, a beloved brother" (v. 16). That members of the nations are now "children of God," like Israel, and can be referred to as "brothers" and "sisters," implies that in Christ there is a new relation between the Jewish people and members of the nations. It should be noted, however, that Paul returns Onesimus to his rightful owner. Paul does not seem interested in revolutionizing every social relationship.

EQUAL STANDING BEFORE GOD

In my view, what makes Paul a radical thinker is his idea of how Jews and non-Jews should interact socially. We need to appreciate that non-Jews in general were considered morally impure because of their involvement in Greco-Roman cults. From a Jewish perspective, this was considered idolatry

---

[12] See e.g., Gen 14:1; Hos 1:10; 11:1; Jer 3:4, 19.

and social relations between Jews and non-Jews were subject to a variety of regulations in order to prevent Jews from becoming morally defiled. Paul, however, seems to argue that non-Jews, who have been freed from slavery to sin to become slaves of righteousness, who have been adopted into the family of Abraham through Christ, who have become children of God, can actually be trusted. Through the master-slave metaphor, and by arguing that non-Jews are adopted into the family of Abraham, Paul creates a completely new order where gender, ethnicity or social status become irrelevant for determining a person's relation to God.

This, I believe, is what Paul aims at in Galatians 3:28: "There is no longer Jew or Greek, there is no longer slave or free, there is no longer male and female; for all of you are one in Christ Jesus." Concentrating on slavery, we must conclude that Paul indeed recognizes the existence of this institution, and it would be a mistake to believe that he argues for its termination. Paul's revolutionary point is that from God's perspective, things are not what they seem to be. In Christ, gender, ethnicity or social status no longer matter because in Christ everyone is placed on an equal footing.[13]

To summarize: Paul uses the slave-master metaphor positively to make the case that no human being is free. God delivered the Israelites from slavery in Egypt so that they could become God's servants. They are also called God's children. In the same way, through Christ, God has delivered the nations from the bondage of sin, so that they can become slaves to righteousness. But they are actually more than slaves since they have been adopted into the family of Abraham and are also God's children and heirs to the blessing of Abraham. As a result, Jews and non-Jews are equal before the God of Israel. Together they are one in Christ. So far, Paul has not really dealt with slavery as such. The institution of slavery constitutes the background that gives meaning to the metaphor.

REMAIN IN YOUR CALLING

In 1 Corinthians 7:17–24, Paul actually deals with real slavery, among other things:

> Let each of you lead the life that the Lord has assigned, to which God called you. This is my rule in all the churches [ἐκκλησίαις]. Was anyone at the time of his call already circumcised? Let him not seek to remove the marks of circumcision. Was anyone at the time of his call uncircumcised? Let him not seek circumcision. Circumcision is nothing, and uncircumcision is nothing; but obeying the com-

---

[13] Cf. 1 Cor 12:13.

mandments of God is everything. Let each of you remain in the condition in which you were called. Were you a slave [δοῦλος] when called? Do not be concerned about it. Even if you can gain your freedom, make use [μᾶλλον χρῆσαι] of your present condition now more than ever. For whoever was called in the Lord as a slave is a freed person belonging to the Lord, just as whoever was free when called is a slave of Christ. You were bought with a price; do not become slaves of human masters. In whatever condition you were called, brothers and sisters, there remain with God.

In this section, Paul works with ideas that we find in other texts. Jews are to remain Jewish, non-Jews should not convert to Judaism. Since Jews and non-Jews are one in Christ, there is no reason for transcending ethnic borders. Then the issue of slaves is brought up. Paul's first advice is quite uncomplicated: slaves should not be concerned about being slaves. There is, however, a considerable debate on the meaning of the subsequent verse. The problem is that the object to the verb χράομαι, "make use of," is lacking and has to be supplemented from the context. Unfortunately, there are (at least) two possibilities: either Paul means that a slave should make use of the possibility of being manumitted, or he means the opposite—that the slave should make use of their present situation, i.e., remain in slavery. Both interpretations have their defenders,[14] and both are historically possible. Manumission of slaves was quite common, and relatively few spent their whole lives in slavery.[15]

Anthony Thiselton has suggested that Paul is deliberately ambiguous because he in fact wants to stress the importance of the present situation, whatever that may be.[16] Being a slave and a freed person can both be used in the service of God. A Christ-believing slave is in reality a slave of Christ but so is a free person who puts their trust in God. This would be in perfect accordance with Paul's way of reasoning in some of the other texts we have looked at.

Summary—Paul on slavery

It is fair to conclude that slavery is predominantly a positive metaphor in Paul. Stressing the "servant aspect" of the concept, he applies the term to himself. Paul is Christ's servant as Jesus is God's servant. Furthermore, Paul probably makes use of the Exodus motif in emphasizing that no hu-

---

[14] For an overview, see Thiselton, op. cit. (note 4), 553–59.

[15] Ibid., 564–65.

[16] Ibid., 560.

man is free. The decisive question is who one's master is. God saves the Israelites from slavery in Egypt so that they can be God's people and serve God instead of Pharaoh, a process that culminates at Sinai, where the Jewish people are given the Torah. We have noted that there is a certain confusion in the LXX's translation of Leviticus 25:55 between "slave" and "child." The people of Israel are indeed God's slaves, but they are also God's children or part of God's household.

Paul uses this slave–master metaphor to explain the new status of non-Jews who put their trust in Jesus-the-Messiah. They were formerly slaves to sin, which is a negative thing, but have become slaves of righteousness. In fact, they are more than slaves. Through Christ, non-Jews have been adopted into the family of Abraham. They have become children, or to be precise, "sons," meaning that they have become heirs. The fact that the nations have been brought into a covenantal relationship with the God of Israel significantly affects the relation between Jews and non-Jews. Where there was previously distrust and enmity, there is now friendship and trust. From God's perspective, Jews, Greeks, slaves, free, men and women are one in Christ.

As for the institution itself, Paul never questions its existence and seems indifferent to the possibility of a slave to be free. The important thing is to make the most of the present situation.

CONCLUDING DISCUSSION—PAUL'S HERMENEUTICS

The recent development in Pauline studies may help us analyze Paul's hermeneutical strategy. Over the last twenty years, Pauline studies have undergone a virtual revolution. Until the end of the 1970s, almost all scholars worked from the fundamental assumption that Paul opposed Judaism and especially the Torah. Ancient Judaism was believed to be a legalistic religion in which the individual strove to achieve righteousness through fulfilling empty commandments in the Torah. It can easily be shown that this view of ancient Judaism was heavily dependent on normative theology, especially the Protestant dichotomy between "law" and "grace" or "faith" and "deeds."[17] During the nineteenth century, normative theology and the incipient biblical scholarship merged and created a powerful frame for the interpretation of Paul, admittedly creating a fairly intelligible picture of his theology.

However, this view of Paul was almost entirely founded on the idea of Judaism as a legalistic religion. The traditional readings of Paul as a former

---

[17] On the development of Pauline studies, especially Paul's relation to Judaism, see Zetterholm, *Approaches to Paul,* op. cit. (note 8).

Jew, who come to realize that the Torah cannot bring life since no one can live up to God's demand for perfect Torah observance, in fact presumes that Judaism really was a religion of strict works righteousness. This view of ancient Judaism was severely challenged when E. P. Sanders published his monumental *Paul and Palestinian Judaism* (1977). Sanders read the ancient Jewish texts anew and reached a completely different conclusion than scholars before him. According to Sanders, Judaism was (and is) a religion of grace. God does indeed punish transgressions and rewards good deeds, but the Torah itself contains a system of reconciliation by which a broken relation between God and human beings can be restored. Judaism is hence a religion of grace and forgiveness and Jews do not observe the commandment of the Torah in order to earn their salvation, but to express their willingness to remain in a covenantal relation with the God of Israel.

This new view on ancient Judaism created significant problems for traditional Pauline scholarship. If Judaism was a religion of grace, characterized by forgiveness and love, what was it, in short, that Paul found wrong with it? From the beginning of the 1980s until now, Pauline scholars have struggled to understand Paul from the assumption that Judaism does not constitute a dark background to the incandescent Christianity, but as a living religion characterized by grace, forgiveness and love.

Today, an increasing number of scholars work on the hypothesis that Paul in fact was as Jewish as any Diaspora Jew. Accordingly, he observed the Torah and defined himself as a Jewish person. Paul never became a "Christian" simply because "Christianity" did not yet exist. Paul's "religion" was Judaism and his main concern was the Jewish idea of bringing the nations to the God of Israel. Paul thus writes to non-Jews about their relation to Judaism and to God and in so doing it seems clear that Paul creatively uses motifs and themes from his cultural context, as in the case of the master-slave metaphor we have studied in this essay. The fact that Paul can and, in my view, should be seen as a representative of first-century Judaism has interesting implications for how to understand what he is doing, for instance, with the social institution of slavery. Moreover, a Jewish Paul may provide contemporary theologians with creative tools for dealing with complicated texts.

Paul is evidently using one way of describing the relation between Israel and God—the slave-master relation—in order to describe a completely different relation, that between God and the nations. He has also, as we have hinted at, completely reinterpreted the role of Abraham in the history of salvation. What principles guided him and what was his view of the traditions he so creatively re-contextualized?

Regarding ancient Jewish biblical interpretation, James Kugel has suggested that "despite the great variety of styles and genres and even interpretive methods involved, underlying all is a common approach, a common set of assumptions concerning the biblical text."[18] First, the Bible is a cryptic document, meaning that the text has a deeper meaning. It may very well speak about X, but in reality it means Y. This may sound strange but when combined with the second assumption it actually makes sense; thus, secondly, the Bible is a book of instruction, i.e., it is a relevant text. For ancient Jewish biblical interpreters, the Bible was not predominantly a history book, but a text that spoke of present conditions. Thirdly, the biblical text is perfect and perfectly harmonious. This means that everything in the Bible is exactly the way God intended it to be. There are no superfluous repetitions and every detail is important. This is, lastly, because all of Scripture is divinely sanctioned and divinely inspired.[19]

An important effect of returning Paul to his Jewish context is the conclusion that, as a Jew, Paul undoubtedly shared the four fundamental assumptions of biblical interpretation as outlined by Kugel. We can see this when Paul uses elements from the Exodus story and reinterprets them to fit his present situation—non-Jews in slavery under sin. From Paul's perspective, the Exodus story and slavery have a deeper meaning pertaining to the contemporary situation. This interpretation of the text is divinely sanctioned. The same is true with regard to Abraham. Paul's reading of what he considers to be a divinely inspired text that speaks to his present situation, leads him to the conclusion that God intended non-Jews to be heirs to the promise of Abraham. Paul's hermeneutics is Jewish and offers a creative strategy also for contemporary Christianity to handle complicated biblical texts.

It should come as no surprise that the Bible advocates views on various issues—same-sex relationships, slavery, the role of women, to name a few—which many today find obsolete and even dangerous. Institutionalized slavery, which seems to have been taken for granted by Paul (and Jesus), is completely unacceptable, even repulsive, for every decent human being. However, if we take seriously the fact that Paul, and the early adherents to the Jesus movement were Jews, who had no intention of leaving Judaism, since they considered the belief in Jesus-the-Messiah to represent true Judaism, Jewish hermeneutical strategies could serve as guidelines for contemporary Christian biblical interpretation. Consequently, simply to adopt views found in the Bible on slavery, same sex-relations, gender or any other issue would, from Paul's perspective, be entirely "unbiblical," since for Paul and other Jews it was clear that the Holy Scriptures

---

[18] James L. Kugel, *The Bible as it Was* (Cambridge: Belknap Press of Cambridge University Press, 1997), 17.
[19] Ibid., 17-23.

had to be given new interpretations to match new circumstances, even if this new interpretation completely alters what appears to be the original meaning of the biblical text. A parable from the midrash *Seder Eliahu Zuta* 2 develops this idea:

> By what parable may the question [of the difference between Scripture and oral tradition] be answered? By the one of a mortal king who had two servants whom he loved with utter love. To one he gave a measure of wheat and to the other he gave a measure of wheat, to one a bundle of flax and to the other a bundle of flax. What did the clever one of the two do? He took the flax and wove it into a tablecloth. He took the wheat and made it into fine flour by sifting the grain first and grinding it. Then he kneaded the dough and baked it, set the loaf upon the table, spread the tablecloth over it, and kept it to await the coming of the king. But the foolish one of the two did not do anything at all. After a while the king came into his house and said to the two servants, "My sons, bring me what I gave you." One brought out the table with the loaf baked of fine flour on it, and with the tablecloth spread over it. And the other brought out his wheat in a basket with the bundle of flax over the wheat grains. What a shame! What a disgrace! Need it be asked which of the two servants was the more beloved? He, of course, who laid out the table with the loaf baked of fine flour upon it.[20]

According to this ideology, God expects human beings to partake in developing what has been revealed to them through Scripture, and the meaning of a given text can consequently change over time. For instance, it is not entirely clear whether or not the so-called *lex talionis* ("eye for an eye, a tooth for tooth")[21] was ever implemented literally,[22] but it is quite evident that the Rabbis reinterpreted the text to mean economic compensation.[23] From this perspective, also "complicated" texts, which reflect ideologies and moral values no longer acceptable in a post-Enlightenment world, are divinely sanctioned. They speak to the present situation and have a deeper meaning. The church's task is to find this deeper meaning that makes the text relevant in a present-day situation.

---

[20] Quoted from Karin Hedner Zetterholm, *Jewish Interpretation of the Bible: Ancient and Contemporary* (Minneapolis: Fortress, 2012), 5.

[21] Exodus 21:23–25; Leviticus 24:17–21; Deuteronomy 19:18–21.

[22] See the discussion in Umberto Cassuto, *A Commentary on the Book of Exodus* (Jerusalem: Magnes Press, 1983 [1967]), 275–78; J. Philip Hyatt, *Exodus* (Grand Rapids: Eerdmans, 1983 [1971]), 234.

[23] Hedner Zetterholm, op. cit. (note 20), 3–4.

READING PAULINE TEXTS AND CONTEXTS

Paul on Charismata (1 Corinthians 12-14): The Principles of Diversity and Community Edification

Rospita Deliana Siahaan

Introduction

In the past, speaking in tongues was largely confined to the Pentecostal churches; today, however, this is no longer the case. Because of the rapid growth of the charismatic movement in the 1960s, this phenomenon has spread not only to the Protestant churches—Presbyterian, Baptist and Lutheran—but also the Roman Catholic Church. Unfortunately, charismatic and non-charismatic churches often judge one another by pointing to particular biblical texts. Charismatics criticize non-charismatics for having no profound spiritual experience and no charismata, and this in turn is evidence for the lack of the Holy Spirit. Non-charismatics criticize charismatics for "disorderly" worship that is against the nature of God (cf. 1 Cor 14:33, 40) and too focused on personal experience (cf. 1 Cor 12:7; 14:4; 16-17, 27).[1]

Attacking one another on the basis of biblical texts is humiliating. Biblical texts can be ambiguous in how they point to the power of the Holy Spirit and pneumatic gifts. Therefore, despite the ambiguity of biblical perspectives, I shall look at 1 Corinthians 12-14, the longest passage that discusses charismata, in order to understand the way in which Paul argues:

---

[1] This phenomenon has also spread in Indonesia and Malaysia. Pdt. Dr. Darwin Lumbantobing, *Teologi di Pasar Bebas* (Pematangsiantar: L-SAPA, 2007), 177–236; Deshi Ramadhani, SJ, *Mungkinkah Karismatik Sungguh Katolik?: Sebuah Pencarian* (Yogyakarta: Kanisius, 2008). Wilfred J. Samuel, *Charismatic Folk Christianity: Reflection on Post Charismatic Trends,* revised edition (Sabah: Sabah Theological Seminary, 2013).

what does Paul actually say to the Corinthian congregation and what can his argument mean for Christian communities and churches today?

Paul and the problem in 1 Corinthians 12–14

Most scholars agree that in 1 Corinthians 12:1 (περὶ δὲ τῶν πνευματικῶν— concerning spiritual gifts), the Corinthians asked about spiritual gifts (cf. 7:1, 25; 8:1; 16:1, 12). However, regarding Corinthian worship practice, "Paul's answer is intended to be corrective, not instructional or informational."[2]

The Corinthians valued glossolalia much more than other charismata and used this as a status indicator of being truly spiritual. Those who spoke in tongues regarded themselves as truly spiritual people, and this boasting disrupted the unity of the congregation. Their high assessment of glossolalia led to abuse. The problem in chapter 12-14 is "the overvaluing and abuse of the gift of tongues."[3]

In order to overcome this problem, Paul does not question the authenticity of glossolalia as charisma. He acknowledges that it is truly a charisma which he himself possesses (14:18). However, Paul helps the Corinthians to understand that "the source and content of an utterance are all-important, not the fact of its inspiration."[4] Therefore, although speaking in tongues is more attractive due to its ecstatic and exalted nature, it is meaningless due to its unintelligibility unless it is interpreted. To achieve his aim of disallowing the Corinthians from speaking in tongues in public worship, he reveals to them the diversity and equal value of charismata and their function in terms of building community (1 Cor 12:4-7; 14:4, 5, 12, 26).

Charismata: diversity and equality

The structure of 1 Corinthians 12

In 1 Corinthians 12, Paul talks about the charismata by distinguishing them on the one hand, and by emphasizing their equal status on the other. This we see in the way in which the lists of charismata in 1 Corinthians

---

[2] Gordon D. Fee, *The First Epistle to the Corinthians*, The New International Commentary on the New Testament (Grand Rapids: Eerdmans, 1987), 570-71.

[3] Roy E. Ciampa and Brian S. Rosner, *The First Letter to the Corinthians*, The Pillar New Testament Commentary (Grand Rapids: Eerdmans and Nottingham: Apollos, 2010), 574.

[4] Frederick F. Bruce, *1 and 2 Corinthians*, New Century Bible Commentary (Grand Rapids: Eerdmans and London: Marshall, Morgan&Scott, 1971), 117.

12 are structured and by analyzing Paul's evaluative interpretation. In 12:12–13, Paul argues that the Spirit works not only through supernatural and ecstatic speech. The confession "Jesus is Lord" is spoken in a natural condition, but it is absolutely the work of the Holy Spirit. From this perspective, all believers are spiritual because all believers confess Jesus' lordship.[5] Verses 1–3 provide basic information about the Spirit's work as a starting point to talk about the special manifestations of the Spirit in charismata. In verses 4–6, Paul argues that the Spirit works through diversity and equality. There are many types of charismata, yet all of them come from the same source, the Spirit. For emphasis' sake, "varieties," διαιρέσεις and "the same," ὁ αὐτός are repeated in three consecutive verses with parallels both in terms of style and content.

The repetition of the word ὁ αὐτός when referring to the source of the diverse charismata (the same Spirit, the same Lord, and the same God) in verses 4–6 is Paul's rhetorical strategy to counteract the Corinthians' belief in the higher status of glossolalia. His point is that even though charismata are various, they come from the same source, and therefore have equal value; the sameness of the source implies sameness of status. This equality is emphasized even more strongly in 12:11 with the phrase τὸ ἓν καὶ τὸ αὐτὸ πνεῦμα "the one and the same Spirit." Adding the word "one" reinforces the sameness of the source.

Paul lists nine charismata in 12:7–11 and twice as many in 12:28–30 to explain that the Spirit grants particular charisma to particular people. The three lists vary in terms of numbers, order and form as can be seen in the table below:

12:8–10	12:28	12:29–30
utterance of wisdom	apostles	apostles
utterance of knowledge	prophets	prophets
faith	teachers	teachers
charismata of healing	deeds of power	work of miracles
working of miracles	charismata of healing	charismata of healing
prophecy	forms of assistance	speak in tongues
discernment of spirits	forms of leadership	interpretation
various kinds of tongues	various kinds of tongues	
interpretation of tongues		

Robertson and Plummer, like many other scholars, categorize the nine charismata in 12:8–10. First, those associated with intellect, then with faith

---

[5] David E. Garland, *1 Corinthians*, Baker Exegetical Commentary on the New Testament (Grand Rapids: Baker, 2003), 567.

and thereafter with glossolalia.[6] Likewise, but with a different structure, Ciampa and Rosner analyze the charismata in an A B A' B' order. That is A: speech (wisdom and knowledge); B: wonder (faith, healing, miraculous powers); A': speech, but more spectacular than A (prophecy, distinguishing of spirit): B': wonder, but more spectacular than B (glossolalia and its interpretation).[7] All efforts at categorizing are not successful because the categories overlap. A charisma that is categorized in a particular category can also belong to another category. "Distinguishing spirits" is an example: as a charisma it is characterized by faith according to Robertson and Plummer, but it also fits as a charisma characterized by intellect.[8]

The three lists contain both extraordinary and ordinary charismata without any hierarchy. This mixture suggests that, for Paul, a charisma that manifests itself in an extraordinary manner is no more special than a charisma that manifests itself in an ordinary manner. Paul never states which charismata are extraordinary and which are ordinary; it is the interpreters, not Paul, who claim such diverging levels. Paul's purpose in presenting the three lists is neither to make an exhaustive list nor a category or hierarchy of charismata. He just gives some examples to demonstrate that there are various charismata given by God to the church in order to support diversity. The divergent order and outline of charismata mentioned in all three lists specifically underline the multiplicity of charismata.

METAPHORICAL LANGUAGE

To reinforce his teaching about diversity and equality, Paul presents an analogy of the body, a very common analogy in his time (12:12–26).[9] The goal of this analogy is explicitly stated in 12:25 so "that there may be no dissension within the body, but the members may have the same care for one another." In the first small unit, 12:12–14, Paul "pictures the church

---

[6] Archibald Robertson and Alfred Plummer, *The First Epistle of St Paul to the Corinthians*, The International Critical Commentary (Edinburgh: T&T Clark, 1929), 265. Their analysis is based on the changing of ἄλλῳ to ἑτέρῳ in verses 9 and 10, by which ἑτέρῳ marks a new category.

[7] Ciampa and Rosner, op. cit. (note 3), 572-73.

[8] Donald A. Carson, *Showing the Spirit: A Theological Exposition 1 Corinthians 12-14* (Grand Rapids: Baker, 1987), 37.

[9] The fable of Menenius Agrippa (ca. 494 BC), recorded in Livy, *The Early History of Rome*, 2.32.9-12, transl. by Aubrey de Sélincourt with an introduction by R. M. Ogilvie (Middlesex, England: Penguin Books, 1971), 141-42; Margaret M. Mitchell, *Paul and the Rhetoric of Reconciliation: An Exegetical Investigation of the Language and Composition of 1 Corinthians* (Kentucky: Westminster/John Knox, 1993), 158, n. 557: Dio Chrysostom records a similar fable of Aesop.

not as a body of Christians but as the body of Christ. There is unity in plurality, but not uniformity. Individual integrity remains."[10] This analogy focuses on the affiliation of the church's members. In the second (12:15-20) and third (12:21-26) small units of the body metaphor, Paul develops his analogy by portraying some body parts as talking to another part. In the first picture, Paul presupposes that some members who feel inferior say to other parts that they are not an integral part of the body. In the second picture, Paul presupposes that some members who feel superior say to other parts that seem weaker that they do not need the weaker parts. Then, in each picture, Paul stresses that God designs the diversity among the members of the body (verses 18, 24).[11] The first picture serves to awaken those who feel inferior to the awareness that they make up the whole body. The second picture serves to awaken those who feel superior to the realization that they need others and, moreover, if they are indeed superior, they are actually responsible for showing more respect to those who are apparently inferior. Both pictures confirm that "diversity is necessary for a body to function, but the body is unified as each member is interrelated and interdependent."[12] Paul's ultimate purpose in this analogy is to negate division in the church by sustaining equality in honor and concern for all members of the body, regardless of their position or role.

Afterwards, Paul applies the body metaphor to the context of charismata using μή as rhetorical questions (vv. 29-31), which he answers with "no": not all are apostles; not all are prophets; etc. This is to reaffirm the argument in 12:28 and 12:7-11: each member has their own charisma; there is no uniform charisma in the church. As Herman Ridderbos rightly points out, "The general purport of the 'charismata chapter,' 1 Corinthians 12, is simply to reject any hierarchical distinction between what is to be valued in the gifts and service in the church as more and less 'pneumatic'."[13] Paul argues against hierarchies among the various charismata—all are to be accepted equally within the community. No charisma is more spiritual or more honorable than the others. Accordingly, just as the members of the body are interrelated and interdependent and cooperation is the condition for the body to remain healthy, various charismata should be interrelated and cooperate so that the church remains harmonious and united. According to Paul, diversity in harmony creates unity.

---

[10] Garland, op. cit. (note 5), 590.
[11] Ciampa and Rosner, op. cit. (note 3), 596-97.
[12] Garland, op. cit. (note 5), 588.
[13] Herman Ridderbos, *Paul: An Outline of His Theology* (Grand Rapids: Eerdmans, 1975), 442.

Charismata: Building up community—1 Corinthians 14 in its literary context

Ecclesiology is Paul's major concern in 1 Corinthians where he extensively discusses the church's life and unity. Of the 46 occurrences of *ekklēsia* in the undisputed Pauline letters, 22 are in 1 Corinthians with ten occurring in 1 Corinthians 12-14. In the context of chapters 12-14, Paul understands *ekklēsia* as the Corinthian assembly with the purpose of worship.

In chapter 13 Paul develops a "love" argument to "open[s] up the possibility of treating the spiritual phenomena ethically."[14] Closing chapter 12 with the statement to show a more excellent way, Paul opens chapter 13 by describing the fruitlessness of all abilities other than love. Glossolalia, prophecy, understanding of mystery and knowledge, faith to move mountains and even bodily sacrifice—all are in vain without love (13:1-3). Verses 4-7 reveal how love should be put into action in fifteen ways that portray various kinds of misconduct of the Corinthians; this description implies that the major matter in Corinthians is the lack of love.[15] Correctly Fee points out that "Paul sets out to put their zeal for tongues within a broader ethical context that will ultimately disallow un-interpreted tongues in the assembly. In chapter 14 love will be even more specified in terms of 'building up' the church."[16] The insufficiency of love causes them to seek only personal benefit. Practicing love, in contrast, will strengthen, unite and build up the community, and will thus be of benefit to it. However, Paul constructs 1 Corinthians 14 with a "community up building"[17] argument (14:26-40), where knowing/understanding is the primary condition (14:6-25). Paul's aim in this chapter is to reject considering speaking in tongues as the higher status charisma and to persuade the Corinthians to practice prophecy for the sake of edification instead of speaking in tongues.

Already in 12:7 Paul described the edifying function of charismata by defining charismata as a common good. Paul's clarity about the interdependence and equality of all community members forces them to be involved in the project of ecclesial edification. In chapter 14, Paul returns to this thought (verses 1-5).[18] Therefore Paul prioritizes prophecy over

---

[14] Oda Wischmeyer, "1 Corinthians," in Oda Wischmeyer (ed.), *Paul: Life, Setting, Work, Letters* (London and New York: T&T Clark, 2012), 167.

[15] Garland, op. cit. (note 5), 607.

[16] Fee, op. cit. (note 2), 627.

[17] Up building (οἰκοδομή, οἰκοδομέω) occurs 7 times, along with 9 occurrences of *ekklēsia*, in 1 Corinthians 14.

[18] The first three occurrences of "church" in chapter 14 are alongside "up building" within the same verse: "but those who prophesy build up the church" (verse 4b); "[...] One who prophesies is greater than one who speaks in tongues, unless

glossolalia: prophecy can edify the community while glossolalia only edifies the (individual) speaker, not the community. Paul's argument refers to the criterion of understanding: understandable words are the condition for community edification with regard to speaking in public worship. For the sake of edification, the Spirit works through the human mind to foster understanding. The mind yields understanding, and understanding yields edification, particularly in congregational meetings. This is precisely in line with the basic understanding of the Spirit that it is not all about ecstatic experience and power—as in glossolalia—but about the presence of God in the Spirit's deed.[19]

Paul gives three arguments for this (14:6-25). The first argument is based on the analogies of three musical instruments and a foreign language. It is fruitless to play musical instruments and to speak in a foreign language when no one understands (14:6-13). The second argument is that although Paul himself could speak in tongues, he chose not to do this in church (14:14-19). The last and most authoritative argument, the argument from Jewish Scripture, is that glossolalia produces alienation and drives outsiders away and, conversely, prophecy produces repentance and draws in outsiders (14:20-25). As a last step (14:26-40), Paul gives practical guidelines in communal worship about practicing speaking in tongues and prophecy and women's participation (14:27-36). Within the framework of public worship these practical guidelines serve for the mutual "building up" (14:26) of community and "all things should be done decently and in order" (14:40) .

The emphasis on the need of understanding for mutual benefit does not suggest that Paul ignores the importance of emotions or spiritual experience in worshipping God. He recognizes the importance of both mind and spirit (1 Cor 14:15). "Paul is, of course, not a philosopher who conceives of the spiritual life as a rational comprehension of the truth. He desires his converts to be emotionally gripped by the truth of the gospel; but the path to the emotions is through the mind, not around it."[20] To worship God implies not only worshipping with mind, nor only with spirit; both are needed.

Let us finally briefly look at 1 Corinthians 8-10 where Paul has already discussed the need of ecclesial edification. Paul presents the argument

---

someone interprets, so that the church may be built up" (verse 5b); "[...] strive to excel in them for building up the church" (verse 12b). The first two verses explicitly state that the church up-building is carried out by prophecy and not by glossolalia.
[19] Joseph A. Fitzmyer, *First Corinthians*, The Anchor Yale Bible, vol. 32 (New Haven and London: Yale University, 2008), 80.
[20] Thomas R. Schreiner, *Paul, Apostle of God's Glory in Christ: A Pauline Theology* (Illinois: InterVarsity Press and Leicester: Apollos, 2001), 353, 355.

of the responsibility of all community members in 1 Corinthians 8 and 10 to build up the community when he deals with eating sacrificed food. The argument of ecclesial edification is thus not only applied to worship activity but also to an ethical attitude in practical life. Accordingly, the function of understanding and knowing is valued differently than in 1 Corinthians 14: since it is on the basis of knowledge that the strong eat the sacrificed meat without regarding the weak, knowing alone can lead to the careless attitude of betraying community edification.[21] Even though Paul strengthens those who know that idols do not exist, their behavior is regarded critically: since they do not prioritize ecclesial edification they should not depend only on that knowledge but, rather, care for the mutual edification of the community. In conclusion, Paul urges them not to eat the sacrificed food for the sake of the weak, which is for the sake of the community's common edification (8:1; 10:23).

MARTIN LUTHER'S INTERPRETATION OF 1 CORINTHIANS 12–14

Although there is no special lecture or sermon on 1 Corinthians 12-14, Luther acknowledged and stressed the diversity of charismata as the work of the Holy Spirit and the importance of accepting this diversity. In his discussion on the fingers of the Lord in creating the sky, the moon and stars in Psalms 8:3, he applied Psalms 8:3 to charismata where he defines the fingers as the Holy Spirit. The plural form, "fingers" does not refer to the plurality of the Spirit, but the Spirit's manifestation in charismata.[22] He also applied the royal opulence and fragrance in Psalm 45:8-9 to the diverse charismata in 1 Corinthians 12:8, 4 and Romans 12:6. Luther claimed that the various charismata are God's ornaments that "spread the loveliest fragrance" in the world; this serves to spread the gospel.[23] Further, in his discussion on embroidered garments in Psalms 45:14, Luther underscores that no part of the body can be another part; no one can have all the diverse charismata. Using the body metaphor in 1 Corinthians 12:14ff., he criticizes those who wanted to be everything. He also refers to Ephesians 4:11 and 1 Corinthians 12:8ff. to state that the Spirit bestows different charismata to different people. Accepting this diversity will prevent disunity and result in harmony.[24]

---

[21] Josef Pfammatter, "οἰκοδομέω," in Horst Balz and Gerhard Schneider (eds), *Exegetical Dictionary of the New Testament*, vol. 2 (Grand Rapids: Eerdmans, 1991), 497.

[22] *LW* 12, 118.

[23] Ibid., 250.

[24] Ibid., 294-95.

Luther's understanding of the diversity of charismata shows us retrospectively how Paul's approach to the topic has helped much later interpreters to look at the diversity and unity of pneumatic gifts. What did Paul achieve? In 1 Corinthians, Paul's main focus is on ecclesiology. Particularly in chapters 12-14, Paul highlights how the church should not be split because of the practice of charismata. Paul emphasizes that the diverse charismata come from the same spirit and, therefore, each charisma has the same value, regardless of whether it is ordinary or extraordinary. The decisive criterion is that charismata are to be regarded as spiritual gifts when they are practiced with love to build up the congregation. As Paul sees it, charismata should have a unifying rather than a separating effect on community life.

In the light of Luther's interpretation of charismata, what can Paul's argument in 1 Corinthians 12-14 mean in practice for life in contemporary Christian communities? If we apply the Pauline hermeneutics of diversifying and evaluating charismata to our present time, as Luther did, we might reach the following conclusion: churches should not judge each other in terms of practicing charismata. Different churches may have and practice different charismata. While it is up to the churches and communities to choose how they want to celebrate their worship, it is definitely not up to them whether or not they want to practice love and community edification. The commitment to ecumenism serves the global project of edifying the Christian *ekklēsia*. Accordingly, diverse churches and Christian communities have to respect differences and accept each other, including the practice of spiritual gifts and inspiration. While diversity is allowed and needed, love, mutual edification and church unity are the undisputed and indisputable values of unifying churches and communities. This is why for Paul agape is the highest hermeneutical principle in all kinds of ecclesial debates.

CREATION AND RECONCILIATION IN 2 CORINTHIANS 5: IMPULSES FROM PAUL AND LUTHER

Roger Marcel Wanke

INTRODUCTION

Creation and reconciliation are central themes of Christian theology. In contexts of prevailing chaos, where rivalry and enmity dominate inter-personal relationships, it becomes increasingly necessary to speak about creation and reconciliation. This has been so throughout the biblical and different ecclesial traditions. In postmodernity, speaking about creation and reconciliation provides important impulses for living in and preserv-ing the world created by God and to promoting reconciliation.

In this article, I shall outline what the biblical tradition, especially Paul, teaches us about creation and reconciliation. I shall furthermore reflect on the church's and theology's responsibility in this world, namely to see, judge and act there where creation and reconciliation are being threatened. Finally, I shall present challenges and perspectives to bring hope to the world and to the human being created and reconciled to God in Jesus Christ.

CREATION AND RECONCILIATION IN 2 CORINTHIANS 5

Paul, and to an even lesser extent Luther,[1] speaks very little about reconciliation in his letters, even if we take the discussion in the deutero-Pauline Epistles

---

[1] Martin Luther, *WA* DB 7, 138-39; *LW* 35, 380-83. Among Luther's writings we only find the lectures on 1 Corinthians 7 (*WA* 12, 94-142; *LW* 28, 5-56] and on 1

into consideration. In his preface to the second letter to the Corinthians (1546), Luther compares Paul's two letters to the community at Corinth. In the first epistle, says Luther, Paul is hard and censures the community by applying bitter wine onto the wounds. But, already in 2 Corinthians, Paul proves himself to be a comforting preacher, one who also applies oil to wounds. Luther does not specifically mention the content of 2 Corinthians 5 but, from the reference to oil onto wounds, we can deduce that he refers to Paul's efforts to reconcile himself with the Corinthian community, which is in a state of crisis. The reason for this crisis in the relationship between Paul and the Corinthians was the fact that the legitimacy and essence of the apostle's ministry had been questioned. A member of the community must have challenged Paul and become the leader of a group opposed to Paul's authority (cf. 2 Cor 5-6).[2] After visiting the community in order to try to resolve the situation, Paul decided to retire and write a letter of apology, urging the Corinthians to be reconciled to him (letter of apology, 2 Cor 1:4-7:4). The main topic of the letter is Paul's apostolic life.[3] It is interesting that Paul identifies himself with Jesus by referring to glory (2 Cor 3:7-4:6) and suffering (2 Cor 4:7-5:10), which are part of the apostolic ministry. For Paul, the realities of the crucified and resurrected are paradoxical characteristics of apostolic life; in other words, the tension between weakness and strength. Paul knows that he is called by God (2 Cor 2:16; 3:5) to proclaim the message of reconciliation (2 Cor 5:11-21). He is convinced that the apostolic ministry is part of God's reconciliation in Jesus Christ. If he can be considered an ambassador of reconciliation, then to accept reconciliation with God is to accept Paul's ministry. Comblin suggests that here Paul refers to the doctrine of reconciliation and applies it practically to his relationship with the Corinthian community. He states that "[t]he reconciliation with God implies reconciliation with Paul."[4] Despite the discussion about its appearance,[5]

Corinthians 15 (*WA* 36, 478-696; *LW* 28, 59-213).

[2] About Paul's opponents in Corinth, cf. Hans-Josef Klauck, *2. Korintherbrief*, Die Neue Echter Bibel: Kommentar zum Neuen Testament (Würzburg: Echter, 1988), 10-12; José Comblin, *Segunda Epístola aos Coríntios* (Petrópolis: Vozes; São Paulo: Imprensa Metodista; São Leopoldo: Sinodal, 1991), 18.

[3] Udo Schnelle, *Einleitung in das Neue Testament*, 6th edition, UTB 1830 (Göttingen: Vandenhoeck & Ruprecht, 2007), 107.

[4] Comblin, op. cit. (note 2), 91-93.

[5] 2 Corinthians is marked by various literary problems. Already Semler (1725-1791) is of the opinion that this letter is in truth a compilation of several distinct parts, written at different times [*Teilungshypothese*]. Cf. Christian Wolff, *Der zweite Brief des Paulus an die Korinther*, Theologischer Handkommentar zum Neuen Testament (Leipzig: Evangelische Verlagsanstalt, 1989), 1-3; Comblin, op. cit. (note 2), 13-18; Colin Kruse, *II Coríntios: Introdução e Comentário* (São Paulo: Vida Nova, 1994), 29-58. Trends in recent research presented by Schnelle continue to point to sev-

the letter can basically be divided into five parts: (a) prologue (2 Cor 1:1–11); (b) defending his ministry (2 Cor 1:12–7:16); (c) the offer to the community of Jerusalem (2 Cor 8:1–9:15); (d) defending his ministry (2 Cor 10:1–13:10); (e) epilogue (2 Cor 13:11–13). There is general agreement that the block within which the pericope is located (2 Cor 2:14–7:4) is cohesive and constitutes a literary unit. In the following, I will focus on verses 7–21 because they are key with regard to the context of 2 Corinthians 5.

CREATION: BE A NEW CREATURE IN CHRIST

Creation and new creation are not main themes in the Bible but act as a framework for the Bible as a whole. Therefore, to speak about a theology of creation, especially in the Old Testament, is, in the words of Gerhard von Rad, to speak of its importance as a servant of the history of salvation.[6] Both the Jewish and the Christian Bible start with creation. In the Bible, confessing a creator God must be understood as a consequence of a redeeming God. In the Old Testament, for example, creation is resorted to in situations of crisis.[7] The use of motifs from a theology of creation is understood as a "symbol of trust in lament" [*Vertrauensmotiv in der Klage*]. [8] God intervenes in creation and history to save human beings.[9]

Unlike the Old Testament, creation does not have a prominent place in the New Testament, but that does not make it irrelevant. On the contrary, all

---

eral distinct letters, which form the second letter of Paul to the Corinthians. Cf. Schnelle, op. cit. (note 3), 96–104; 108–109.

[6] Gerhard von Rad, "Das theologische Problem des alttestamentlichen Schöpfungsglaubens," in Gerhard von Rad, *Gesammelte Studien zum Alten Testament*, TB 8 (München: Chr. Kaiser Verlag,[2] 1958), 136–47.

[7] Hans J. Boecker, *Das Lob des Schöpfers in den Psalmen* (Neukirchen-Vluyn: Neukirchener, 2008), 22–24. Cf. also Othmar Keel and Silvia Schroer, *Schöpfung: Biblische Theologien im Kontext altorientalischer Religionen* (Göttingen: Vandenhoeck & Ruprecht, 2002).

[8] Otto Kaiser, *Der Gott des Alten Testaments. Wesen und Wirken. Theologie des Alten Testaments*, vol. 2: *Jahwe, der Gott Israels. Schöpfer der Welt und des Menschen* (Göttingen: Vandenhoeck & Ruprecht, 1998), 210ff.

[9] Especially Deutero-Isaiah and the Psalmen point to this issue. Already the Book of Job presents an inverted use of the theology of creation. Cf. Roger M. Wanke, *Praesentia Dei. Die Vorstellungen von der Gegenwart Gottes im Hiobbuch*, BZAW 421 (Berlin/Boston: de Gruyter, 2013), 217–31, "Die Beschreibung der Macht Gottes in der Schöpfung dient als Rahmen für die Verzweiflung Hiobs. Gott ist Hiob durch seinen Zorn so nah und so zur Bedrohung geworden, dass er sich von Hiob entfernt und entfremdet hat. Hiob hat keinen Rettergott gefunden, und der Schöpfergott will ihn als zorniger Gott zerstören," 231.

New Testament texts assume that the world is God's creation. What is new, however, is that the New Testament speaks of creation as a matter related to Christology (Jn 1:1-3; Col 1:15-17; Heb 1:2). This is evident in verse 17 in which Paul approaches the concept of the new creation from the prophetic tradition, especially the school of Isaiah (cf. Isa 65:17; 66:22) and the apocalyptic tradition. The cosmic dimension of a new heaven and a new earth is now presented as a reality. For Paul, the new creature is defined as being in Christ, that is, anchored in Christ's death and resurrection. Within the context of the letter, the concept of a new creation is directly related to the new covenant (3:6), with the daily renewal of the inner person (4:16) and the size of the image of Christ reflecting the glory of God (4:4). In this context, the new creature in Christ has its own image, which had been lost by sin, restored. God's creative power is manifested in us (4:6), for just as God said, "Let there be light," God makes God's glory shine in us through Christ.

Reconciliation: Be reconciled through Christ

Contrary to what one might think, there are only few references to the concept of reconciliation in the New Testament. In those of Paul's letters that are considered authentic, God's salvific action in Jesus Christ is described as reconciliation in two passages only: 2 Corinthians 5:18-20 and Romans 5:10-11. In the context of the deutero-Pauline Epistles, the Pauline concept of reconciliation appears in Colossians 1:20-22 and Ephesians 2:16.[10] Two things attract our attention in this text: first, when referring to reconciliation, Paul did not use religious terminology but drew on terminology from Hellenistic diplomacy.[11] In the Hellenistic context, the noun [καταλλαγή] and the verb [καταλλάσσω] are used to talk about the resolution of conflict between people or nations. Although Paul's terminology has no religious background, his argument points to the religious aspect. While Paul presents God's reconciliation in terms of human reconciliation, the basis is entirely theological. I agree with Hofius, who connects Paul's concept of reconciliation more closely to Isaiah 53.[12] The other interesting aspect

---

[10] James D. G. Dunn, *The Theology of Paul the Apostle* (Edinburgh: T&T Clark, 1998), 228-29; Otfried Hofius, *Paulusstudien* (Tübingen: Mohr, 1989), 1.

[11] There has been a lengthy discussion about the background to the history of the tradition of Paul's concept of reconciliation. Cf. Hofius, ibid., 9-14; Wolff, op. cit. (note 5), 133-37; Ralph Martin, *2 Corinthians* (Waco: Word Books, 1986), 146-47.

[12] Hofius, op. cit. (note 10), 11-14; Cf. Nikolaus Walter, "Alttestamentliche Bezüge in christologischer Ausführungen des Paulus," in Udo Schnelle (ed.), *Paulinische Christologie: Exegetische Beiträge. Hans Hübner zum 70. Geburtstag* (Göttingen: Vandenhoeck & Ruprecht, 2000), 246-71.

of this text is the eschatological background to Paul's discussion from the beginning of chapter 5. The resurrection of the dead is a central theme in Paul's two letters to the Corinthians (cf. 1 Cor 15; 2 Cor 5). It underlies the new creation as well as the reconciliation of human beings. Both his ministry as well as his relationship with the community of Corinth are seen in light of the resurrection and God's judgment (cf. 1 Cor 15:56-57; 2 Cor 5:11-21). Let us now briefly look at some aspects of verses 18-21 in order better to understand Paul's concept of reconciliation.

As we have seen, in verse 17 Paul's approach to reconciliation is based on the new eschatological reality of the believer as a new creature in Christ. In verse 18 he shows how this reconciliation takes place. For Schnelle, Paul develops his concept of reconciliation both theologically and christologically. For him, "all this is from God" and reconciliation happens "through Christ."[13] The forgiveness of sins and reconciliation are God's initiative through God's act in Christ. The new life of the human being in Christ and reconciled through Christ is the work and gift of God.[14] In Romans 5:10, Paul refers to the human being, thought to be the actual goal of God's reconciliation, as the enemy of God. According to Hofius, this expression appears along with other similar terms such as impiousness (v. 6) and sinfulness (v. 8), human acts of rebellion against God to end their relationship with God.[15]

While in verse 18 Paul highlights the personal and individual aspect of reconciliation, in verse 19 he broadens his approach. Through Christ, God reconciled the world. As Comblin states, "Our reconciliation is part of a general reconciliation that involves the whole world. The world is the totality of being involved in the relationship between God and humanity."[16] There is general agreement on the existing parallels between verses 18 and 19:[17] Paul did not only have the reconciliation of human beings in mind but, in light of the fall of the human being (Gen 3), speaks of a new creation in Christ as something that includes the universe as a whole. If "all this is from God," then "all things" are in the process of being reconciled through the cross of Christ.

In verse 20, Paul realizes his concept of reconciliation, taking up what had already been said in verse 18 about the ministry of reconciliation. Being part of the new creation shaped by Christ means to be restored from the old

---

[13] Udo Schnelle, *Theologie des Neuen Testaments*, UTB 2917 (Göttingen: Vandenhoeck & Ruprecht, 2007), 231.

[14] Hofius, op. cit. (note 10), 2.

[15] Ibid., 4.

[16] Comblin, op. cit (note 2), 92.

[17] David Turner, "Paul and the Ministry of Reconciliation in 2 Cor 5:11-6:2," in *Criswell Theological Review* 4.1 (1989), 84-85.

creation, ruined by the fall of Adam, through God. For Schnelle, God founded the office of reconciliation on the act of reconciliation [*Amt der Versöhnung*]. "The act of reconciliation on the cross enables the announcing of the message of reconciliation. At the same time, reconciliation with God takes place and the Word is present in the salvific event."[18] Schnelle understands that Paul connects the Word of God on the cross with the apostolic message of reconciliation.[19] Thus, Paul presents himself as Christ's ambassador, the logical and practical consequence of being a new creature in Christ and reconciled with him.

Finally, in verse 21, Paul grounds theologically how reconciliation promoted by God happens in Christ. "For our sake he made him to be sin who knew no sin, so that in him we might become the righteousness of God." Here Paul once again alludes to the image of the suffering servant of Isaiah 53,[20] describing Jesus Christ as the one who knew no sin. Paul identifies a parallelism in their arguments: God made Christ sin and made us the righteousness of God. Paul, therefore, says that God reverses the retributive logic of reconciliation. The price we should pay, Jesus has already paid for us (cf. Rom 3:21-26; Phil 3:7-9; Isa 53:4-6, 12).

THE RELATIONSHIP BETWEEN CREATION AND RECONCILIATION: GOD WAS IN CHRIST

For Paul, creation and reconciliation are connected; they are distinct, but related and based on Christology. To be in Christ is a reality, both of the new creation as well as for reconciliation. For God was in Christ reconciled to the world and human beings (v. 18) and anyone who is in Christ is a new creature (v. 17). Thus, God's being in Christ is crucial for the human being's being in Christ. For Niebuhr, "the message of the death and resurrection of Jesus is God's call to accept reconciliation. Thus, believers participate in the consummation of creation (5:17)."[21]

Udo Schnelle briefly compares 2 Corinthians 5 and Romans 5 and points to four Pauline settings for reconciliation and their relationship to the new

---

[18] Schnelle, op. cit. (note 3), 7: "Die Versöhnungstat am Kreuz ermöglicht die Verkündigung der Versöhnungsbotschaft, zugleich ereignet sich in dieser Verkündigung die Versöhnung mit Gott, im Wort ist das Heilsgeschehen present."

[19] Ibid., 107.

[20] Paul's intertextual dialogue with Isaiah 53 is identified by many scholars. Cf. Kruse, op. cit. (note 5), 137-38; Martin, op. cit. (note 11), 157.

[21] Karl-Wilhelm Niebuhr, "Die Korintherbriefe," in Karl-Wilhelm Niebuhr (ed.) *Grundinformation Neues Testament: Eine Bibelkundlich-theologische Einführung*, UTB 2108, 3rd edition (Göttingen: Vandenhoeck & Ruprecht, 2008), 235.

creation.[22] First, reconciliation is only an act of God, who is both the subject and object of reconciliation; second, reconciliation is an event of universal peace, because it is not restricted to the Jew or Christian, but reaches all of humanity within creation; third, reconciliation happens concretely in the acceptance of the gospel message of reconciliation; and, finally, this acceptance transforms the human being as a whole. Therefore, it can be a new creature. Schnelle's four considerations help us to understand how the relationship between creation and reconciliation is understood in Paul. It is interesting to note that various Protestant scholars[23] interpret Paul's concept of reconciliation in its relationship with creation, making use of Luther's formulation of the "joyous exchange."[24] Jesus took away the sin and the sinner receives the righteousness of God.

It is worth remembering that in Luther's lecture on Genesis[25] creation is always related to reconciliation. For him, being created in the image and likeness of God is related to God's righteousness, that is, to full communion with God and complete obedience to God, for which the human being was created.[26] Interestingly, Luther mixes the reality of sin and the need for reconciliation and justification already in the interpretation of Genesis 1 and 2, that is, before the biblical account of the fall. While he states that this image of God in the human being is totally corrupted by original sin, he states categorically that:

> But now the Gospel has brought about the restoration of that image [.] And so the Gospel brings it about that we are formed once more according to that familiar and indeed better image, because we are born again into eternal life or rather into the hope of eternal life by faith, that we may live in God and with God and be one with Him, as Christ says. And indeed, we are reborn not only for life but also for righteousness, because faith acquires Christ's merit and knows that through Christ's death we have been set free.[27]

---

[22] Schnelle, op. cit. (note 13), 232.

[23] Cf. Hofius, op. cit. (note 10), 5.

[24] WA 31/II, 435, 11; 40/I, 443, 23. Cf. Philip S. Watson, *Um Gottes Gottheit–"Let God be God." Eine Einführung in Luthers Theologie*, 2nd edition (Berlin: Lutherisches Verlagshaus, 1967), 141–66.

[25] WA 42–44; *LW* 1.

[26] *LW* 1, 55–68. Cf. Bengt Hägglund, "Luthers Anthropologie," in Helmer Junghans (ed.) *Leben und Werk Martin Luthers von 1526 bis 1546. Festgabe zu seinem 500. Geburtstag*, vol. 1 (Leipzig: Evangelische Verlaganstalt, 1983), 70–71; Roger M. Wanke, "Antropologia em Lutero a partir de sua preleção de Gênesis," in Paulo Buss (ed.) *Lutero e a Antropologia: Potencialidades e Limites*, 6º Simpósio Internacional de Lutero (São Leopoldo: Concórdia, forthcoming).

[27] *LW* 1, 64.

For Luther, turning away from God constitutes sin. The transgression of the divine commandment (Gen 2:17) leads to the destruction of spiritual life.

THE CHURCH AND THEOLOGY: RESPONSIBLE FOR A NEW AND RECONCILED WORLD

As we have seen, in biblical and theological terms, creation and reconciliation are God's works for humanity. This is a crucial message for a world guided by the principles of autonomy and self-sufficiency. Human beings, who especially in today's postmodern world are accustomed to being the subject and protagonist of their actions and to boast of them, are powerless in the face of creation and reconciliation. The church must always remember that it is not the church that reconciles the world, even if human beings appear as creators and cocreators and agents of reconciliation in interpersonal relationships. What we usually forget is that this is just the result of God's action in us in the first place. This is the great discovery that we can make in 2 Corinthians 5:17–21. God is the subject of creation and reconciliation, but calls the church in God's name to announce it to the world.

This has concrete implications for the church's role in today's global context: reconciliation becomes a permanent task for the church in the world. The church neither owes its existence to itself nor exists for itself. The church has a task defined by the Lord: to proclaim the message of reconciliation. This includes the call to faith, not as an order, but a plea. In view of 2 Corinthians, the church's task of reconciliation can be deduced on two fronts: a homiletic-missionary task and a diaconal one. These two tasks are not mutually exclusive, but complement each other, because the word of reconciliation and the ministry of reconciliation belong to the same definitive saving action of God in Christ in favor of the human being and, therefore, the world. Only the church has a message: it takes the human being beyond the reality of suffering and death by announcing the reconciliation through the death of Jesus and the new creation through his resurrection. Paul had an eternal rather than a temporal perspective and taught the communities to do the same. Those who believe in eternal life can engage themselves for the world. When Paul says that God has given to him the ministry of reconciliation, he intends to act as a preacher of peace (cf. Ralph Martin).[28] Those who proclaim forgiveness have the duty to denounce sin. In his interpretation of Genesis 3, Luther affirms that "the

---

[28] Martin, op. cit. (note 11), 155.

more you minimize sin, the more will grace decline in value."[29] Therefore, sin, as we know, is much more than a social or moral dilemma or a wrong choice that has been made. The Lutheran church is known worldwide as the church of the word. This word is the word of forgiveness, reconciliation and the promotion of the new creation in Christ. This preaching should be echoed in concrete situations. For Comblin, "the gospel is far from forgetting the concrete reality of human beings."[30] The proclamation of the gospel is always in service to the human being and the world. If the Lutheran Reformation is to have any meaning and to have made a contribution to the world, then here, in Paul's words in 2 Corinthians 5, it finds its foundation and strength.

THE HOPE BEFORE THE CROSS: FURTHER PERSPECTIVES

If Lutheran theology is essentially a theology of the cross then Luther's hermeneutics could not have another point of departure or arrival. Luther teaches us not only to interpret the biblical text in light of the cross, but also the reality in which we live. Therefore, Lutheran theology provides an answer for this world. It takes its point of departure in the word and ministry of reconciliation. The message of reconciliation invites the human being to the cross. Through the resurrection of Christ the human being is given new life. Not only is Luther's theology a theology of the cross but his anthropology also is an anthropology of the cross. Therefore, speaking of the relationship between creation and reconciliation is to speak of the hope that the human being and this world have before God, their creator and redeemer.

The gospel testifies to the power of God and proclaims the good news. The message is powerful (Rom 1:16-17). It proclaims the reconciliation of God in Jesus Christ to the world—a reconciliation of cosmic dimensions since it includes the whole reality of creation. But the modern concept of autonomy has led human beings to the postmodern concept of individualism. Recently Euler R. Westphal said that "in postmodernity dehumanization is seen as an expression of humanism."[31] Unfortunately, postmodernity can be described as a post-Christian era.[32] While the world asks, Where it God?,

---

[29] *LW* 1, 142.

[30] Comblin, op. cit. (note 2), 27.

[31] Euler R. Westphal, "A Pós-modernidade e as verdades universais: a desconstrução dos vínculos e a descoberta da alteridade," in Nadja de Carvalho Lama e Taiza Mara Raeun (eds), *(Pro)Posições Culturais* (Joinville: Univille, 2010), 16.

[32] Cf. Westphal, ibid.; Gianni Vattimo, *Depois da Cristandade: Por um cristianismo não religioso* (Rio de Janeiro; São Paulo: Record, 2004).

it also claims that God is dead. This has led to feelings of abandonment, loneliness and depression and the world also asks, Where is the human being? Dietrich Bonhoeffer said that the human being needs communion.[33] Communion presupposes reconciliation; this has anthropological implications. Anthropology today is one of the most developed sciences.[34] Why, then, do human beings keep asking the question about God and themselves and do not seem to find an answer? We are living in an anthropological aporia *ad absurdum*. Human beings want to solve their problems by severing their relationships; these are not long lasting and it is easy to disconnect. The human being has become a commodity. Modern science defines the human being as useful and useless, claiming its independence from morality and external regulations in order to control scientific practices.[35] Not least, this anthropological aporia manifests itself, when the human being is affected by the reality of suffering.[36] Which anthropological concept provides the minimum conditions for human beings to be what they are in the world in which they live?

Christian theology proclaims the gospel to all humankind. How can we be agents of reconciliation in a hostile world? This has practical pastoral implications. Providing pastoral care in a world marked by suffering may be one of the greatest challenges the church faces today. Brakemeier suggests that there are three possibilities for ending conflict in the world and promoting reconciliation, but that only one of them is an effective means of reconciliation. Crime, conflict and retribution are ineffective means of reconciliation and contrary to the gospel and "sin is not eliminated through a 'blackout' as the suppression of memory and retribution does not repair but causes a new wound, crying out for revenge."[37] Sin cannot be solved at the social or psychological level because it is not in essence a

---

[33] Dietrich Bonhoeffer, *Life Together and Prayer Book of the Bible*, Dietrich Bonhoeffer's Works, vol. 5, ed. by James H. Burtness and Geffrey B. Kelly (Minneapolis: Augsburg Fortress Publishers, 2004).

[34] Cf. Gerald Krughöffer, *Der Mensch–Das Bild Gottes*, Biblische-theologische Schwerpunkte, vol. 16 (Göttingen: Vandenhoeck & Ruprecht, 1999), 13.

[35] Cf. Euler R. Westphal, *Ciência e Bioética: Um olhar teológico* (São Leopoldo: Sinodal, 2009), 22–36, 82; Euler R. Westphal, *Bioética* [Série para entender] (São Leopoldo: Sinodal, 2006), 23–30; Euler R. Westphal, *O Oitavo Dia: na era da seleção artificial* (São Bento do Sul: União Cristã, 2004); Gottfried Brakemeier, *O ser humano em busca de identidade: contribuições para uma antropologia teológica*, 2nd edition (São Leopoldo: Sinodal; São Paulo: Paulus, 2005), 129–71.

[36] Cf. Gottfried Brakemeier, *G. Sabedorias da fé num mundo confuso* (São Leopoldo: Sinodal, 2014), 7–20.

[37] Gottfried Brakemeier, *Panorama da Dogmática Cristã* (São Leopoldo: Sinodal, 2010), 82–83.

purely social or psychological problem. For Brakemeier, the only effective means of reconciliation is forgiveness, "that does not reward or forget, but removes what blocks the communion; this implies starting afresh."[38] Because Brakemeier bases what he calls the doctrine of reconciliation on human sin as the cause of conflict between human beings and God and human beings and their neighbor, forgiveness is the decisive factor in processes of reconciliation. In its pastoral care the church must proclaim forgiveness—one that only theology and the church may announce. Thus, the theme has direct implications on soteriology. "Sin separates us from God, alienates and creates enmity between humans. So reconciliation is necessary because there is a tragic conflict between creature and creator."[39]

All this becomes clear in the words of Jacqueline A. Bussie,

> The Christian word of hope in the twenty-first century takes suffering and injustice as seriously as redemption [...]. Luther provides us with the theological resources so as not to shirk away from this paradox, but to confront it with the necessary theological honesty, the lived tension that is the result of hope versus rationality.[40]

In light of the antagonism that we experience in this world, which leads us to question God's creative, reconciling and healing presence, the announcement that God in Christ reconciled the world constitutes the power of the gospel. In Brazil, when we speak of creation and reconciliation, we point to issues of social injustice that destroy God's creation and threaten reconciliation such as: the divide between the rich and the poor; men and women; racism; religious intolerance; environmental degradation and the destruction of the environment. In situations such as these, the gospel brings us hope. Luther leaves us his legacy:

> But without doubt, Just as at that time God rejoiced in the counsel and work by which man was created, so today, too, He takes pleasure in restoring this work of His through His Son and our Deliverer, Christ. It is useful to ponder these

---

[38] Ibid., 83.

[39] Ibid., 82. Starting from Wilfried Härle, *Dogmatik 3*, revised edition (Berlin/New York: de Gruyter, 2007), 322, Brakemeier distinguishes between subjective reconciliation that refers to God's unconditional forgiveness and objective reconciliation, which requires some form of compensation. Both take place in the event of Jesus Christ. He dies for our sins to give him unconditional forgiveness of God. The forgiveness of sins comes at a price. Cf. Bakemeier, op. cit. (note 37), 83–86.

[40] Jacqueline Bussie, "A esperança de Lutero para o mundo. Discurso cristão responsável hoje," in Christine Helmer (ed.), *Lutero: Um teólogo para tempos modernos* (São Leopoldo: Sinodal, 2013), 147.

facts, namely, that God is most kindly inclined toward us and takes delight in His thought and plan of restoring all who have believed in Christ to spiritual life through the resurrection of the dead.[41]

Therefore, if anyone is in Christ, the new creation has come: The old has gone, the new is here! All this is from God, who reconciled us to himself through Christ and gave us the ministry of reconciliation: that God was reconciling the world to himself in Christ, not counting people's sins against them. And he has committed to us the message of reconciliation. We are therefore Christ's ambassadors, as though God were making his appeal through us. We implore you on Christ's behalf: Be reconciled to God (2 Cor 5:17–20).

---

[41] *LW* 1, 68.

Towards an Intersectional Hermeneutics: Constructing Meaning with and not of Galatians 3-4

Marianne Bjelland Kartzow

Introduction

> There is no longer Jew or Greek, there is no longer slave or free, there is no longer male and female; for all of you are one in Christ Jesus (Gal 3:28).

What did and does it imply when Paul says "for all of you are one in Christ Jesus"? Is this a timeless message of equality to be interpreted anew in each context?

My point of departure is the following assumption: to understand a text is to understand oneself in a dialogue. For over ten years, I have been working with feminist hermeneutics in my research as a way critically to read the New Testament, with the expressed aim of establishing patterns of power and gender in texts, interpretations and reception processes. In this essay, I will build on some of these perspectives and focus on how they may impact the "real readers'" potential use of Galatians 3-4 through a lens I have called intersectional hermeneutics. This, I will argue, is a further step in the feminist interpretation of the Bible, with the potential to impact the broader Lutheran interpretation and reception of sacred texts.

First, a brief look at the context and background. It has been argued that the Reformation was a biblical movement: the Word of God was now free to all. All believers—educated and uneducated alike—should read Scripture and find in it guidance for their everyday lives. The printing press and schools for the laity contributed to reaching this goal. There was optimism that the principle of *sola Scriptura* would make the text speak clearly and directly into people's lives, no longer "filtered" by the church's authority or power of the clergy. This fascinating enthusiasm, prior to the invention of the hermeneutical circle, was perhaps a bit naïve in relation to the complex act of reading or the role of the reader in constructing meaning of a text.

The lack of tools to let the text speak clearly was perhaps the reason why the exegetical method of historical criticism was developed.[1] Within a theological framework, the first generations of exegetes tried to reconstruct the original historical context and meaning of the texts. Implicitly or explicitly the aim was to discover the clear message of Jesus' or Paul's words.

Since the 1970s, literary theories and impulses from the social sciences have contributed new perspectives. The New Testament scholar is no longer necessarily a believer reading Holy Scripture. An interdisciplinary group of researchers have continued to study these texts as part of various historical, literary or ideological projects. A variety of different feminist interpretations can be found among such approaches, starting with Elisabeth Schüssler Fiorenza's groundbreaking book, *In Memory of Her*, in 1983.[2]

There are countless ways to read, use and interpret the New Testament. This wide range of possibilities obviously influences the way in which different churches read the Bible; the Lutheran church is no exception. Among recent developments, I will let the Reformers' enthusiasm for what role biblical texts can play in people's everyday lives be an inspiration. I have two concrete cases in mind:

The intent of contextual Bible studies, modeled in particular in Pietermaritzburg, South Africa and the Ujamaa center, but exported globally, is to read biblical texts with poor and marginalized people, arguing that their interpretations have epistemological privilege. The center describes itself as follows:

> The Ujamaa Centre is an interface between socially engaged biblical and theological scholars, organic intellectuals, and local communities of the poor, working-class, and marginalised. Together we use biblical and theological resources for individual and social transformation.[3]

---

[1] See Clare K. Rothschild, "Historical Criticism," in Joel B. Green (ed.), *Methods for Luke* (Cambridge: Cambridge University Press, 2010), 9–41.

[2] Elisabeth Schüssler Fiorenza, *In Memory of Her: A Feminist Theological Reconstruction of Christian Origins* (London: SCM Press Ltd., 1983).

[3] See ujamaa.ukzn.ac.za/Homepage.aspx. The methodology has been tried out in a variety of contexts, from unemployed workers in Baltimore, USA, to various communities in Europe. Similar projects have also been developed in various Latin American countries. For an attempt to transfer this approach to a Norwegian context, see Anders Martinsen, Jan Christian Kielland, and Stine Kiil Saga, *Tekster til forandring: Et Bibelstudieopplegg* (Oslo: Verbum, 2010).

This way of reading the Bible for liberation and transformation has encouraged researchers from different fields to set up Bible study groups in order to access how today's "real readers," for example widows in Kenya or sex workers in the USA, make meaning of these texts.[4] A recent development in the field of interreligious hermeneutics is to combine readings of biblical texts with sacred texts from other traditions, for example the Qur'an or the Hadith.[5]

I shall argue that both contextual Bible studies and ethnographic work with "real readers" of the sacred texts have challenged traditional exegeses in a number of ways, in particular when it comes to questions of what the texts may mean. Gender issues have been a part of these challenges. How do we understand what the Ujamaa Centre calls the "interface" between the academy and the marginalized reader? How do we meet the global expectation that biblical texts constitute sources for liberation and transformation?

The role of the discipline's research knowledge, hypothesis and traditional exegetical tools in such Bible studies or ethnographic approaches is a much discussed topic. Has scholarship become irrelevant for "real readers"? Is academic knowledge just one among many possible ways of receiving biblical texts? Do we have to accept that the New Testament texts can mean anything to any reader or do we have something to offer?

In the following, I shall argue that taking a closer look at New Testament texts, using recently developed interdisciplinary tools to understand marginality and complexity, may have the potential to be relevant and to build a bridge between the academy and the "ordinary" reader of the Bible. I will use Galatians 3–4 as a source, and present intersectional hermeneutics as a resource for such studies.

In a hermeneutical process, the slow reading of and deep reflection on Pauline texts are important, although I would suggest that we do theology with and not of the text.[6] By trying to make sense of two selected passages in Galatians 3–4, I will investigate how historical, narrative and theological perspectives are at work. The famous credo of Galatians 3:28 is my first text passage, read together with the story of Hagar and Sarah in Galatians 4:21–31. I shall read the texts through the lens of intersectional hermeneutics.

---

[4] Loreen Maseno and Marianne Bjelland Kartzow, "Queering the Widow and the Judge in the Lukan Parable," in *Journal of Gender and Religion in Africa* 18, no. 1 (2012), 29–41; Avaren Ipsen, *Sex Working and the Bible* (London: Equinox, 2009).
[5] Anne Hege Grung, *Gender Justice in Muslim-Christian Readings: Christian and Muslim Women in Norway: Making Meaning of Texts from the Bible, the Koran, and the Hadith* (Amsterdam: Brill Rodopi, 2015).
[6] Professor Dale B. Martin, Honorary Doctor at the University of Copenhagen, held a lecture on 20 November 2015 entitled, "Theology WITH (not OF) the New Testament."

INTERSECTIONALITY AS A FEMINIST APPROACH

Today, feminist readings of the New Testament vary significantly, with different perspectives, tools or aims. Since Schüssler Fiorenza's contribution of feminist theories in the early 1980s, the interdisciplinary dialogue within women's studies, feminism and gender studies has further developed. Among the many recent approaches, I shall focus on theories that insist that gender cannot be studied in isolation, as a further development within feminist studies. A woman, for example a woman mentioned in the New Testament, is always something more: she is rich or poor (or something between), educated or not, has a skin color, bodily ability, age, religion, social status, etc. I am interested in how such perspectives can influence the way in which we study women in the Bible.

Intersectionality as a theoretical concept has only very recently been applied to biblical scholarship,[7] although the basic ideas and concerns have been articulated by African American scholarship and womanist biblical interpreters for some years.[8] The core idea is the following: instead of examining gender, race, class, age and sexuality as separate categories of oppression, intersectionality explores how these categories overlap and mutually modify and reinforce each other. Intersectionality is an essential element within recent race and gender theory:[9] Two of the leading journals in gender studies have recently published separate theme issues on intersectionality.[10]

---

[7] Elisabeth Schüssler Fiorenza, "Introduction: Exploring the Intersections of Race, Gender, Status, and Ethnicity in Early Christian Studies," in Laura Nasrallah and Elisabeth Schüssler Fiorenza (eds), *Prejudice and Christian Beginnings: Investigating Race, Gender, and Ethnicity in Early Christian Studies* (Minneapolis: Fortress Press, 2009), 1-23; Marianne Bjelland Kartzow, "Asking the Other Question: An Intersectional Approach to Galatians 3:28 and the Colossian Household Codes," in *Biblical Interpretation* 18, no. 4-5 (2010), 364-89; "Intersectional Studies," in Julia M. O'Brien (ed.), *The Oxford Encyclopedia of the Bible and Gender Studies* (New York: Oxford University Press, 2014).
[8] See various articles in Brian K. Blount et al. (eds), *True to Our Native Land: An African American New Testament Commentary* (Minneapolis: Fortress Press, 2007). See also numerous works by Schüssler Fiorenza and for example Kwok Pui-lan, "Finding a Home for Ruth: Gender, Sexuality, and the Politics of Otherness," in Robert M. Fowler, Edith L. Blumhofer, and Fernando F. Segovia (eds), *New Paradigms for Bible Study: The Bible in the Third Millennium* (New York: T&T Clark, 2004), 135-54.
[9] See for example, Gudrun-Axeli Knapp, "Race, Class, Gender: Reclaiming Baggage in Fast Travelling Theories," in *European Journal of Women's Studies* 12, no. 3 (2005), 249-65; Leslie McCall, "The Complexity of Intersectionality," in *Signs: Journal of Women in Culture and Society* 30, no. 3 (2005), 1771-91.
[10] Ann Phoenix and Pamela Pattynama (eds), *European Journal of Women's Studies* (Issue on Intersectionality), vol. 13 (2006); Sumi Cho, Kimberle Williams Crenshaw, and Leslie McCall, "Toward a Field of Intersectional Studies: Theory, Applications, and

A Scandinavian scholar even talks about "the intersectional turn."[11] I use this theory because I believe that feminist biblical interpretation should not limit itself to look at one socio-anthropological pattern only (such as gender), but rather examine diverse historical and contextual connotations influencing power structures in texts and interpretations.

The characters described in ancient texts experienced complex social relations. A man is never only a man: he belongs to a social group or class, with complex ethnic, religious and cultural implications, and the same could be said about a child or a slave. The Ethiopian eunuch in Acts 8, for example, represents a social position that requires an intersectional sensitivity in order not to miss out on any of the categories used to construct his complex identity.[12] As the "sixteenth-century Christian Reformers found in [Paul's] letters new language and ideas on how to revitalize the church and order human relations in society"[13] we are in an ongoing process of finding ways to communicate the relevance and complexity of these letters.

The genealogy of the theory of intersectionality may explain some apparently obvious but still nuanced concerns. When white Western feminists in the 1960s and 1970s started to criticize male-centrism, their insights about oppression "as a woman" tended to conflate the experiences of one particular group of women with those of all women. In the early 1980s, scholar-activists, in particular, started to question the hegemony of white women within the feminist movement. They argued that the experiences of African-American women are not only shaped by race, but also by gender, social class and sexuality. Awareness of how different social divisions cannot be understood in isolation, but mutually modify and reinforce each other, is central to intersectional studies.[14]

Mari Matsuda argues that intersectionality enables interpreters to "ask the other question" and thereby to make visible categories that otherwise are overseen.[15] When she sees a woman she asks about class or sexuality;

Praxis," in *Signs* 38 (Theme Issue: Intersectionality: Theorizing Power, Empowering Theory), no. 4 (2013), 785-810.

[11] Katarina Mattsson, "Genua Och Vithet I Den Intersektionella Vändingen," in *Tidsskrift för genusvetenskap* 1-2 (2010), 7-22.

[12] Gitte Buch-Hansen, Marianne Bjelland Kartzow, and Anna Rebecca Solevåg (eds), *Metodemangfold Og Det Nye Testamentet: I Fotsporene Til Den Etiopiske Evnukken* (Oslo: Cappelen Damm Akademisk, 2013).

[13] See www.lutheranworld.org/content/power-gospel-developing-pauline-hermeneutics

[14] Catharine A. MacKinnon, "Intersectionality as Method: A Note," in *Signs* 38, no. 4 (2013), 1019-30.

[15] She argues: "The way I try to understand the interconnection of all forms of subordination is through a method I call "ask the other question." When I see

when she sees a child she asks about race or gender. Her insights are compelling and her concern is with oppression and marginalization. Her way of questioning may be applied to this essay: When I read about women I ask, What role do class or ethnicity play here? When I read about slaves I ask, Were there any men among them? When I read about Greeks or Jews I ask, Could slave women or children be counted among them?

The complexity of liberation: Galatians 3:28

Insights from intersectionality may offer some useful perspectives in order to understand the type of social situation Paul deals with in Galatians. Galatians 3:28 reflects a complex web of social categories,[16] related to ethnicity/religion, social status and gender.[17] In particular, the meaning and implication of Ἰουδαῖος οὐδὲ Ἕλλην have been scrutinized by several interpreters.[18]

Paul's arguments in this verse are disputed.[19] One possible interpretation is that the existing social hierarchy is of less importance in baptism, since all are one in Christ Jesus. Using categories such as free over slave and male over female, which in social life expressed relatedness in a rather fixed and given hierarchical structure, Paul seems to construct a differ-

---

something that looks racist, I ask, "Where is the patriarchy in this?" When I see something that looks sexist, I ask, "Where is the heterosexism in this?" When I see something that looks homophobic, I ask, "Where are the class interests in this?" See Mari J. Matsuda, "Beside My Sister, Facing the Enemy: Legal Theory out of Coalition," in *Stanford Law Review* 43 (1990), 1187. See also Jennifer C. Nash, "Re-Thinking Intersectionality," in *Feminist Review* 89 (2008), 12.

[16] Gal 3:28: οὐκ ἔνι Ἰουδαῖος οὐδὲ Ἕλλην, οὐκ ἔνι δοῦλος οὐδὲ ἐλεύθερος, οὐκ ἔνι ἄρσεν καὶ θῆλυ· πάντες γὰρ ὑμεῖς εἷς ἐστε ἐν Χριστῷ Ἰησοῦ.

[17] Sheila Briggs, "Slavery and Gender," in Jane Schaberg, Alice Bach, and Esther Fuchs (eds), *On the Cutting Edge: The Study of Women in Biblical Worlds: Essays in Honor of Elisabeth Schüssler Fiorenza* (New York: Continuum, 2004), 171–92, here 175.

[18] I use the NRSV translation "Jew or Greek" here although the adequate terms to be used are contested. See overall discussion in Anders Runesson, "The Question of Terminology: The Architecture of Contemporary Discussions on Paul," in Mark D. Nanos and Magnus Zetterholm (eds), *Paul within Judaism: Restoring the First-Century Context to the Apostle* (Minneapolis: Fortress Press, 2015), 53–77.

[19] See, for example, Elisabeth Schüssler Fiorenza, *Discipleship of Equals: Critical Feminist Ekklesia-Logy of Liberation* (London: SCM Press LTD, 1993). Lone Fatum, on the other hand, came to another conclusion, in Lone Fatum, "Images of God and Glory of Man: Women in the Pauline Congregations," in Kari Elisabeth Børresen (ed.), *Image of God and Gender Models in Judaeo-Christian Tradition* (Oslo: Solum, 1991), 56–139.

ent reality.[20] The effect of this argument, however, might be that he also emphasizes that although all are one "in Christ Jesus," they are separate, different and unequal in all other areas of life; this may be one way of understanding Martin Luther's interpretation.[21] From this perspective, Paul does not challenge the social hierarchy of his society, but slightly modifies it in order to construct a new spiritual world order. Nonetheless, the text's destabilizing potential has been noted by later interpreters, not least in the last decades' feminist movements.

In contrast to the parallel texts in 1 Corinthians 12:13 and Colossians 3:11, Galatians 3:28 mentions "male and female." For decades, scholars have discussed whether or not this verse is "good news" for women,[22] but when using intersectionality I am more concerned about what kind of women were potentially included in this category. In the interpretative tradition of Galatians 3:28, nationality/ethnicity, class and gender are often seen as three separate sets of categories.[23] But what if we deconstruct them with the help of intersectional hermeneutics? If the categories in Galatians are combined in novel ways, a more complicated structure appears.[24] Using

---

[20] Betz writes: "Surprisingly, v. 28 leads to the field of political and social ideals and practices. The first part (v 28a-c) contains three parallel statements in the present tense, which define the religious, cultural, and social consequences of the Christian initiation." Hans Dieter Betz, *Galatians: A Commentary on Paul's Letter to the Churches in Galatia*, Hermeneia: A Critical and Historical Commentary on the Bible (Philadelphia: Fortress Press, 1979), 189.

[21] Peter Matheson, "Luther on Galatians," in Michael Lieb, Emma Mason, and Jonathan Roberts (eds), *Reception History of the Bible* (Oxford: Oxford University Press, 2011), 627-28.

[22] See Mary Ann Beavis, "Christian Origins, Egalitarianism, and Utopia," in *JFSR* 23, no. 2 (2007), 37 and 39.

[23] In Betz, op. cit. (note 20), 192-95, the second relationship pair in Galatians 3:28b is translated as "neither slave nor freeman." In his analysis of this relationship pair, he does not discuss gender, overlooking the important difference between male and female slaves. See Elisabeth Schüssler Fiorenza, *Rhetoric and Ethic: The Politics of Biblical Studies* (Minneapolis: Fortress Press, 1999), 155-56. She writes: "In order to understand and translate Gal. 3:28-29, one needs to ask, for instance, whether the expressions 'Jew/Greek, slave/free' mean only men or whether they include wo/men so that wo/men as a matter of course belong to these groups."

[24] Note, however, that while the two first relationship pairs connect the dual elements by the use of *oude*, male and female are connected by the use of *kai*. If the ethnicity category as well as the class category are meant to be complementary, what does the "and" mean in the last relation? Could a person be either Jew or Greek, either slave or free, but both male and female? See suggestions to queer interpretations of this verse, in Dale B. Martin, *Sex and the Single Savior: Gender and Sexuality in Biblical Interpretation* (Louisville, Ky.: Westminster John Knox Press, 2006), 77-90.

Matsuda's methodology, we may ask, What gender or social class could Jews or Greeks have? Were ethnic categories applied to slaves? I have found eight new hypothetical categories: Jewish slave male; Jewish slave female; Jewish free male; Jewish free female; Greek slave male; Greek slave female; Greek free male; and Greek free female.

These eight combinations allow me to pose new questions to this passage and not only to dealing with the three pairs as isolated parallels. For example, if enslavement, at least legally, severed ties to an *ethnos* and *genos*, as Denise Buell has pointed out, did it make sense to consider a slave as either Jewish or Greek?[25] The relationship between slavery and ethnicity/religion was rather complex.[26] And further, free is above slave as male is above female in the ancient Mediterranean world, but it is not stipulated who holds privilege and who is subordinated in the relation of Jew and Greek.[27] For Paul, are the terms Jew or Greek to be understood for males and females alike as ethnic or religious, national or racial categories?[28] And what do such modern terms (ethnic, religious, national, racial) mean when used on ancient texts?[29]

Could slaves be included in the gender relationship pair? Echoing Genesis 1, the way in which gender is expressed in Galatians includes terms that focus on male and female (ἄρσεν καὶ θῆλυ); these terms are also used to determine animals' bodies, referring not only to "social" difference but also to a "biological" one, to use Betz's distinction.[30] Some interpreters have seen this expression as referring to patriarchal marriage, since the

---

[25] For a discussion of the terms *ethnos* and *genos*, see Denise Kimber Buell, *Why This New Race: Ethnic Reasoning in Early Christianity*, Gender, Theory, and Religion (New York: Columbia University Press, 2005). On Jewish slaves, see e.g., Dina Stein, "A Maidservant and Her Master's Voice: Discourse, Identity, and Eros in Rabbinic Texts," in *Journal of the History of Sexuality* 10, no. 3/4 (2001): 375–97. Tal Ilan, *Jewish Women in Greco-Roman Palestine: An Inquiry into Image and Status* (Tübingen: Mohr, 1995), 205–11.

[26] Catherine Hezser, *Jewish Slavery in Antiquity* (New York: Oxford University Press, 2005). See also Sandra R. Joshel and Sheila Murnaghan (eds), *Women and Slaves in Greco-Roman Culture: Differential Equations* (London: Routledge, 1998), 1.

[27] See Briggs, op. cit. (note 17), 182. She makes this point reflecting on how Jews were frequently persecuted and despised.

[28] Again, what kind of category this may be is important to question. See also discussion on women and conversion in Judith M. Lieu, "The 'Attraction of Women' in/to Early Judaism and Christianity: Gender and the Politics of Conversion," in *JSNT* 72 (1998), 5–22.

[29] Paula Fredriksen, "Mandatory Retirement: Ideas in the Study of Christian Origins Whose Time Has Come to Go," in *Studies in Religion* 35, no. 2 (2006), 231–46.

[30] In Betz, op. cit. (note 20), 195. He writes: "In contrast to the preceding statements, this one names the sexes in the neuter, which indicates that not only the social difference between man and woman ('roles') are involved but the biological

sex distinction achieved its highest purpose in marriage.[31] However, the terms used to express gender here are not "husband and wife," as in the household codes of Colossians and Ephesians. Another context in which it made sense to talk about the relationship pair of male and female was reproduction, involving also slaves who normally could not marry.[32]

This way of mapping is not giving us clear answers as to how Paul's social environment reflected in Galatians 3:28 was constructed, but with the help of the other question we see a more complex picture. Intersectional hermeneutic helps us to be aware of unresolved dilemmas in our research: Could women really be insiders? Were slaves forced to belong to their owner's ethnicity or religion? Who could be considered as a Jew?

Making meaning with Galatians 3:28 is to be able to hold two thoughts in our mind at the same time: the verse has liberating potential while being heavily embedded in its own social, cultural and political environments, in which some positions were more important than others. To grasp the complexity of liberation in texts considered sacred is one important step. Intersectional hermeneutics may help us to construct theology with this verse.

Mapping Hagar: Galatians 4:21–31 in context

If readers find inspiration in Galatians 3, maybe we should recommend that they stop reading before they come to the last part of chapter 4. Or, Can Paul's rhetorical play or ploy with Hagar belong to a similar metanarrative as Galatians 3:28, if read with intersectional hermeneutics? What if we try to use Galatians 3:28 to map Hagar's role in this story?

In many of Paul's letters to the various early Christian groups of the Roman Empire, familiar characters from the Jewish tradition and the Hebrew Bible function as models to explain community building and theological reasoning. In two of the letters, Romans and Galatians, the forefather Abraham and the two mothers of his first two sons function as rhetorical tools (ἅτινά ἐστιν ἀλληγορούμενα) to describe how not all those who claim to belong to God are real children of Abraham. The story in Genesis 16

---

distinction." See also the Liddell-Scott dictionary's entries on these terms, "The Perseus Digital Library," at www.perseus.tufts.edu.

[31] The late Krister Stendahl pointed out that "male and female" seems to allude to Genesis 1:27, emphasizing men and women's role in procreation, understood as referring to marriage; see the discussion in Schüssler Fiorenza, *Rhetoric and Ethic*, op. cit. (note 23), 56–57. See also Briggs, op. cit. (note 17), 178–79.

[32] See Briggs, op. cit. (note 17). Also Marianne Bjelland Kartzow, "Navigating the Womb: Surragacy, Slavery, Fertility and Biblical Discources," in *Journal of Early Christian History* 2, no. 1 (2012), 38–54.

and 21, where Abraham and Sarah were childless, is obviously familiar to the readers and hearers.[33] But we meet a different Hagar and a different narrative of motherhood and slavery.

According to Genesis, Hagar flees to the wilderness twice and disappears from the story, while Sarah, Abraham and their son Isaac are counted as the founding family of the Jewish covenant.[34] The most stable factor in this family story is that Abraham is the father of the two boys. He is also said to name both (Gen 16:15 and 21:3), indicating that, at one level, he acknowledged them both as sons. When it comes to circumcision, it was only Isaac who passed this rite of passage at the age of eight days, as required (Gen 21:4). The oldest brother Ishmael, on the other hand, underwent circumcision together with Abraham and the slaves of the house.

When the story of Hagar and Sarah and their children appears in the Pauline letters, something has happened to the different mothers and their sons. Paul operates with two different kinds of motherhood for Ishmael and Isaac: One of Abraham's sons, that is the one he had by the slave woman Hagar is "born according to the flesh" (κατὰ σάρκα γεγέννηται), while Isaac, who he had by Sarah, is "born through the promise" (ἐκ τῆς ἐλευθέρας δι' ἐπαγγελίας) (Gal 4:23). What has happened to Sarah who intended to let Hagar give her a son? Hagar is reduced to flesh only, and her son is reduced to a slave: "[I]t is not the children of the flesh who are the children of God, but the children of the promise are counted as descendants" (Rom 9:8). "Drive out the slave and her child; for the child of the slave will not share the inheritance with the child of the free woman" (Gal 4:30). For Paul, the slave woman's son was only born according to the flesh, not an heir, not a real son, not a boy to belong to the category of "Jew." Hagar had no role in the community and could therefore be used as a symbol of the outsider. The slave status and the foreign Egyptian origin of Ishmael's mother strengthen their marginal position.

But the picture is not consistent: the characterization of Hagar becomes rather ambivalent when she is likened to Mount Sinai, the present Jerusalem, terms overloaded with associations to the Jewish tradition (Gal 4:25). She is, however, in slavery with her children since she is not of the Jerusalem

---

[33] More on my earlier works on Hagar "On Naming and Blaming: Hagar's God-Talk in Jewish and Early Christian Sources," in John T. Greene and Mishael M. Caspi (eds), *In the Arms of Biblical Women*, Biblical Intersections 13 (Piscataway: Gorgias Press, 2013), 97–119; Marianne Bjelland Kartzow, *Destabilizing the Margins: An Intersectional Approach to Early Christian Memory* (Eugene, Oregon: Wipf and Stock Publishers, 2012), see chapter 11 on Hagar.

[34] Shaye J. D. Cohen, *The Jewish Family in Antiquity*, vol. no. 289 (Missoula: Scholars Press, 1993).

from above. If we apply the distinctions of Galatians 3:28 then, as a female slave, what role could she have in the Jew–Greek-pair?

Paul chose to use Hagar and her son to argue against those who require that men had to be circumcised to join the Jesus group. If he had followed his own vision some verses earlier, "Here are neither Jew nor Greek, neither slave nor free, neither male and female, you are all one in Christ Jesus," Hagar, a foreign slave woman, could have represented an ideal character. If "you are all one in Christ Jesus," negotiated categories of religion/ethnicity, social position and gender, as a standard interpretation of Galatians 3:28, Hagar and her son who was not properly circumcised could really embody the ideal of the new covenant. They are obviously persons of low status in the narrative, but since ethnicity, class and gender seem to be downplayed and "all are one in Christ," Paul's use of Hagar and Ishmael may come as a disappointing surprise. Paul reduces Hagar to a foreign female slave, although connected to the present Jerusalem, since her child was born according to nature. According to this Pauline biblical interpretation and reception, they were not part of the promise of the religious community, but to be driven out and excluded. Hagar, as a woman of the New Testament, is mentioned by name and remembered from the Jewish tradition. Her role in Galatians 4 however seems like a paradox in contrast to the credo in Galatians 3:28. How is that paradox solved? Or, is it left in the text as a challenge to the interpreter?

To study marginalized women is one important task for feminist theology. Rather than blaming Paul or Luther or other men from the past for overlooking and marginalizing women, it is crucial that sacred texts are read with a hermeneutic of suspicion. Interpreters must do theology with the text and not of it.

Galatians 4 ends with a statement and challenge: διό, ἀδελφοί, οὐκ ἐσμὲν παιδίσκης τέκνα ἀλλὰ τῆς ἐλευθέρας. ("So then, friends, we are children, not of the slave but of the free woman"). But who are these *adelfoi*? Who belongs to the group Paul is addressing? Is it not a bit misleading when modern translations use inclusive terms such as siblings or friends and not brothers here? As we have seen: all categories of women or slaves were not included.

So what happened to the liberating and destabilizing potential of Galatians 3:28? How can an intersectional hermeneutics help us construct meaning with Galatians 4?

INTERSECTIONAL HERMENEUTICS

In this essay I have aimed to show how a close and critical reading with the help of intersectional hermeneutics of two central passages from

Galatians 3-4 can provide valuable tools to construct meaning with the texts. The limits of intersectional theories have been pointed out by several feminists.[35] What categories are relevant? Is intersectionality, although aiming at including and destabilizing categories, nevertheless reinscribing stereotypes?[36] At its best this theory can help us realize, when approaching texts with a hermeneutics of suspicion, that "women in the Bible" is not one fixed and unified group.

To understand a text is to understand oneself in a kind of dialogue. Theories developed to understand marginality and discrimination can help us to see patterns, dilemmas and nuances in ancient texts that we otherwise might have overlooked. Since this publication is primarily concerned with hermeneutics and the power of the gospel in Pauline texts, I will point at three possible directions in which this analysis may take us:

- The use of historical and literary knowledge: an approach to Galatians 3-4 with the help of intersectional hermeneutics may open up new spaces for readers with experience of intersecting marginalization and discrimination. The text is nomadic; the purpose is to construct meaning with the text, not merely to look for Paul's intended meaning as open and clear, but let the text invite readers to share. We can use intersectional perspectives to suggest an hypothesis of what the text may have meant in its social, cultural and religious environments, and to see if this new mapping has any connection to our global world today. Accordingly, we are not asking for what the text means once and for all but what it can mean for various readers. This may contribute to construct the academy as a relevant dialogue partner within contextual Bible studies of the New Testament.

- The power of the gospel: it is completely acceptable and to be encouraged that "real readers" take Galatians 3:28 as a liberating vision for all people today, regardless of what we think its historical origin may have been. We can look for destabilizing potential and metanarratives of freedom and love. Applying intersectional hermeneutics we have found gaps, breaks and new possible connections in Galatians 3:28

---

[35] Erica Burman, "From Difference to Intersectionality: Challenges and Resources," in *European Journal of Psychotherapy and Counseling 6*, no. 4 (2003), 1 293-308; Shuddhabrata Sengupta, "I/ME/Mine-Intersectional Identities as Negotiated Minefields," in *Signs: Journal of Women in Culture and Society* 31, no. 3 (2006), 629-39; McCall, op. cit. (note 9).

[36] Randi Gressgård, "Mind the Gap: Intersectionality, Complexity and 'the Event'," in *Theory and Science* (2008), 67-83.

and otherwise hidden complex subject positions. When examining text and context, historically and today, the intersecting structures of marginalization and discrimination become clear. We cannot read Galatians 4 and conclude that the story is gender inclusive since Sarah is given a prominent position, while Hagar is paid no attention. This has a contemporary parallel: modern slavery and the stories of the endless line of immigrants hide similar structures of power and privilege, indeed also related to gender patterns.

• The travelling memory of Hagar: the biblical character of Hagar may have disappeared from the narrative of the Bible, but she plays an impressive role elsewhere. Women like her can be put on the map in the credo of Galatians 3:28, whatever role Paul gives her in the following chapter. Her memory has had the power to travel elsewhere: a lot is said of her in other ancient texts (Rabbinic, Jewish historians, Church Fathers, etc.) and she has come to symbolize the female slave in African and African American culture. As the mother of the Prophet Ishmael and wife of Ibrahim, she holds a prominent position in the Islamic traditions in particular and is thus a "shared character" in the three Abrahamic traditions. The story from Galatians 4, where Paul uses her as a foreign female slave "to think with" and to discuss insiders and outsiders, can encourage conversations about ambiguous memory, women at the margins, or injustice. A shared interest in Hagar can open the way to read religious texts that are unfamiliar to us. An intersectional hermeneutical approach to the Pauline letters may offer some useful resources in such interreligious encounters.

PAUL ON CITIZENSHIP: PAULINE HERMENEUTICS IN PHILIPPIANS 1:27 AND 3:20

Lubomir Batka

The notion of citizenship appears twice in Paul's letter to the Philippians. The first time it appears in the form of the verb, πολιτεύομαι (Phil 1:27), the second time as a noun, πολίτευμα ἐν οὐρανοῖς, in Philippians 3:20. There is only one further occurrence of the word in the New Testament, and that is in Acts 23:1.

This article will deal with three questions: What does the concept of citizenship mean in the letter of the Apostle Paul to the Philippians? Does Paul's understanding of citizenship in his letter to the Philippians serve as a hermeneutical instrument? If so, can it be used as such today?

CONTEXT

The first appearance of πολιτεύομαι in Philippians 1:27a is in the form of an imperative: "Only, live your life in a manner worthy of the gospel of Christ [...]." Raymond Brewer has pointed out that this term is used "when conduct relative to some law of life—political, moral, social, or religious—is signified"[1] (cf. Acts 23:1). We could translate it as a direct command: "Let your way of life be worthy of the gospel of Christ!" As free citizens in the Roman colony of Philippi, Christians are to "live as citizens" a life fitting this calling.

---

[1] Raymond Brewer, "The Meaning of Politeueste in Philippians 1.27," in *Journal of Biblical Literature 73* (1954), 76–83, here 80.

The Philippians knew very well that Paul was a Roman citizen, unjustly imprisoned (probably in Ephesus). Paul had not sought his own prosperity, but had served to advance the gospel in the proclamation of Christ (Phil 1:18) in Philippi during his second mission trip (49–50 CE). Paul makes clear that the real foundation for advancement rests outside of oneself. Everything is based on Christ's steadfast suffering, depicted in the Christological hymn in Philippians 2:5–11, not only as an example but the real source of unity and love (Phil 2:1–4). Christ suffered so that the Philippians can be united and love one another in their suffering.

For the congregation in Philippi to "live as citizens worthy of the gospel of the Christ" thus implied, like Paul, conducting their lives as citizens, both in the Roman colony and the believing community, despite their suffering in "sharing in the gospel" (Phil 1:5). Paul feels compelled to but hindered from preventing the distortion of the gospel and the destruction of the congregation, and stresses proper Christian conduct until he returns to Philippi. The Philippians are to prove themselves as being true to their calling (cf. Acts 23:1) by Christ.

In Philippians 3:20 the notion of citizenship occurs for a second time. Here, the specific political and civic connotations are even more obvious. In comparison to most other cities or colonies, Philippi was interesting in terms of its unusual ethnic and social structure. It surpassed other cities in its "Romanness."[2] "In Philippi, the Romans ruled without the medium of any Greeks, and Latin ruled unchallenged until well into the third century."[3] This means that for the Greeks of Philippi the experience of empire was far more acute than in other Greek towns. Citizens were granted Roman citizenship, with the right to self-governance and freedom from tribute payments to Rome—typical for a place where military veterans lived as well. According to *Lex Porcia* and *Lex Julia*, Roman citizens were under the protection of the Caesar and thus protected from crucifixion and torture.[4]

In Philippians 3:20, Paul contrasts the Philippians' earthly and heavenly πολίτευμα (citizenship). The term itself is not Paul's invention. Its use in the books of Maccabees, or by Philo and Josephus allows one to conclude that Paul knew the term in its Jewish context as referring to being a part of the Jewish nation (cf. Eph 2:12). According to Miller, "Paul thus employs

---

[2] Peter Oakes, "Remapping the Universe," in *Journal for the Study of the New Testament* 27.3 (2005), 308–309. See Peter Oakes, *Philippians. From the People to Letter* (Cambridge: CUP, 2001), 74–75.

[3] Ibid., 74.

[4] Gerhard Friedrich, "Der Brief an die Philipper," in Jürgen Becker, Hans Conzelmann, Gerhard Friedrich, *Das Neue Testament Deutsch*, *NTD* 8 (Göttingen: Vandenhoeck, 1981), 125–75.

this traditional Jewish language to describe the Philippian community as an alternative *polis* in contrast to that earthly Roman city in which the Philippian believers reside."[5]

A deeper understanding of Paul's meaning is revealed when looking at the purpose of the Pauline epistle in its entirety. The congregation in Philippi was originally formed by the Greeks (Phil 1:28). Readers of the letter are warned to beware of those praising circumcision (Phil 3). Even though there probably was a small group of Jews in Philippi (cf. Acts 16:13), they were not a problematic group as such; the opponents of Paul were a group of Jewish-Christian missionaries, perhaps of the Petrine type.[6] Friedrich draws a subtle comparison between Philippians and 2 Corinthians and suggests that there are "close parallels" between both letters.[7] These missionaries strongly emphasized their Jewish origin and boasted about their own circumcision. According to Klaus Berger, "What the Judaizers hope to achieve by Gentile circumcision is to bring them into the privileges of belonging to God's ancient people, 'Israel's race.'"[8]

Paul argued against this by addressing the value of circumcision (cf. Phil 3:3; Rom 2:28; Rom 3:1ff.; Gal 5:6). According to Paul, these missionaries do not serve God in spirit, because they do not boast in Christ, since they still trust in the flesh. His rhetoric sounds harsh; he calls them "dogs" and "liars," the opposite of what they want to be. In the Jewish context, these unclean animals (Mt 7:6 and 2 Pet 2:22) represented paganism (Mt 15:26, Rev 22:15). Their emphasis on the external (flesh) is worthless, because circumcision is considered a mutilation (Phil 3:2; cf. Gal 5:12). Paul turned their argument upside down and portrayed the Jewish-Christian missionaries as "pagans." They do not represent a higher form of Christian excellency: they hope to boast spiritually about Christ, but actually they boast "according to the flesh" and therefore destroy and do not edify.

But Paul could also boast according to "the flesh" (Phil 3:3–5; cf. 2 Cor 11:18, 22). He insists that as a model Jew he could have more confidence in the flesh than anyone else (Phil 3:5–6). Paul's brash recalling of his Jewishness as a Pharisee "as to the law (κατὰ νόμον)" (Phil 3:5) stands in striking contrast to his warning to the congregation to "beware of those who mutilate the flesh (κατατομήν)" (Phil 3:2). Paul reports that he was, "as to zeal a persecutor of the church; as to righteousness under the law, blameless" (Phil 3:6).

---

[5] Ernst C. Miller, "πολιτεύεσθε in Phil 1:27: Some Philological and Thematic Observations," in *JSNT* 15 (1982), 86–96.

[6] Klaus Berger, *Theologiegeschichte des Urchristentums* (Tübingen: Francke Verlag, 1994), 468.

[7] Friedrich, op. cit. (note 4).

[8] Berger, op. cit. (note 6), 481. C. even as a "sign of nobility," ibid., 481.

As a result, Paul warned the congregation to beware of those calling them to be circumcised. The believers are metaphorically "the circumcision" in their conduct, the ones who worship God in Christ Jesus spiritually, rather than placing confidence "in the flesh," as do those who undergo physical circumcision (Phil 3:3-4; cf. 2 Cor 10:17). This argument is relevant for the concept of citizenship, since Paul points to the social meaning of circumcision—making one a member of a particular group.

SOCIAL STATUS AND PRIVILEGE

Paul, himself a Jew, was a Roman citizen with the city rights of Tarsus (Acts 21:39) and Rome (Acts 22:25-28; 23:27, cf. Acts 16:37ff.). Dual citizenship was allowed during Caesar Claudius's reign[9] and Paul had been bestowed this privilege at birth (Acts 22:28). Paul had a higher social status than the tribune Claudius Lysias, who had had to purchase his citizenship (Acts 23:26). Likewise, when dealing with his Jewish compatriots, Paul could use his Jewish origin as a way of achieving a higher social status: "The tribe of Benjamin stood high in Jewish estimation—it had within its borders the city of Jerusalem and with it the temple (Judg 1:21)—and so it was regarded as a special privilege to belong to it."[10]

What is the purpose of boasting of one's status? Or, is this merely a reflection of Paul's character, one that might even be problematic? Klaus Berger observed that one of the "pillars of Paul's theology" is "social prestige." "No other early church thinker is so insistent on the dimension of social status as Paul is, the worth one attributes to oneself and to others and oneself in front of others and in front of God."[11] According to Berger, the reason for this is Paul's Jewish origin and the fact that he was not fully accepted as an apostle among the rest of the apostles.

However, this trait in Pauline theology can also be seen from another perspective. According to Berger, boasting is not primarily negative. It is an "elementary human act in human social life," a kind of *prudentia* and it is "normal, that everyone seeks their own advantage."[12] Therefore, it would be "stupid" to boast about something that does not have a value in

---

[9] Rainer Riesner, *Die Frühzeit des Apostels Paulus* (Tübingen: Mohr Siebeck, 1994), 131. For the town Tarsus, see 236f. and Jürgen Becker, *Paulus. Der Apostel der Völker* (Tübingen: Mohr Siebeck, 1989), 34-41. Also worth reading is Riesner, "Das römische Bürgerrecht des Paulus," in Riesner, ibid., 129-39.

[10] Peter T. O'Brien, *Commentary on Philippians* (Grand Rapids: Eerdmans, 1991), 371.

[11] Berger, op. cit. (note 6), 451.

[12] Ibid.

itself. It has to be something that grants prestige. In all instances (2 Cor 10:13; 2 Cor 7:14; 2 Cor 9:2; Phil 2:16; 2 Cor 1:14; 1 Cor 1:31; Rom 2:17; Rom 2:23; 2 Cor 5:12; 1 Thess 2:19) Paul never used the verb to mean "to boast of oneself." Paul sets an example. Wherever he asks his readers to imitate him (Phil 3:17; Phil 4:9; 1 Cor 4:16; 1 Cor 11:1; 1 Thess 1:6; 2 Thess 3:7; Gal 4:12), he encourages them to accompany him on his journey toward obtaining citizenship in heaven, trusting in Christ who lives in him and is powerful in him. This is not an absolute worth but, rather, a relative one *coram hominibus*. The goal is to acquire social prestige.

The issue of status is closely linked to the Roman colonial system. Status implied an individual's rank within a particular group, accompanied by certain expectations for a particular behavior. Peter Oakes showed that "throughout the Greek East, the arrival of Rome reinforced the importance of status and made the hierarchy of status more rigid. The maintenance of status and the proper observation of distinctions of statuses were imperatives of society."[13] As already mentioned, the town of Philippi was socially diverse; compared to Greeks, Romans were in the minority, but they belonged to a higher social class and lived out their social status. In practical terms, as Berger suggests, this indicates that not only for Paul societal relationships went hand in hand with perception of status and origin. The social importance of status is interwoven with the idea of privilege. According to Paul, status is not self-serving but its purpose is to grant and foster a privileged position. In addressing the social connotations of "citizenship," Paul's other bold theological move becomes visible.

Paul addressed his adherents with harsh words: by prioritizing circumcision they are prioritizing the "glory" and not the humiliation of the flesh on the cross.[14] How can they truly be missionaries of Christ when they avoid the cross? Therefore, they are actually "enemies of the cross of Christ" (Phil 3:18). Eventually their position will be overthrown and their whole glory will become blame (Phil 3:19; Phil 1:20).

Ironically, Paul's proposal is much harder to follow and grasp, because choosing the cross and not being circumcised led to contempt and loss of status. As former heathens, choosing to refuse circumcision resulted in having an inferior status to Jews. As Roman citizens, choosing the cross meant loss of privilege when compared to the Romans. This two-fold humili-

---

[13] Oakes, *Philippians*, op. cit. (note 2), 74–75.

[14] With "ὧν ὁ θεὸς ἡ κοιλία" (Phil 3:19) Paul is not tackling some sort of sensualism or bodily hedonism but, as Friedrich argues, the "belly" as "hearth" is the center of the human being, their thinking and egocentric way of life looking for personal benefit. In this way, they are still fleshly and boasting about fleshly things. They do preach Christ as well, but without the cross. Friedrich, op. cit. (note 4), 125–75.

ation is the negative mirror of the new citizenship. This "Pauline theology of the cross" is explained in Philippians 2:5–11. The Jews regarded Christ as having been cursed; the Romans regarded him as having been humiliated, without honor in the "form of a servant" (Phil 2:7). Despite the double humiliation *coram mundo,* in essence he truly belongs to God.[15]

Thus the Philippians, even without circumcision as a sign of prestige in the eyes of the Jews and without honor and privileges in the eyes of the Romans, shall trust that as true believers they are elected by God to a new glorious (heavenly) citizenship.[16] A similar theme is pursued in the depiction of the penitent thief on the cross (Mk 15:27). From the perspective of the onlookers he was dying without honor *coram deo* and *coram mundo.* But, regardless of his status in the eyes of the people, having reached rock bottom, Christ granted him the highest possible honor and dignity of heavenly citizenship, as we read in Philippians 1:21. Only those who have reached the very bottom are on their way to the highest glory.

Paul's proposal is a very complex one, since parallel to this dual perspective on the individual there is also a positive use of status in Philippians. Paul plays out his status as a Jew and a Roman citizen and both have to be taken into account simultaneously. Paul does not doubt that he has dignity *coram deo* as a Jew. Likewise, Paul as a Roman citizen by birth has the status *coram mundo.* In other words, *coram deo* he has status as a Jew and as a Christian. *Coram mundo* he is humbled as a Jew and as a Christian, but has status as a Roman citizen. This explains why, as a result, Paul does not want to boast with the "flesh." This dual aspect appears in Philippians 3:4: it could be useful *coram judaioi,* but it is nothing *coram deo.* Rather, according to Philippians 3:10 (cf. Phil 4:12), Paul and pagan Christians regard the humiliation of the cross as a curse in light of the Jews and shame in light of the Roman citizens. In this way, they become the truly circumcised and therefore endowed with a new status *coram deo* that makes them superior to Jews and Romans. The reason for "boasting in Christ Jesus" is not the "flesh" but the "gospel of Christ." Similar to Paul, the Philippians are also in this dual position: as Christians and as Roman citizens.

ROMAN CITIZENSHIP OF PHILIPPIAN CHRISTIANS—A TWOFOLD HONOR

In Philippians 3:20 we see the twofold honor Paul was thinking of. As citizens of the Roman Empire, Philippians have a higher status than

---

[15] Luther's remark in *WA TR* 6, 79.20–31 (Nr. 6615).
[16] Berger, op. cit. (note 6), 481.

Jews; as citizens of heaven and God's children (Phil 2:15) their status is higher than that of the Judaizing missionaries in Philippi. Therefore, it would be futile not to conduct their Christian life according to the calling they received through the gospel (Phil 1:27). Paul does not overstate the importance of mundane citizenship as such; it does not matter who the person is or what other earthly citizenship they may have. What matters is citizenship in Christ.[17]

What place does citizenship take in Pauline hermeneutics? Paul's missionary work concentrated on larger cities, the capitals of several provinces (Antiochy at Orontes, Thessaloniki, Ephesus, Rome) and Roman colonies (Pisidian Antioch, Iconium, Lystra, Troas, Philippi, Corinth). Citizenship is not only a topic for Paul. In the New Testament we read that there were several Roman citizens close to him. Citizenship could be endowed by Caesar as a reward for special services to Rome, e.g., after long military service, but could also be acquired as a gift in the form of *manumissio*, the free decision of the slave owner. There was no official procedure or permission from the state.[18] It is probable that Paul's father acquired his Roman citizenship as a freed Jewish slave for free. Paul, as the son of a *liberus/libertinus*, would have had full citizenship and it would be generally accepted as ingenuous (inborn). In contrast to the notion of the gift of liberty stands a verb used in the mercantile context.

The verb "gain" might be related to the town with its market place[19] and financial accounting terminology. The audience hear that whatever were "gains" for Paul with regard to his Jewishness (Phil 3:5–6; Phil 1:21–23) is now "shame." And Jesus' "shame" now becomes the true gain. The idea of *manumissio*, however, is very close to Philippians. Paul uses a common social notion of prestige to show that citizenship, granted as free gift, is the largest "gain." Everything else, no matter how worthy in its origin, is in the end only "shame."

Another characteristic of the notion of citizenship is the fact that citizens are free but live under one Caesar. Even the *liberus* owed longtime loyalty to the *patronus*. This social hierarchy is not only a precondition of

---

[17] The Pauline understanding of "new creation" means the abolishment of differences between circumcised and uncircumcised (Gal 6:15)—but always with the precondition that it happens in Christ. Cf. 1 Corintians 7:19—no difference, if keeping the commandments of God is fulfilled. Cf. Galatians 3:28—no difference, as long as Christians are one in Christ. And in Colossians 3:11—no difference, as long as Christ is the Lord.

[18] Riesner, op. cit. (note 9), 135.

[19] On the marketplace metaphors in 3:7–8, see Richard S. Ascough, *Paul's Macedonian Associations: The Social Context of Philippians and 1 Thessalonians* (Tübingen: Mohr Siebeck, 2003), 118–20.

governance. The state or city consists of free individual citizens but also of *artes et ordines* who rank higher in the hierarchy (cf. Phil 1:1).[20]

Similar to Roman citizens who were free but under Caesar's lordship, Christians live as free, or freed citizens of heaven under one Kyrios (lord) (Phil 2:10-11, Phil 3:8). The political connotation of the use of this title of Roman Caesars cannot be excluded beforehand.[21] In Philippians there are eight occurrences of the phrase ἐν Χριστῷ, five occurrences of ἐν κυρίῳ and five of mixed formulations. It can mean local (as a description of what heavenly citizenship is) but, likewise, it can be understood in instrumental terms (things happening through Christ). This answers the question how, according to Paul, a human being can become a citizen of heaven. Similarly to Philippians 3:8, knowing Christ not only means having subjective knowledge of something but also the objective fact of being known by God. God's knowledge is God's election of God's people and it means that God's people will live a worthy and loyal life according to their new status. The life of a Christian is similar to a city built on a hill that cannot be hidden (Mt 5:14-16). To be a free citizen does not imply being free to do whatever one pleases but having the freedom to participate in the law (*Recht*).[22] In this complex structure a citizen knows that to participate (*participare*) does not mean to govern (*principari*), but to fulfill one's "civic" responsibilities. In Pauline hermeneutics it means that the Philippians ought to take seriously their civic responsibilities in the new "polis" of the believing community. Christ is the source of love as expressed in the lives of his citizens—Christians (Phil 1:8).

The third important aspect of the notion of citizenship is the societal level as expressed in fellowship and unity. Paul's definition of status and privilege differed from Aristotle's, who defined πολίτευμα primarily as the ruling aspect in a society. According to Paul, citizenship includes fellowship; individual citizens do not function alone. A city does not consist of one person but is a communion of many. Even cities could only grow

---

[20] The image of church as a body comes close to this, Romans 12:4-5, 1 Corinthians 12:12. Scholars such as Richard Ascough argue that the Macedonian Christian communities functioned in ways analogous to those of collegia, associations. Associations had hierarchies that to some extent reflected those of cities. In a Roman colony such as Philippi, the hierarchy of the city reflected, in turn, that of Rome. Roman power relations might thus be partially replicated in those of a Christian community. Ascough, ibid., 160-61, 190.

[21] Oakes, "Remapping ... ," op. cit. (note 2), 314.

[22] Luther reflects a similar way of thinking in 1528 in his treatise "Vom Abendmahl Christi," *WA* 26, 425.25-35 ("Confession concerning Christ's Supper," in *LW* 37, 283) where he used Philippians 3:20 to explain the presence of the kingdom of heaven on earth.

together by trade for instance. The Christians in Philippi are to realize that they are fellow sharers, "brothers and sisters" (Phil 1:12),[23] closely aligned with Paul, who is deeply concerned for their welfare.

Naturally, fellowship strives for unity. Unity is given by the "one Spirit" (Phil 4:1; cf. 1 Cor 16:13; Gal 5:1; 1 Thess 3:8). Unity in faith is important so that the congregation can withstand external pressure. In Philippi, external persecution probably came from the non-Christian citizens of Philippi (Phil 1:28). The idea of citizenship serves Paul to express his will that Philippians shall struggle together in unanimous conviction (σύμψυχοι) by standing united in one Spirit (ἐν ἑνὶ πνεύματι), struggling together (cf. Eph 2:19) with one mind (μιᾷ ψυχῇ) for "the faith of the gospel" (Phil 1:27).

The fourth aspect of citizenship is its exclusiveness. To speak about citizenship as fellowship raises the question about who is excluded from that fellowship. There were always people who were not citizens of a particular city. In Philippi that could be farmers, shepherds, villagers, as well as external enemies. This should not only be understood in the negative sense of exclusion or war. Based on the gospel in Philippians 1:5 and in references to the gospel throughout the first portion of the letter, it can also be interpreted as a mission mandate to attract outsiders to the message of Christ through conduct and suffering (Phil 1:27) and verbal proclamation (Phil 1:28).

Finally, the fifth possible use of the notion of citizenship points to a typical characteristic of city life: days of festivities and joy for all citizens. In Philippians this is the final day, the Day of Joy. The last day (the ἡμέρα in its references to the eschatological day) will be like the triumphant march of the Kyrios into the city. This serves as a model for the *parousia* of Christ, the day of redemption (Phil 1:6; 3:21). In Philippians, Christ is depicted as a savior and not as a judge. Until the coming of the Kyrios God will continue to perfect the good work that God began in Philippians. With the assurance of divine assistance they shall live in joy (Phil 1:6) and to the glory and praise of God (Phil 1:11). The epistle to the Philippians is a letter of joy (Phil 4:5).[24] But to be a citizen of a heavenly city does not lead to triumphalism, pride and arrogance. In the opening verses (Phil 1:1-2),

---

[23] According to BDAG, 18, the plural "brothers" can also mean "brothers and sisters." On the meaning of "brothers" for Paul, Johannes Beutler (EDNT 1.28) states: "The prevailing sense in Paul is that of fellow Christians, the foundational statement being Rom 8:29: the redeemed are conformed to Christ the 'first-born among many brethren.'"

[24] John P. Heil, *Philippians: Let Us Rejoice in Being Conformed to Christ* (Atlanta: SBL, 2010), 142–50.

for example, Paul and Timothy, the senders of the letter, are characterized as obedient "slaves" under the authority of Christ Jesus.

THE APPLICABILITY OF PAULINE HERMENEUTICS

Even though the actual word "citizenship" occurs only rarely in the Pauline letters, the concept as such is ever present. Citizenship points to God who in God's creative activity made Philippians into citizens in and through Christ. This precondition did not change and is valid universally for every human being in faith in Christ. Paul's understanding of citizenship serves as a hermeneutical instrument. It has the following key characteristics:

- Citizenship is an exclusive term and concept. The Hellenistic-Roman world was syncretistic in many aspects but not in the context of πολίτευμα. Slaves, wanderers and foreigners were not included. In Paul's hermeneutical use it implies that "the opposite" has to be abandoned. Monotheism is an exclusive religion, demanding the strict denunciation of other gods (Phil 2:15) and compromises with gods and the ways of life of the "fleshly" (old) world are not acceptable. Everything that does not fit the form of heavenly life has to be given up and a new way of life has to be taken up.

- Until today, the term citizenship implies status and privilege. According to the Pauline understanding, such an honor can be achieved through a process of being humbled and emptied to the depths of disgrace and shame (*kenosis*, cross). Confidence "in Christ Jesus" means trusting that Christ can grant every human the highest possible honor and dignity of heavenly citizenship as is expressed in Philippians 1:21, "living is Christ and dying is gain." Only those who have reached the nadir are on their way to the highest glory. Both perspectives—looking at an individual from the perspective of God on the one hand and the world on the other—have to be taken into account simultaneously.

- The term citizenship carries a message of joy about the blessed city of eternal life where blessed citizens live. The passage in Philippians 3:20 means: your country is in heaven and it has an impact on your conduct. It is not "local" (since it is where Christ is), but is not a way of conduct only. Rather, it is a divine realm that influences human conduct. It is the realm of the risen Christ, where he extends his power with serious ecclesiological implications. Citizenship serves as a metaphor for the persuasive invitation to live according to the privilege of being a member (Phil 3:16). *Politeuma* means the realm of power (and is similar to *basileia*), as the new homeland standing above all worldly political structures.

IS SUCH A PAULINE HERMENEUTICS APPLICABLE TODAY?

In Philippians 1:27 and 3:20, Paul bases his argument on a notion that people knew, understood and could relate to. This kind of argument belongs to the realm of common sense. A similar example is his use of the "olive tree" in Romans 11:24. It is contrary to nature to graft a wild branch onto a cultivated tree. Common sense tells us to graft good branches onto a wild tree and it is therefore understandable that good branches will be grafted onto a good tree. Similarly, it makes sense that citizenship, a coherent civil concept, is used in a theological context. For Lutheran hermeneutics it is helpful to illustrate such New Testament passages that are based on common sense with present day examples. The common sense argument has its firm place in Lutheran hermeneutics.

Paul's concept of citizenship not only answers the question of how to become a "citizen" but also how one can be a "good citizen." It is a life led in accordance with love as the highest principle (Phil 2:3-4). This is actually a formulation that expresses the Golden Rule (Mt 7:12; Mt 22:39; Rom 13:8-10; Gal 5:14) as the meaning of what the commandment of love means. It might be helpful if we were to exercise more caution when addressing the meaning of this ethical principle in current ethical debates. Even more so, because the Golden Rule is not a particular revealed Christian knowledge, but a general principle understandable for every rational citizen—heavenly or otherwise, regardless of political conviction.

For Paul, citizenship does not equal "living in." There are several groups of people who do not have citizenship but nevertheless live together with the citizens. This applies to and is important for certain societies, such as European ones for instance. For Paul, status and privilege do not and cannot mean an unfriendly, proud and boastful life. Paul states several clear imperatives: to live honorably, commendably (Phil 4:8; cf. 1 Thess 4:12),[25] according to the order a city is organized by. The starting line is not the pride in status and boasting about our freedom, but the relativization of all privileges (Phil 3:8) and humility before *coram deo* and *coram hominibus*, leading to the highest possible status of heavenly citizenship.

---

[25] Similarly: To do good works to all people (Gal 6:10), not to pay evil with evil (Rom 12:17) or keeping peace with all (Rom 12:18). This is actually the content of natural law.

APPLYING PAUL'S THEOLOGY AND HERMENEUTICS TO CHURCH AND SOCIETY

The Paradox of Reading Paul in the Context of the Lutheran Churches in Africa

Faustin Mahali

Introduction

The "Lutheran" missionary emphasis on a distinct Christian identity divorced converts from some of their cultural practices. In the process of reinforcing the churches' identity, stringent church discipline was introduced that took the place of African "ethics." The theological burden carried by African Lutheran churches today lies in the emphasis on the doctrine of justification by faith without the works of the law.[1] In practice, the Lutheran churches have been betrayed by the excessive observation of ecclesial ordinances which, in turn, promote sectarianism.[2] The Lutheran doctrine of justification by faith alone (by grace) stands in total contradiction to the churches' daily ecclesial and pastoral practices.[3] This casts doubt on whether Lutherans in Africa understand Paul's and Luther's interpretation of the doctrine of justification.

---

[1] Brighton Mufuruki Katabaro, *Rechtfertigung und Erfolg. Pfingstcharismatische Lehre und Praktiken als Herausforderung für die Lutherische Rechtfertigungslehre in Tansania* (Göttingen: Cuvillier Verlag, 2009), 107.
[2] MikaVähäkangas, "On the (ir)relevance of Lutheran Theology: Teaching Lutheran Theology in Tanzania," in *Dialog: A Journal of Theology* 47, 2 (2008), 173-74.
[3] Wilhelm Richebaecher, *Religious Change and Christology: Christian Theology in East Africa Set against the Background Processes of Religious Synthesis* (Neuendettelsau: Erlanger Verlag für Mission und Oekumene–Makumira Publication Seventeen, 2007), 202-203.

It is the assumption of this paper that the general hermeneutical key of Lutheran justification by faith alone has superficially taken root in the African Lutheran churches. This affects also the reading of the letters of Paul. In order for Africans to read Paul's letters they need to review the Lutheran hermeneutical key of "justification by faith alone" so that it resonates with their hermeneutical positions of well-being in their respective contexts.

CONTEXT

The first Lutheran churches in southern Africa were founded in 1780.[4] Assisted by German colonial occupiers the vibrant and vigorous growth of Lutheranism continued throughout the nineteenth century.[5] Subsequent contexts in which Lutheran churches were established and consolidated were based on these first missionary encounters of Lutheran missionaries with different communities in Africa.

The socio-cultural and religious dynamics of African communities during this epoch relate to an epoch in which Christianity was introduced and gained its hermeneutical vigor. Lutheran missionaries encountered local communities with well-established social and religious systems[6] and their attitude toward local religious practices was influenced by their aim to convert.[7] The conjecture that in evolutionary terms African culture was primitive and uncivilized undermined the comprehensive contextualiza-

---

[4] Hanns Lessing et al. (eds), *The German Protestant Church in Colonial Southern Africa: The Impact of Oversees Work from the Beginnings until the 1920s* (Wiesbaden: Harrassowitz, 2012), 15, at www.harrassowitzverlag.de/dzo/artikel/201/004/4216_201. pdf?t=1347530205.

[5] Philippe Denis, "African Indigenous Christianity in a Geo-Historical Perspective," in *Studia Historiae Ecclesiasticae* 38, 2 (2012), at uir.unisa.ac.za, 4; Carl-Erik Sahlberg, *From Kraft to Rugambwa: A Church History of Tanzania* (Nairobi, Kenya: Evangel Publishing House, 1986), 23–29; Per Hassing, "German Missionaries and the MajiMaji Rising," in *African Historical Studies* 3, 2 (1970), 373–89, at www.jstor. org/stable/216222; MuteroChrenje, "Church, State, and Education in Bechuanaland in the Nineteenth Century," in *The International Journal of African Historical Studies* 9, 3 (1976), 401–18, at www.jstor.org/stable/216845, 104; Faustin Mahali, "Becoming the Church in Tanzania," in *Lutheran Forum* (Delhi, NY: The American Lutheran Publicity Bureau, Spring 2009), 47–53.

[6] John S. Mbiti, *African Religions and Philosophy* (Nairobi, Kenya: Heinemann, 1969), 1–5; Ukachukwu Chris Manus, *Intercultural Hermeneutics in Africa: Methods and Approaches* (Nairobi Kenya: Acton Publishers, 2003), 9.

[7] John Parrat, *Reinventing Christianity: African Theology Today* (Grand Rapids, Michigan: William B. Eerdmans Publishing Company, 1995), 7–13; Kwame Bediako, "Africa and Christianity on the Threshold of the Third Millennium: The

tion of African worldviews into Christianity. Even there where Lutheran missionaries enthusiastically strove to integrate cultural values and belief systems into the process of evangelization, the problem of reducing these values and customs to mere social structures persisted.[8] Western Christians were trapped in the strict dichotomization of African societies as purely communal in relation to individualistic Western social structures.[9] Thus, African communities ironically had to be protected from the spoils of modernity in the course of the missionary activities, which used the same parameters of Western civilization to do mission.

It is plausible today to think that in their attempt to Christianize Africa, missionaries harbored ethnocentric views toward local culture(s).[10] According to Bénézet Bujo, the African context was supposed to integrate "anthropocentric, cosmic, and theocentric relational network."[11] Misconceptions such as that the environment was primitively socialist and uncultured contributed to the inadequate contextualization of Christianity into African culture. This initial stage affected the contextualization of evangelization in the Lutheran churches in Africa.

While missionary reports are rich in quantifying the achievement of baptizing and converting people to Christianity as part of their civilization project, they underestimate the thrust of traditional cultural and religious values that directly or indirectly remained embodied in the worldviews of Christian converts.[12] First-generation local Christians, who pioneered the establishment of indigenous Lutheran churches, carried with them African cultural attributes that shaped these churches. However, because of the legacy of the earlier missions, Africa continued to be regarded as an "uncivilized and underdeveloped" continent. Later, European and North American Lutheran churches became

---

Religious Dimension," in *African Affairs* vol. 99. no. 395 (2000), at www.jstor.org/stable/723811, 303–23.

[8] Bruno Gutmann, *Das Dschaggaland und seine Christen* (Leipzig: Verlag der Evang.-Luth. Mission, 1925), 119–22, here 131.

[9] Ernst Jaeschke, *Bruno Gutmann, His Life—His Thoughts—and His Work: An Early Attempt at a Theology in an African Context* (Erlangen: Verlag der Evang.-Luth. Mission, Makumira Publications, 1985), 83.

[10] Sjaak van der Geest and Jon P. Kirby, "The Absence of the Missionary in African Ethnography, 1930-65," in *African Studies Review* 35, 3 (1992), 59–103, at www.jstor.org/stable/525128, 91.

[11] Bénézet Bujo, *Foundations of an African Ethic: Beyond the Universal Claim of Western Morality* (Nairobi, Kenya: Paulines Publications Africa, 2003), 20.

[12] Norman Etherington, "Mission Station Melting Pots as a Factor in the Rise of South African Black Nationalism," in *The International Journal of African Historical Studies* vol. 9. no. 4 (1976), 592–605, here 596–97.

asymmetrical partners of the local churches.[13] The objectives of partnership were aimed at the "cheap" evangelization of African communities, using old models of modernity, and not necessarily striving to establish a strong basis for contextual theology and diaconal practice.

Furthermore, the uniqueness of the Lutheran churches in Africa is rooted in their teachings. The identity marker of a Lutheran Christian is affirmed during baptism as follows: "I renounce the devil and all its deeds and dealings. I submit to you God, the Father, and the Son, and the Holy Spirit, so that I totally depend on you and trustfully serve you until death."[14] When a baptized person has affirmed this they become a member of the Lutheran church that constitutionally confesses the Word of God through the Old and New Testaments, the Apostles, Nicene and Athanasian creeds, the unaltered Augsburg Confession and Martin Luther's catechism as the only "correct" explanation of the Word of God.[15] The use of the word "correct" instead of "pure"[16] appearing in many Swahili Lutheran constitutions gives rise to confusion and encourages a literal understanding of the Bible and the traditions of the church. Thus, the two aspects of baptismal and scriptural teaching constituting the Lutheran churches' identity, while plausible, ignite hermeneutical concerns in terms of teaching and living out the Word of God.

Lutheran churches encounter any attempt to integrate cultural values into Christianity with suspicion. The notion of justification by faith is used erroneously to discredit any positive consideration of the contextualization of the gospel. The root cause of the Christian stigmatization of African cultures lies in the sectarian Christian consideration of other cultures and religions, hatched by an evolutionary theory of civilization, and not

---

[13] Eila Helander and Wilson B. Niwagila, *Partnership and Power: A Quest for Reconstruction in Mission*, Makumira Publication Seven (Erlangen: Verlag der Evang.-Luth. Mission, 1996), 57–63.

[14] A direct paraphrase of baptismal promise of the baptized from *Katekisimo na Ufundisho wa Kikristo kama alivyofundisha Dr. Martin Luther* (Catechism and Christian Teaching According to Dr Martin Luther), Evangelical Lutheran Church in Tanzania, 1962, republished 1996, 21. This is also common in other Lutheran churches in Swahili speaking areas in East and Central Africa.

[15] *Katiba ya Kanisa la Kiinjili la Kilutheri Tanzania*, Toleo la Mwaka 2007 (The Constitution of the Evangelical Lutheran Church in Tanzania, 2007 edition). Due to the influence of ELCT in East and Central Africa, Swahili speaking Lutheran churches have adopted the same wording.

[16] About the clarity of Scriptures, Martin Luther, "The Bondage of the Will, 1536," in *LW* 33, 24–28. Cf. *Constitution of the Lutheran World Federation* (as adopted by the LWF Eighth Assembly, Curitiba, Brazil, 1990, including amendments adopted by the LWF Ninth Assembly, Hong Kong, 1997 and by the LWF Eleventh Assembly, Stuttgart, 2010), at www.lutheranworld.org/content/resource-lwf-constitution-and-bylaws.

simply from the teaching of justification by faith. When African Lutherans are allowed to contextualize justification by faith, they are likely first to resolve the puzzle of practiced rigorous church discipline. This also allows us to trace the practice of moral discipline back to the traditional religious interpretation of life as holistic and harmonious well-being.

Paul's views on justification and the quest for the covenantal inclusion of Gentiles

Traditionally the African Lutheran Christian was formed by the Lutheran doctrine of justification by faith. This Lutheran doctrine is derived from Paul's understanding of justification, which is linked to the understanding of salvation.[17] The African Christian identity, linked to justification, draws its impetus from the *praeparatio evangelica*.[18] This concurs with the current discourse in Pauline theology on the inclusion of all nations in God's salvific promise. Since such discourse touches the very heart of Lutheranism, it does not escape the hermeneutical strategy of integrating the identity of the African Lutheran Christian with Pauline theology as suggested by theologians throughout the history of reformation.

Recent studies have affirmed ethnocentric biases resulting from the Christian interpretation of the Jewish–Gentile rhetoric in Paul's letters. An intensive analysis of the rhetoric and context of Romans 9–11 has spawned new insights into the question of salvation for both Jews and Gentiles. Alan Segal considers Paul's thinking to be sectarian and based on the rabbinic teaching on the Messianic expectation paradigm of his time.[19] In Romans 9–11, Paul writes to both Jews and Gentiles and maintains that only those few (remnants) who have remained faithful until the end will be saved (cf. Lk 2:25–26; 36–38).[20] So, Paul emphatically identifies himself with Jewish Christians (Rom 11:1; cf. Phil 3:5–6)

---

[17] Norvald Yri, "Luther Speaks to Africa: The Question of Salvation," in Samuel Ngewa, Mark Shaw, and Tite Tienou (eds), *Issues in African Christian Theology* (Nairobi: East African Educational Publishers, 1998), 186–91.

[18] John S. Mbiti, *Bible and Theology in African Christianity* (Nairobi: Oxford University Press, 1986), 11; Yong Seung Han, *The Understanding of God in African Theology: Contributions of John Samuel Mbiti and Mercy Amba Oduyoye* (PhD diss., University of Pretoria, 2013),163–67, at repository.up.ac.za/bitstream/handle/2263/33006/Han_Understanding_2013.pdf; cf. Kwame Bediako, "Roots of African Theology," in *International Bulletin of Missionary Research* (April 1989), 60–62, at www.internationalbulletin.org/issues/1989-02/1989-02-058-bediako.pdf.

[19] Alan. F. Segal, *Paul the Convert: The Apostolate and Apostasy of Saul the Pharisee* (New Haven: Yale University Press, 1990), 281.

[20] Ibid., 278–79.

who profess justification on the grounds of their faith in Jesus Christ through whom they await the granted salvation (Rom 10:13). Paul's belief in God's impartiality toward Jews and Gentiles is centered on his belief in the faithfulness of Jesus Christ who is the only entry point to salvation.[21] In other words, all Jews and Gentiles must be converted in order to belong to a new Christian community that transcends ethnic boundaries. Ethnic groups that have not accepted Christianity automatically become inferior to those that have.

Moreover, the over-particularization of Christianity against Judaism has an impact on the interpretation of the gospel in relation to its cultural context. This is demonstrated in the translation and interpretation of Romans 10:4. According to Segal, the failure of the Jews to believe in Jesus Christ marks an explicit discontinuity with the Jewish Torah and Jewish culture.[22] In this respect, Segal translates Romans 10:4 to mean that the Torah and its practices come to an end with the belief in Christ.[23] Here Segal presents a notion of Jewish Christians breaking away from Judaism. Segal excommunicates Paul from his ethnic group for embracing Christianity at the expense of Judaism and attempts to respond to the stigma that Christians attach to Judaism as an "achievement religion."[24] By affirming Paul's misconception of Judaism, Segal detaches Paul from it and therefore justifies Christianity as a sect built on the wrong premises of Judaism.

Contrary to Segal's perspective, Stanley K. Stowers indicates a quite different view with regard to the Jew–Gentile inclusion in God's saving event in Jesus Christ. Stowers suggests that despite Paul's Jew–Gentile rhetoric the addressees of his letter to the Romans remained Gentiles.[25] In Romans 9-11, Israel's failure is attributed to its failure to perceive Abraham's faithfulness as synonymous with Jesus' faithfulness.[26] The subjective translation attributed to the faithfulness of Abraham and Jesus impacts how we read Romans 9-11, especially Romans 10:4, and also Romans 1:16-17.[27] Similarly to Abraham's faithfulness in the past, Jesus' faithfulness now

---

[21] Ibid., 279–80.

[22] Ibid., 278–79.

[23] Ibid., 278–79. Rom 10:4 "τέλος γὰρ νόμου Χριστὸς εἰς δικαιοσύνην παντὶ τῷ πιστεύοντι" is translated, "For Christ is the end of the law so that there may be righteousness for everyone who believes."

[24] On the term "achievement religion" as opposed to a religion of grace, see Heikki Räisänen, *Jesus, Paul and Torah: Collected Essays,* Journal for the Study of the New Testament Supplement Series 43, transl. by David E. Orton (London: Sheffield Academic Press, 1992), 45–47.

[25] Stanley K. Stowers, *A Rereading of Romans: Justice, Jews, and Gentiles* (New Haven: Yale University Press, 1994), 288.

[26] Ibid., 286.

[27] Ibid., 286.

becomes the condition for salvation. In Judaism, the observation of the law is considered as an instructional tool (Gal 3:24).[28] That tool leads to the fullness of righteousness in Jesus Christ and therefore does not become an end in itself.[29] The meeting point of both Jews and Christians is God's faithfulness to the whole of creation through the faithfulness of Jesus Christ.[30] Both Jews and Gentiles—being descendants of Abraham from whom the promise of salvation originates—are accountable before God based on the faithfulness that is in Jesus and not on their written and unwritten laws.[31]

Segal and Stowers agree that Paul identifies himself as a Christian Jew. According to Segal, Paul is a deviant and sectarian Jew who, together with other Jews who had converted to Christianity and identify themselves as the remnant of Israel, would ultimately convert other Jews to Christianity as the only way to salvation. According to Stowers, Paul's identification with Jewish culture serves as a continuation of God's fulfillment to save all nations without discrimination. Therefore, Paul becomes a Christian Jew and is equally entitled to salvation like any other Christian of any ethnic origin so long as all believe in the faithfulness of Jesus Christ, manifested through his life, death and resurrection (Rom 5:8–11; cf. Phil. 2:8). Although Christians embody different ethnic identities, they should stand faithfully and be responsible before God. Thus, according to Stowers, Christians of Paul's time are not divorced from their cultural identities, but become transformed into the newness of life; the life, death and resurrection of Jesus Christ.

The outcome of this reading of Paul concurs with the struggle of African scholars who seek their identity against a predominantly ethnocentric and, more precisely, a euro-western-ethnocentric Christianity.[32] In the African context, the notion of *preparatio evangelica* fits the Pauline idea of continuity according to Romans 9–11. God incarnates to renew life of the whole creation. This not only creates a positive view of culture and human beings as God's creation, but makes all Christians appear equal before God, regardless of gender, ethnicity, social status and any other peculiarity (Gal 3:28). In addition, such an interpretation reduces the stigma imposed on African Christianity as being legalistic and based on African customs and rules.

---

[28] Paul L. Owen, "'Works of the Law' in Romans and Galatians: A New Defense of the Subjective Genitive," in *Journal of Biblical Literature* vol. 126. no. 3 (2007), 553–77, especially 559, at www.jstor.org/stable/27638452.

[29] Stowers, op. cit. (note 25), 287.

[30] Ibid., 292–93.

[31] Ibid., 298.

[32] Cf. George Tinker, "Decolonizing the Language of Lutheran Theology: Confessions, Mission, Indians, and the Globalization of Hybridity, " in *Dialog: A Journal of Theology* 50/2 (2011), 193–204.

PAULINE–LUTHERAN THEOLOGY OF
JUSTIFICATION BY FAITH FOR AFRICANS

The Western ethnocentric Christianization of Africa galvanized forensic ecclesial rules that diminished the force of a theory of justification by faith according to Paul, which intends good or newness of life for all of creation. The practice of church discipline in the Lutheran churches in Africa is interpreted as forensic and not in line with justification by faith. This is so since the premises for judging the practice are wrong. A justification–salvation theory in Paul should be measured against the holistic universalistic-cosmic view of goodness of the African worldview and not necessarily from the pessimistic anthropological point of view. Such a view is likely to accommodate Paul's and even Luther's theological keys of justification as an inherent condition of God's saving event.

The Lutheran encounter of the justification–salvation correlative syntaxes is emphatically anthropological.[33] Lutherans affirm that a human being (who is regarded as a sinner) is graciously (*sola gratia*) awarded divine righteousness through faith (*sola fide*) in Jesus Christ. According to Martin Luther, it is only God revealed in Jesus Christ who possesses the power to remit sins and grants us the power of faithfulness ("made believers") to do God's will.[34] However a trace of this justification–salvation model in Paul's understanding of justification makes for a twofold consideration. The two Lutheran dimensions summarize the meaning of Paul's *dikaiosune tou Theou,* namely, "God-adjudicated righteousness," or righteousness as "primarily a reference to God's saving activity [...] as a divine activity manifesting divine power."[35] The latter dimension originates in a pessimistic anthropological view of justification and leads to the understanding that justification should be perceived as the powerful action of divine salvation inherent in God's saving event through the entire life of Jesus Christ.

In his work, *Bondage of the Will,* Luther describes hermeneutical principles that are imperative for ascertaining the divine nature of "justification by faith." In his vehement disapproval of the human free will, Luther asserts that "God foreknows nothing contingently, but that he foresees and purposes and does all things by his immutable, eternal, and infallible will."[36] Furthermore, Luther

---

[33] Theo A. Boer, "Is Luther's Ethics Christian Ethics?" in *Lutheran Quarterly* Volume XXI (2007), 414-15, at www.pthu.nl/over_pthu/Medewerkers/boer/Boer_2007_Lutheran_Quarterly.pdf.

[34] Martin Luther, *Commentary on the Epistle to the Romans,* transl. by J. T. Mueller (Grand Rapids, Michigan: Zondervan Publishing House, 1954), 60-64.

[35] William S. Campell, "Ernst Kaesemann on Romans: The Way Forward or the End of an Era?" Romans through History and Cultures Seminar, SLB, 2007, 5-6, at www.vanderbilt.edu/AnS/religious_studies/SBL2007/Campbell.pdf.

[36] *LW* 33, 37.

believes the Scriptures to be the only source of God's free will" and internally and externally clear.[37] This internal clarity is a result of the fact that the Holy Spirit helps to interpret it, and the external clarity is drawn from the Word (of) God as manifest in the preaching of the earthly Jesus Christ.[38] These are significant biblical theological hermeneutical principles. According to Luther, it is God's free will that determines everything lived in God and all works are the result of God's will.[39] What is required of human beings is faithfulness and submission to the law of God.[40] However, even staying faithful depends on God's grace.[41]

It should therefore be understood that God restores a sinful person into the newness of life through God's gracious providence of life manifest in the life, death and resurrection of Jesus Christ.[42] Through faith, if Luther is interpreted correctly, a human being is endowed with these divine qualities because it is God's will that a human being retains these qualities through a responsive faith that also originates from God. It is not through our faith but through Christ's faithfulness that we are endowed with righteousness and forgiven for our sins.[43]

An African way of thinking, according to which the human being's inherent divine force strives toward a progressive and transcendental good life on earth for all its creatures through ancestral divine mediation, is consistent with justification as the manifestation of God's power. In the African context, a disturbance of one part of God's creation is perceived as a disturbance of the whole.[44] According to Bujo, the universe is held in a balance and personal well-being is identified with the whole while being responsible and accountable.[45] This concept fits well with Paul's understanding of salva-

---

[37] Ibid., 24–28.

[38] Luther argues, "For the Spirit is required for the understanding of Scripture, both as a whole and in any part of it." Ibid., 28.

[39] Luther says, "The sort of person I am, and the spirit and purpose with which I have been drawn into this affair, I leave to Him who knows that all these things have been effected by his free choice, not mine—though the whole world itself ought to have been long ago aware of this." Ibid., 73.

[40] Luther insists, "It is thus shown in that first man, as a frightening example and for the breaking down of our pride, what our free choice can do when it is left to itself and not continually and increasingly actuated and augmented by the Spirit of God." Ibid., 124.

[41] Ephesians 2:8.

[42] Romans 6:11, 23; 8:2; 1 Corinthians 15:22; 2 Corinthians 5:17, 19; Galatians 3:14, 26, 28; Galatians 5:6.

[43] Hung-Sik Choi, "πίστις in Galatians 5:5–6: Neglected Evidence for the Faithfulness of Christ," in *Journal of Biblical Literature* vol. 124, no. 3 (Fall, 2005), 467–90; cf. Charles L. Quarles, "From Faith to Faith: A Fress Examination of the Prepositional Series in Romans 1:17," in *Novum Testamentum* vol. 45, fasc. 1 (Jan. 2003), 1–21.

[44] Bénézet Bujo, *Ethical Dimension of Community: The African Model and the Dialogue between North and South* (Nairobi: Paulines Publications Africa, 1997), 25.

[45] Ibid., 28.

tion that takes on board the fate of the whole of creation (Rom 8:18–28). It also fits the "Lutheran" perspective of a total dependence on God's will that ultimately endows the human being with divine qualities.[46]

Luther's rereading of the Bible was influenced by his search for spiritual authenticity in the way in which God justifies humanity. For him justification by faith, God's gracious free gift of salvation in Jesus Christ, was an alternative to the manipulated endowment of justification manifest in the payment of indulgences. Luther's doctrine of justification by faith explicitly opposed the payment of indulgences and hence freed Christians from the burden of the extravagant and unjust expenditures of the papal church.[47] This liberating paradigm is holistic and makes it possible for the Lutheran churches to accommodate a holistic view of life and to challenge individual, social and religious structures that threaten life.

In this case, the interpretation of Pauline texts in relation to the holistic cosmic view of the correlation between justification and salvation is made possible. The African concept of justification and well-being of the community rests on reconciling individuals who have offended each other.[48] Moreover, a harmonious coexistence with the environment is envisaged since creation is considered to be in divine harmony with the needs of human beings.[49] For Paul, the central text for linking justification and salvation identifies reconciliation as the binding power of the present and future expectations of the whole creation that lie in trusting the faithfulness of Christ manifested in his life, death and resurrection (Rom 5:8–11). For Paul, the implication of Luther's hermeneutical key of total submissiveness to God's law as is manifested in Jesus Christ brings the whole creation to God's gracious gifts and life in abundance.

---

[46] Martin Luther, "Fifth Sunday after Epiphany: The Glorious Adornment of Christians, Colossians 3:12-17," in *Sermons on Epistle Texts for Epiphany, Easter and Pentecost*, transl. by John Nicholas Lenker, Minneapolis, 1909, at www.martinluthersermons.com/Luther_Lenker_Vol_7.pdf.

[47] Martin Luther, "Disputation of Doctor Martin Luther on the Power of and Efficacy of Indulgencies," in *Works of Martin Luther*, vol. 1 (Albany: The Ages Digital Library Collections, 1995), 27–35.

[48] Kizito Menanga, "Ethical Foundations for African Traditional Reconciliation Mechanisms: A Case Study of the Ugandan *Mato Oput* [traditional] Process [of reconciliation]," a paper presented at the interdisciplinary session (Uganda: Catholic University of East Africa, 2008), 8–13, at www.urbanleaders.org%2F655LandRights%2F05LocalResponses%2FNairobi%2FMato%2520-%2520Oput%2C%2520Fr.%2520Kizitodoc.doc

[49] Clement Dorm-Adzobu & Peter G. Veit, *Religious Beliefs and Environmental Protection: The Malshegu Sacred Grove in Northern Ghana* (Nairobi Kenya: World Resources Institution [WRI], 1991), 12–13, at pdf.usaid.gov/pdf_docs/PNACA562.pdf.

The human manifestation of power through faith to salvation is in God's act of dying for our sins and resurrection (Rom 5:8–9). God makes a self-expiatory act through Jesus' death in order to cleanse human beings and their cosmic requirements from evil forces (Rom 5:9). God's sacrificial act reconciles opposing parties (including cosmic elements); the reconciled creatures are brought to life and remedy lost relationships. Salvation simply means accepting, believing or trusting that God's sacrificial act brings reconciliation and life. This means that as human beings we confess our sins and are ready to adhere to the qualities of reconciliation and forgiveness that produce righteousness or justification (Rom 1:16–17; Rom 5:8–11).

Thus, as a point of departure into a viable contextualization, it should be taken seriously that, according to the African Christian perception, faith accommodates in it an act of human trustfulness and obedience to God. Obedience is associated with Abrahamic trustfulness that has maintained the participation of both Jews and Gentiles in God's promise that transcended into the faithfulness of Jesus Christ.[50] Jesus Christ's emphasis on faithfulness as a participatory condition for both Jews and Gentiles in the promise of salvation rejects God's impartiality (Rom 1–11). This breaks through all bondages of ethnocentrism and opens new avenues for the Christian encounter with different ethnicities, identities and cultures.

THE AFRICAN "LUTHERAN" DOCTRINE OF JUSTIFICATION/SALVATION AND ITS RESPONSE TO AFRICAN HEALING MINISTRIES

From an African perspective, well-being is holistic. An individual should exist in harmony with the whole of creation. The "Lutheran" doctrine of justification/salvation largely adheres to this logic if Luther's understanding of total dependence on and submissiveness to God is taken seriously. It follows then that the ethical dimensions as a consequence of this theological principle would reflect how such a human being, endowed with divine and spiritual qualities, responsibly participates[51] in taking care of God's creation.

The forensic practice of church discipline in African Lutheran churches has strong roots in the African concept so that the prosperity of communal life should never be divorced from the interests of an individual or an element. Anything that disturbs this equilibrium commits an offense and becomes subject

---

[50] Romans 3:22, 26; Galatians 2:16; 3:22.

[51] William J. Wright, *Martin Luther's Understanding of God's Two Kingdoms: A Response to the Challenge of Skepticism* (Grand Rapids, Michigan: Baker Academic, 2010), 17–31, esp. 22.

to corrective measures. Such remedial measures are designed in such a way that at the end of the day the offender (human being) and the victim (human being or object) are brought together in order to reconcile and to start afresh.[52]

The excommunication from the community is not necessarily based on a person's introspection but to what extent one disturbs the principles and customs that promote a harmonious life and the well-being of the whole creation. In this respect there are many pastoral qualities that can be reinvented and integrated to counteract the excessive and rigorous practice of church discipline in the African Lutheran churches. The pastoral paradigm for ethical procedures should challenge those practices of church discipline that do not promote effective reconciliation among members of the church and society at large.

Another area where the Lutheran churches in Africa could reconsider their role in promoting the well-being of their communities is their position on healing ministries. For decades such ministries have been considered as being opposed to the scientific and medical cause and effect paradigms. One of the missionary achievements in Africa was the introduction of health facilities employing modern medical expertise. Anything that did not meet the criteria of modern medical treatment was discredited as being primitive and ineffective. As a result, many Lutheran Christians in Africa and elsewhere think that healing ministries are irrelevant and ineffective.

However, recent studies have pointed to another direction in the therapeutic understanding of diseases. In order for healing to have a holistic meaning, one should differentiate between "sickness" and "illness."[53] Medical sociology distinguishes between illness and sickness. Illness is the objective diagnosis that an external impartial observer is able to make based on the constellation of symptoms that the patient presents. Sickness is the social role that the patient adopts as the patient and how other concerned stakeholders, in relationship with the patient, interpret the meaning of the illness. While for a long time medical professionals have considered medical treatment from the perspective of sickness only, today a more holistic view of disease is taken. Healing deals with a holistic view of a person in relation to their whole environment.[54] Thus, an African (and maybe global) Lutheran concept of healing that is anchored in

---

[52] Jean-Marc Éla, *My Faith as an African*, transl. by John P. Brown and Susan Perry (Nairobi, Kenya: Acton Publishers, 2001), 21–24.

[53] Emilio Voigt, "Zwischen Reich Gottes und anderen Interessen: Die Frage der Suche nach Jesus," in Wolfgang Stegemann and Richard E. DeMaris (eds), *Alte Texte in neuen Kontexten: Wo steht die sozialwissenschaftliche Bibelexegese?* (Stuttgart: Verlag W. Kohlhammer, 2015), 205–21.

[54] The World Health Organization defines health in a very holistic manner and describes, "Health is a state of complete physical, mental and social well-being and not merely the absence of disease or infirmity," at www.who.int/governance/eb/who_constitution_en.pdf.

the diaconal understanding of health and healing from a medical perspective needs to be reviewed in order to integrate new ways of healing.

If this is the case, then an application of an African Lutheran justification/salvation theory is inevitable. Based on the reading of the African context and Luther's propositions, this "justification" or as an outcome of it "salvation" should be drawn from a holistic view of God's saving act in Christ that resonates with the holistic view of life in the African context. Life should be liberated or healed from individual or systemic sin. The involvement of the church in the struggle against such evil forces defines a holistic diaconal ministry and the role of the church as a healing institution. From this perspective, one can easily accommodate and critically reflect on healing ministries in Africa. It is life and not the ability of a person to follow the law that matters. Healing ministries in Africa serve this purpose of saving life that is well rooted in the worldviews of many Africans.

Ultimately this African Lutheran justification/salvation model is expected to respond to the Pentecostal healing ministries that seem to challenge Lutheran models of treatment. Pentecostal ministries, though aiming at individualistic salvation, tend to accommodate African traditional rituals of healing.[55] The Lutheran churches in Africa miss the point when they condemn Pentecostal initiatives as theologically deceptive and baseless. It is a mistake to regard healing and miracle performances as achievement religion or, as it is referred to today, the prosperity gospel, without relating it to the inner philosophy of African life. Having reviewed the inner meaning of justification according to the Lutheran tradition, the integration of the African views of well-being into Paul's and Luther's justification/salvation mystery opens positive avenues for dialoguing with Charismatics and Pentecostals regarding healing practices.

CONCLUSION

It is a theological and practical challenge for members of the Lutheran churches in Africa to regard themselves as gracious Christians based on the interpretation of justification by faith while, at the same time, greatly acknowledging stringent church discipline. The survey of the Lutheran context in Africa indicates that strict church discipline was promoted in an effort to maintain a Lutheran ecclesial identity. In so doing, Christianity strongly embodied Euro-Western ethnocentric perceptions, which to a certain extent stigmatized African cultural realities.

---

[55] Robert Mbe Akoko, "*Ask and You Shall Be Given:*" *Pentecostalism and the Economic Crisis in Cameroon* (Buea, Cameroon: University of Buea, 2007), 18-19.

A reading of Paul on salvation economy has freed Christianity from ethnocentric sentiments. It has allowed the reinterpretation of salvation as God's invitation to all of humanity to participate in the saving event manifested in the life, death and resurrection of Jesus Christ. A comprehensive understanding of salvation that respects God's promise to the continuity of all ethnic and cultural groups permeates African contexts and permits the viable and valid contextualization of the foundations of the Christian faith. This has created a possibility for a direct comparison between Luther and African contexts in relation to the understanding of justification by faith.

It was discovered that Luther's biblical and theological hermeneutical keys of justification by faith resonate with the African view of total dependence on God, mediated through divine personalities and objects. Luther affirms that human freedom is completely dependent on God's free will, from which our faithfulness and deeds originate. The African paradigm of God's giving of holistic well-being and also well-being achieved through stewardship of human beings and objects embodied with God's divine powers, echoes Luther's affirmation of the fruits of gracious faithfulness of human beings resulting from God's endowment of justification to the whole of creation.

Thus, the rigorous practice of church discipline in Africa is mistakenly considered as purely African ecclesial ordinance, without considering its perceived maintenance of a holistic view of the well-being of creation. A direct comparison of Luther's view of salvation/justification and the African view of well-being has opened up a new avenue to reinterpret church discipline practiced by Lutheran churches in Africa as the contextualization of ethical dimensions aiming at sustaining the well-being of the whole of creation. This resolves the paradox of misinterpreting justification by faith as ridged church discipline.

Furthermore, the reinterpretation of the Lutheran justification/salvation doctrine leads the Lutheran churches to consider their role of healing. The adoption of a holistic view on health and healing critiques a diaconal view of health based on strict medical and psychological perspectives. A Lutheran solution to the problem is the reinvention of hermeneutical keys of justification by faith that attributes salvation to God's faithfulness in reclaiming human life from life threatening forces through God's free gift of faith. Such a solution enables the Lutheran churches in Africa to participate in healing projects such as confronting social, economic, gender, ethnic and religious injustice and to eradicate the manipulation of God's spiritual gifts. This will encourage African Lutheran churches proactively to respond to the irresponsible and unethical social, political and economic systems and teachings of some Pentecostal and Charismatic circles through preaching a gospel that promises increased well-being in life without responsibility and accountability.

The Pauline Letters and (Homo)Sexuality: Examining Hermeneutical Arguments Used in the Estonian Discussion

Urmas Nõmmik

The Estonian background

Societal life and the church landscape in Estonia have their own peculiarities. Compared to most other countries, only a relatively small percentage of the population are religiously affiliated. Currently, this varies between twenty and twenty-five percent, and shows a slightly decreasing trend. The majority are Christian and the predominant denominations are the Estonian Orthodox Church of Moscow Patriarchate and the Estonian Evangelical Lutheran Church. Church affiliation among the Russian speaking population (approximately twenty-seven percent of the population) is greater than among the Estonian speaking population; hence, in recent years, the Orthodox Church has become the largest religious denomination in Estonia. However, since the public discussion is predominantly carried out in Estonian, the Russian Orthodox Church does not have a particular influence on the public agenda. Among Estonian speaking Christians, the Lutheran church has historically been the largest Christian denomination, followed by the Estonian Apostolic Orthodox Church (Constantinople Patriarchate). Despite a considerably smaller membership, Baptists and Roman Catholics are very active and influential. The Estonian Council of Churches (ECC) has considerable influence since it unites the fragmented church landscape quite well. It is the only Christian institution in Estonia that receives state funding.

The Christian hermeneutical discussion in Estonia is therefore not only restricted to the Lutheran domain but involves the ECC and, through this, particularly Roman Catholics and Baptists. Within the framework of this institution, the size of the denomination does not matter much.

In the following, I will refer to examples from the Estonian discussion on (homo)sexuality and biblical hermeneutical issues, particularly with regard to Paul's letters. In 2014, for the first time during the Soviet and post-Soviet era, Estonian society became involved in discussions that incorporated religious and specifically Christian arguments. The reason was the Estonian parliament's plan to introduce the new Cohabitation Act, in which Estonian Christians, despite their small number, were actively involved. The fact that biblical arguments and discussions, including biblical hermeneutical questions, reached people outside the churches came as a surprise, particularly in light of the discussion on women's ordination, which remains an entirely inner-church or even inner-clergy matter. The majority of non-Christians in Estonia did not suddenly discover the Bible. Rather, they became aware that sexual, gender and marriage issues are addressed in it. In other words, the Bible is a known entity for Estonians but, due to fifty years of Communist Soviet ideology and no comprehensive religious education in schools, there is considerable religious illiteracy. There is little awareness of the contents of the Bible and the reception of its ideas among the population is fraught with various prejudices. Moreover, there is insufficient hermeneutical reflection. Those reshaping the cultural-philosophical thesis of the decline of traditional (i.e., Christian and Western) values into a strong political statement over the last years, could use this unique opportunity of a renewed interest in the Bible to gain support from certain biblical passages.

I will not discuss the controversy regarding women's ordination, since it is not officially a central issue in the Estonian Lutheran church, despite being hotly debated among the clergy and a focal issue in some neighboring Lutheran churches. However, when examining the biblical hermeneutical arguments regarding homosexuality and same-sex partnership one cannot escape the fact that there are points of contact with the question of women's ordination.[1] The basic question in the vivid discussion on gender and sexual issues is how to interpret certain biblical passages in light of the modern world and modern Lutheran contexts, particularly with reference to the Pauline letters, creation theology and the revelatory character of the Scripture.[2]

---

[1] For background information, see several articles in *Religion & Gesellschaft in Ost und West*, no. 1, vol. 43 (2015), at g2w.eu/zeitschrift/rgow-archiv/2015/1020-rgow-1-2015-politik-und-religion-im-baltikum, particularly Priit Rohtmets, "Die lutherischen Kirchen vor den Herausforderungen der Moderne" (18–21); Alar Kilp, "Kirchliche Reaktionen auf das neue Lebensgemeinschaftsgesetz in Estland" (22–24).

[2] As an introduction to different arguments in regard to both issues, see Jack B. Rogers, "Culture vs. Revelation: Women's Ordination and LGBT Ordination as Parallel Struggles," in *Church & Society*, no. 3, vol. 96 (2006), 97–110; John T. Pless,

DISCUSSION AND SOURCES

Compared to Western societies, the theological discussion on same-sex relationships was initiated only relatively late in the day as a reaction to lobbying by several LGBT activists. In 2005, Mark P. Nelson (Canada), a teacher at the Baltic Methodist Theological Seminary in Tallinn, published an article in the journal of the Methodist Church in Estonia, reflecting on similar debates in the USA.[3] In a short paper in the Lutheran newspaper *Eesti Kirik* [Church of Estonia], New Testament scholar and pastor Vallo Ehasalu reflected on the Bible and homosexuality.[4] A first serious attempt to map the opinion of churches on the question of family, sex and homosexuality was made in 2008, when the ECC published a *Declaration of the Estonian Council of Churches on the Issue of Homosexuality.*[5] In 2011, two Lutheran biblical scholars, Jaan Lahe and Urmas Nõmmik, responded to the declaration in a scholarly article on homosexuality in the Bible.[6] The reactions to this were more or less emotionally charged.

The overall debate was provoked by the Estonian government's plan legally to recognize same-sex unions. While the political procedure was launched already in 2011, from April to October 2014 the coalition was on the way to change the Cohabitation Act. This triggered an intensive debate in society. The Estonian churches' official reaction was univocal and several declarations and memoranda have been published. These include the *Statement of the Estonian Council of Churches on the Issue of the Development of the Cohabitation Act;*[7] the *Declaration of the Estonian*

"The Ordination of Women and Ecclesial Endorsement of Homosexuality: Are They Related?" in *Concordia Theological Quaterly*, no. 3–4, vol. 74 (2010), 343–58.

[3] Mark P. Nelson, "Kirik ja homoseksuaalsus ... Miks nii palju kära?" ["Church and Homosexuality... Why So Much Noise?"], in *Koduteel. Eesti Metodisti Kiriku ajakiri* [*Homeward Bound. Journal of the Estonian Methodist Church*], no. 4 (2005).

[4] Vallo Ehasalu, "Piibli sõna homoseksuaalsuse kohta" ["The Bible's Word on Homosexuality"], in *Eesti Kirik*, no. 51 (15 December 2006).

[5] *Eesti Kirikute Nõukogu seisukoht homoseksuaalsuse küsimuses* (16 October 2008), at ekn.ee/lakitus.php?id=1.

[6] Jaan Lahe and Urmas Nõmmik, "Homoseksuaalsus Piiblis" ["Homosexuality in the Bible"], in *Usuteaduslik Ajakiri* [Theological Journal], no. 1, vol. 62 (2011), 3–21. This article caused a bit of an uproar among clergy and members of several churches; the respective issue was removed from sale at the Christian book store of the Lutheran congregation of St. Paul's Church in Tartu and at the sales desk of the Conference of the Lutheran Clergy in January 2012. However, public interest grew; the issue was quickly sold out and spread electronically, at usuteadus.ee/wordpress/wp-content/uploads/2011%20%2862%29/Nommik-Lahe.pdf.

[7] *Eesti Kirikute Nõukogu arvamus kooseluseaduse väljatöötamise küsimuses* (2012), at ekn.ee/lakitus.php?id=19.

Council of Churches on the Conception of the Cohabitation Act;[8] and the *Public Notice of the Estonian Council of Churches to the Parliament of the Estonian Republic Regarding the Project of the Cohabitation Act.*[9] Furthermore, "a group consisting mostly of lay Catholics who formed the Foundation for the Protection of Family and Traditional Values committed to fight homosexual relations as immoral acts in conflict with 'the law of nature.'"[10] However, particularly in the Lutheran church and among academically qualified theologians, there was considerable opposition to the official theological discourse. A seminar on the new Cohabitation Act, organized by the Legal Affairs Committee of the Estonian parliament on 28 August 2014, included two different Christian voices. The seminar was broadcast on the internet and the recording can be accessed on the committee's homepage. Both papers addressing theological questions were published shortly after the seminar—one by the Baptist biblical scholar Peeter Roosimaa,[11] the other by the author of this article.[12] On the side of the Christians supporting the Cohabitation Act, a series of articles was published in the special issue of the weekly online journal, *Kirik & Teoloogia* [*Church & Theology*].[13] On

---

[8] *Eesti Kirikute Nõukogu seisukoht kooseluseaduse eelnõu kontseptsiooni kohta* (28 September 2012), at ekn.ee/lakitus.php?id=21.

[9] *Eesti Kirikute Nõukogu avalik kiri Eesti Vabariigi Riigikogule seoses kooseluseaduse eelnõuga* (3 October 2014), at ekn.ee/uudis.php?id=147; Cf. also *Eesti Kristliku Nelipühi Kiriku seisukoht homoseksuaalsuse küsimustes* [*Statement of the Estonian Christian Pentecostal Church on the Issues of Homosexuality*] (5 May 2014), at www.eknk.ee/content/fck/File/EKNK%20seisukoht_homoseksuaalsus.pdf.

[10] Alar Kilp, "Religious Nationalism Blocking the Legal Recognition of Same-Sex Unions in the Baltic States," in Srdjan Sremac, R. Ruard Ganzevoort (eds), *Religious and Sexual Nationalisms in Central and Eastern Europe: Gods, Gays and Governments* (Leiden, Boston: Brill, 2015), 113–33, here 125.

[11] Peeter Roosimaa, "Mida ütleb Piibel seksuaalelust" ["What Does the Bible Say on Sexual Life?"], in *Eesti Kirik*, no. 35 (10 September 2014).

[12] Urmas Nõmmik, "Kirikust, teoloogiast, peremudelitest ja kooseluseadusest" ["On Church, Theology, Family Models and Cohabitation Act"], in *Kirik & Teoloogia*, no. 145 (19 September 2014); in abbreviated form published also at *ERR uudised* [*News of the Estonian Public Broad Service*] (23 September 2014), at uudised.err. ee/v/arvamus/de49f050-176a-4f62-85cf-ef89881bb407.

[13] *Kirik & Teoloogia* (www.kjt.ee) is published by an independent NGO; however, most of the editors are Lutherans, many of them ordained pastors. Besides Nõmmik, op. cit. (note 12), at kjt.ee/2014/09/osadus-ja-erisus-nr-145-19-9-2014), included Jaan Lahe, "Kas homoseksuaalse partnerluse hukkamõistmine Piibli alusel on põhjendatud?" ["Is the Condemnation of Same-sex Partnership Justified According to the Bible?"]; an Estonian translation of *Orientierungslinien zur ethisch-theologischen Urteilsbildung am Beispiel der strittigen Bewertung von Homosexualität in christlicher Perspektive.* Texte aus der VELKD, no. 170, by Mareile Lasogga; and Thomas-Andreas Põder, "Quo vadis, EELK? Küsimusi, selgitusi ja ettepanekuid ühenduses

the side of the Christians opposing the Cohabitation Act, one of the most prominent conservative theologians, the pastor of the Lutheran congregation of St. John's Church in Tallinn, Arne Hiob, published a response to Lahe and Nõmmik's article on the internet portal *Meie Kirik [Our Church]*.[14]

By the same token, a discussion on biblical hermeneutics endorsed the debate on homosexuality. Also in this case, Hiob,[15] Lahe and Nõmmik[16] have dominated the public theological discussion.

ISSUES ADDRESSED IN THE ESTONIAN DEBATE

MEANING OF INDIVIDUAL WORDS: HOMOSEXUALS OR NOT, ORIENTATION OR PRACTICE

Among other biblical passages, Lahe and Nõmmik's scholarly article discusses three New Testament passages: Romans 1:26–27, 1 Corinthians 6:9–10, 1 Timothy 1:8–10 and considers the meanings of some strategic lexemes with negative connotations.[17] Against the backdrop of a scholarly discussion on two words, *malakoi* and *arsenokoitai*, in 1 Corinthians 6:9,

---

kirikukogu hiljutise avaldusega" ["Quo vadis, EELC? Questions, Explanations, and Suggestions Regarding a Recent Statement of the Church Council"].

[14] Arne Hiob, "Piiblitõlgendusest, homoseksualismist ja Jumala armastusest" ["On Biblical Interpretation, Homosexuality, and God's Love], in *Meie Kirik* (23 September 2014); in abbreviated form published also at *ERR uudised [News of the Estonian Public Broad* Service] (24 September 2015), at uudised.err.ee/v/arvamus/5398d6fe-18c0-44d3-bb75-3ed0a37be346. *Meie Kirik* (earlier www.meiekirik.ee, now www. meiekirik.net) is edited by Lutheran pastors who openly declare their conservatism and represent the Society of the Augsburg Confession.

[15] Arne Hiob, "Jah, tõesti ajaloolis-kriitiline reduktsioon" ["Indeed, Historical-Critical Reductionism"], in *Kirik & Teoloogia*, no. 115 (21 February 2014); Hiob, "Usk muutuvas maailmas luterliku vaate kohaselt" ["Faith in the Changing World According to the Lutheran View"], in *Kirik & Teoloogia*, no. 113 (7 February 2014); Hiob, *Piibel usu ja teaduse vahel. Universaalne kultuuriraamat tänapäeval [Bible between Faith and Science. Universal Culture Book Nowadays]* (Tallinn: Allika, 2015).

[16] Jaan Lahe, Urmas Nõmmik, "Lühike sissejuhatus ajaloolis-kriitilisse meetodisse" ["Short Introduction to the Historical-Critical Method"], in *Kirik & Teoloogia*, no. 116 (28 February 2014); Nõmmik, "Kas tõesti ajaloolis-kriitiline reduktsioon?" ["Is It Really a Historical-Critical Reductionism?"], in *Kirik & Teoloogia*, no. 114 (14 February 2014).

[17] Lahe and Nõmmik, op. cit. (note 6), 15–17; similarly Lahe, op. cit. (note 13). The author of this paper takes the freedom to refer to his own writings by trying to be as neutral as possible; the fact that he is an Old Testament scholar, and that he has taken some distance to certain details in his writings will help him.

and admitting that a variety of translations, other than the translation "homosexuals" are possible, [18] the article argues that there are considerable cultural differences between the understanding of homosexuality in the Jewish-Hellenistic world and today. There is no direct reference to homosexual orientation in ancient writings; only the issue of homosexual practice was addressed under certain circumstances.

In most Estonian publications citing or referring to 1 Corinthians 6, there is no reflection on the meaning of these two words.[19] The authors largely rely on the conventional Bible translation into Estonian, using *lõbupoisid* "catamites" and *meestepilastajad* "desecrator of men."[20] In the ECC's declaration on homosexuality, 1 Corinthians 9-11 is quoted three times and referred to twice; there is no explanation of the terminology but expressions such as "homosexually inclined men" and "alternative sexual orientation" reflect the interpretation of the given words. Nelson directly adapts the interpretation "homosexuals"; Ehasalu is more precise, using the expression "Greek homosexual relationships"; similarly, Hiob stresses "active and passive homo-practice." In all cases the thrust of the argument does not rely on the exact meaning of the terminology,[21] and hence the next argument needs to be studied. The basic question is, Do *malakoi* and *arsenokoitai* in 1 Corinthians 6 refer to homosexuality in general or to a certain kind of homosexual practice?

---

[18] Works by Peter Arzt-Grabner, Robin Scroggs, Kenneth J. Dover, Christian Wolff, Hans Tiedemann, John Boswell, David F. Wright, Andreas Lindemann, Wolfgang Schrage, Helmut Merklein, Eckhardt J. Schnabel and Jacob Kremer are referred to.
[19] Nelson, op. cit. (note 3); Ehasalu, op. cit. (note 4); *Eesti Kirikute Nõukogu seisukoht homoseksuaalsuse küsimuses,* op. cit. (note 5); *Eesti Kristliku Nelipühi Kiriku seisukoht,* op. cit. (note 9); Hiob, op. cit. (note 14).
[20] The conventional newest reedition of the Bible was first published in 1997 by the Estonian Bible Society; however, the older translation of the New Testament (1989) reused here had originally *poisipilastajad* "desecrator of boys" and was changed to *meestepilastajad.*
[21] Cf. Martti Nissinen, *Homoeroticism in the Biblical World: A Historical Perspective* (Minneapolis: Fortress, 1998), 117: "Whether fully convincing or not, these attempts not only show how difficult it really is to determine the actual meaning of this word in different contexts but also illustrate that our questions do not emerge solely from 'objective' philological interest but from ideological needs as well." For a further overview, see ibid., 113-118, and Dale B. Martin, *Sex and the Single Savior: Gender and Sexuality in Biblical Interpretation* (Louisville, KY: Westminster John Knox Press, 2006).

ROMANS 1:26-27—THE IMMEDIATE CONTEXT

Besides 1 Corinthians 6, the main Pauline passage under discussion has been Romans 1:26-27, also involving its closest context 1:18-32. Romans 1:18-32 focuses on the corruption of the Gentiles. Because of idolatry, God gave the Gentiles up to degrading passions. These are listed in verses 26-27, followed by a catalogue of wicked deeds in verses 29-32.

Lahe and Nõmmik[22] take advantage of the context by concentrating on the argument of idolatry. According to them, Paul stresses the Gentiles' apostasy and divine punishment, which manifests itself in unnatural sexual relations. The passage could also be regarded as an etiology of unnatural sexual relations among the Gentiles. Hence, Paul reflects only on the given situation, not on the admissibility or prohibition of homosexual relations. Thereby, he maintains ancient Judaism's view that idolatry, the Gentiles and unnatural sexual relations are connected to one another (Lev 18-20, Wis 13:1ff, 14:12-14, 22-27).[23] Furthermore, Paul's premise is the same as in the ancient world in general, namely that women and men are naturally heterosexual but they can change their sexual behavior to unnatural acts. Particular attention is paid to the word *homoiōs* at the beginning of verse 27, since the syntactical interpretation is decisive in terms of whether the unnatural intercourse of women in verse 26 is homosexual or not; the authors suggest that nothing in the text itself points in this direction. At the end, the authors suggest that Paul does not exclusively condemn all kinds of sexual relations of all homosexually inclined human beings.[24] Lahe adds that the Pauline design of sexual freedom in Roman society is a caricature that does not exactly reflect reality and, furthermore, Paul's message in Romans 1-2 refers to the sin of all humankind.

The EEC's declaration on homosexuality interprets Romans 1:25-28 as follows:

> In his letter to Romans, Paul teaches with all his apostolic authority that the sexual life of homosexually inclined persons is wrong (cf. Rom 1:28), for "they exchanged the truth of God for a lie" (Rom 1:25), and "received in their own persons the due penalty for their error" (Rom 1:27).[25]

---

[22] Lahe and Nõmmik, op. cit. (note 6), 12-13; and similarly Lahe, op. cit. (note 13).

[23] Works of Jürgen Becker, Klaus Wengst, and Brendan Byrne have been referred to.

[24] Discussion involving publications by Heinrich Schlier, Brendan Byrne, Michael Theobald, Christian Wolff, Jürgen Becker, Martin Stowasser, Klaus Haacker and Ed P. Sanders have been referred to.

[25] *Eesti Kirikute Nõukogu seisukoht homoseksuaalsuse küsimuses,* op. cit. (note 5), both quotations below are from this document.

The passage is further polemically used against the thesis that the Bible condemns violent homosexual practice only[26]—the Bible condemns all kind of homosexuality. The verses in Romans 1:26-27 support the idea that both sides of sexual intercourse do it voluntarily, women as well as men:

> The Holy Scripture disapproves of homosexuality not only as a form of direct violence but in the sense of an unnatural sexual orientation that directs people in their sexual evolution "to a debased mind and to things that should not be done (Rom 1:28).

Similarly, Nelson refers to Romans 1:26-27; his premise is that homosexuality as such is condemned here.[27] Ehasalu takes homosexuality in the context of Romans 1:18-32 as an "exemplary sin" (men and women alike)—through idolatry, "the man 'corrupts' God, and God from God's side corrupts the man."[28] In his paper delivered at the seminar of the Estonian parliament, Roosimaa concurred with Lahe and Nõmmik that in Romans 1:26-27, the emphasis is not on homosexuality but on the Gentiles' apostasy. According to Roosimaa, the fundamental question is whether sin is sin if understood in terms of divine punishment, but he adds a new perspective by focusing on the aspect of the "degrading of the body" (Rom 1:24), which can be neither norm nor example.[29]

In one of his articles Hiob reproaches Lahe and Nõmmik for disregarding the context of Romans 1:26-27. Sin, including homosexuality, is the outcome of idolatry. This outcome is evaluated negatively throughout the passage and in accordance with Jewish thought (Wis 14:22-27). No syntactical operations, such as dividing the sentence in verses 26-27 into different parts, or questioning whether the passage intends only homosexual practice or not, are possible. Paul himself understands both sexes as one in Christ Jesus (Gal 3:28), and so do other New Testament passages (Lk 2:23; Rev 12:5, 13).[30] The basic questions are the following:

- Does Romans 1:26-27 refer to homosexuality in general, to unnatural, i.e., homosexual behavior, or only to male homosexual behavior?

- Can Romans 1:26-27 be used in the discussion on homosexuality since its context is the sin of all humankind, and specifically the idolatry of the Gentiles?

- How do we interpret sin if it is a divine penalty for idolatry?

---

[26] This kind of evaluation has been suggested regarding Genesis 19 and Judges 19 by Lahe and Nõmmik, op. cit. (note 6).
[27] Nelson, op. cit. (note 3).
[28] Ehasalu, op. cit. (note 4).
[29] Roosimaa, op. cit. (note 11).
[30] Hiob, op. cit. (note 14).

THE TORAH'S VALIDITY FOR PAUL AND CHRISTIANS

One of the subjects discussed in the Estonian Christian, and specifically Lutheran, discussion on homosexuality is the question of the validity of the Torah.[31] The debate goes beyond the usual reference to the famous passages in Leviticus 18:22; 20:13, that demand the death penalty for intercourse between men.[32] Particularly regarding Paul, the question has been discussed many times. The ECC's declaration polemicizes the claim of the "advocates of homosexuality" that the "Holy Spirit and the council of apostles have released Gentile Christians from the law of Israel of those days (Acts 15:28-29)." The authors of the declaration answer:

> But it has to be admitted that the decision of the Apostles did not release the Christians from the whole law of the Old Testament but mainly from commandments and prohibitions related to ceremonial holiness. By the same token, "desecration" (Greek *porneias*) being a general designation for sexual sins in the language of the Early Christianity was prohibited verbatim. Neither Jesus nor the New Testament as a whole have exculpated the "abominable" sexual practices described in the Law of Moses. On the contrary, many texts of the Holy Scripture (Rom 1:26-27; 1 Cor 6:9; 1 Tim 1:10; Jude 7-8, etc.) assure that homosexuality is "contrary to sound teaching" and does not belong to the kingdom of God.[33]

Hiob underlines that Paul relied on the Torah and was convinced of its inspired authority (2 Tim 3:16; Rom 1:2). Thus, one has to acknowledge the validity of the Torah behind Paul's arguments, also in cases, such as in Romans 1:26-27, when he does not mention it. There is no need to discuss

---

[31] It has to be noted that due to the lack of specialists and unfavorable historical circumstances, only some classical Lutheran works have been published in recent years: in 2012, a representative set of Martin Luther's writings was for the first time published in Estonian, and was followed by the Lutheran Confessions in 2014. Such important writing for the understanding of the role of Torah as Luther's "How Christians should Regard Moses" (*LW* 35, 161ff.), was for the first time published in *Kirik & Teoloogia*, nos. 217-218 (5 and 12 February 2016).

[32] Nelson, op. cit. (note 3); Ehasalu, op. cit. (note 4); *Eesti Kirikute Nõukogu seisukoht homoseksuaalsuse küsimuses* (note 5); *Eesti Kristliku Nelipühi Kiriku seisukoht* (note 9); Roosimaa, op. cit. (note 11).

[33] *Eesti Kirikute Nõukogu seisukoht homoseksuaalsuse küsimuses*, op. cit. (note 5). One additional remark can be made on *Eesti Kirikute Nõukogu avalik kiri* , op. cit. (note 9)—it is difficult to decide whether the only biblical quotation (Ps 1:1-3) in this document is meant to be understood as some kind of key or not. But since it is positioned right at the end of the document, one cannot avoid feeling that the authors have underlined the Torah's outstanding quality by referring to the meditation on God's law mentioned in verse 2.

whether Paul understood homosexuality as sin or not; he condemns the active and passive practice of homosexuality (1 Cor 6:9–11; 1 Tim 1:9–10). Like Jesus, Paul is aware of the threat that the libidinous glance poses (1 Cor 7:5), and prohibits divorce (1 Cor 7:10ff.).[34]

Even if Roosimaa does not directly integrate the Pauline letters into his argument, he adds in the same context as Paul's writings that the sexual taboos listed in Leviticus 18 and 20 aim to protect the family. The public agenda overrides individual pleasure. It is the result of the condemned practices and not the reason for the prohibitions that were important.[35]

Lahe and Nõmmik pose several critical questions concerning the role of the Torah in Christianity. We need to examine why, if the Bible is to be used as a code of conduct, Leviticus 18:22 and 20:13 are more important than other (sometimes drastic) prohibitions in those chapters? How does the Holiness Code of the Jews relate to Christians? What is the reason for us nowadays not to apply death penalty so often demanded in this code?[36] Lahe examines how to relate to the laws of cultic purity and impurity, and hence to the understanding of human physiology in those prescriptions.[37]

In his presentation to the Estonian parliament's seminar, Nõmmik said the following on the Lutheran interpretation of the Bible:

> At the center is the faith in God and Jesus Christ. This faith says that God has mercy on humankind and redeems it. This inevitably presupposes an answer from the side of humankind. The answer is love; love of God and of neighbor. [...] If this has been realized, then one can also realize why Christians can take the Old Testament law seriously only then when it accords with the commandment of love of God and neighbor. This, in turn, [...] does not allow a word-for-word, literal application of many biblical principles. And to my mind this primarily affects sporadic statements on homosexual practice in the Bible. A homosexual act can be theologically condemned, can be taken for one of the manifestations of the transgression of humankind, among others, but to my mind, it is difficult to find biblical or theological arguments against a positive attitude towards same-sex partnership based on love [...]. The church that wants to be the Church is responsible for all its members; this requires contact and communion with everyone.[38]

---

[34] Hiob, op. cit. (note 14).

[35] Roosimaa, op. cit. (note 11).

[36] Lahe and Nõmmik, op. cit. (note 6), 9. Works of Adrian Thatcher, Thomas Römer, Loyse Bonjour and Martti Nissinen are referred to. Hiob, op. cit. (note 14), answers some of these questions with the thesis of societal development, which surpasses the death penalty, and also refers to Rabbi Bar Rav Nathan and Rabbi Ben Zion Bokser.

[37] Lahe, op. cit. (note 13).

[38] Nõmmik, op. cit. (note 12).

The basic questions are the following:

- Does Paul presuppose the absolute validity of the Torah, or is his understanding to some degree selective?

- Does the Torah still have authority among Christians, and to what extent can the argument concerning current issues be based on the Torah?

- According to the Torah and, hence, according to the Pauline letters, is homosexuality in one way or another a special case?

THE CREATION ORDER AND PAUL

One of the most important biblical arguments against homosexuality or at least against the legalized partnership of homosexuals has been the one of the everlasting and definite divine creation order, which is not abandoned by Paul. The statement in Genesis 1:27 that humankind is created by God in God's image, as male and female, has been interpreted as the basis for the institution of marriage.[39] The statement on constitutional and natural heterosexual marriage by the ECC says:

> The creational definition of human life as male and female surpasses the biological dimension of being a human. This is an ontological category. Hence, homosexuality is not merely a question of morals or juridification. It is literally an existential question or, in other words, a question of the definition of being human as such. The human will cannot change the divine definition of the human world as two sexes.[40]

The ECC's 2008 declaration argues very similarly, but opens with the statement that the human being is a sexual being; still, man and woman separately do not constitute an integral whole. Then 1 Corinthians 11:11-12 is cited.[41]

Hiob claims that Jesus reestablished the original purity of marriage. He reminds us that until the Reformation (and nowadays in the Orthodox and Roman Catholic churches) marriage was or remains a sacrament, i.e.,

---

[39] Ehasalu, op. cit. (note 4); *Eesti Kirikute Nõukogu arvamus*, op. cit. (note 7); *Eesti Kristliku Nelipühi Kiriku seisukoht*, op. cit. (note 9).

[40] *Eesti Kirikute Nõukogu arvamus*, op. cit. (note 7).

[41] *Eesti Kirikute Nõukogu seisukoht homoseksuaalsuse küsimuses*, op. cit. (note 5). In *Eesti Kirikute Nõukogu arvamus*, op. cit. (note 7), this line of thinking is followed by the statement not to discriminate against homosexual people who, like all other human beings, share in God's grace and human dignity. But sin is still sin.

a mystery based on the creation order, and that this was originally referred to by Paul (Eph 5:31–33).[42]

Without referring to the Pauline letters, Lahe and Nõmmik, and the latter in a separate article on the exegesis of Genesis 1,[43] try to relativize the importance of Genesis 1:27, since the whole Priestly account of creation in its own right is aimed at defining the Sabbath, the cult of the one and only God, the fertility of humankind—their reproductive ability—and the creation of humankind in God's image. This implies that human beings are the administrators of and responsible for what has been created by God.

In addition, Nõmmik remarked at the seminar of the Estonian parliament that the Bible does not demand any kind of sexuality or family model but presupposes them. And this has hermeneutical consequences for our discussion nowadays when presuppositions have changed.[44] The basic questions are as follows:

- Are two sexes an ontological category according to Genesis 1?

- Can marriage be regarded as a sacrament in the Lutheran context?

- Does Genesis 1:27 have a definite and constitutional character, particularly in light of changing cultural and societal circumstances?

BROADER HERMENEUTICAL ISSUES, SOCIOCULTURAL CHANGE AND THE RELEVANCE OF THE RESULTS OF HISTORICAL-CRITICAL STUDY

As we have seen, the understanding of the authority of the Bible, including the authority of the Pauline letters, is a central issue. Nelson rightly points to the need to clarify the premises:

> In other words—the real problem does not lie in the way how one relates to homosexuality, but the question is, how one theologically understands the essence of God and God's communication with humankind, particularly through the Bible. This is exactly the problem that needs to be discussed but has not yet been debated in the framework of discussion on homosexuality.[45]

---

[42] Hiob, op. cit. (note 14). He adds in footnote 5 that the question of Paul's authorship does not play any role here, and the negative thesis has never been proven anyway.
[43] Lahe and Nõmmik, op. cit. (note 6); Urmas Nõmmik, "Mida küll väidab Piibli esimene loomislugu?" ["What Does the First Creation Account of the Bible Tells Us?"], in *Kirik & Teoloogia*, no. 88 (16 August 2013).
[44] Nõmmik, op. cit. (note 12).
[45] Nelson, op. cit. (note 3).

The ECC felt the need to underline Paul's authority since in the 2008 declaration the authors dedicate a chapter to this issue.[46] They refer to some passages where Paul does not rely on the Lord's command but on his own opinion (1 Cor 7:12, 25), and underline that Paul still has the Spirit of God (7:40). But concerning the Pauline passages regarding homosexuality, there is no doubt that Paul teaches with full apostolic authority.

The authors of the declaration indicate that they are aware of changing cultural circumstances, providing the example of the idea of long hair, which according to Paul degrades a man (1 Cor 11:14). Further, the authors address slavery as something accepted by the early Christians as an unnatural situation enforced by the Roman Empire (cf. Titus 2:9). According to contemporary Christian ethics, humankind in the image of God is and has to be free of slavery. The authors immediately add that sexual practices are not comparable to changing trends in fashion; Paul evaluates homosexuality as sin and, thus, also humans of both sexes have to be freed from the addiction to homosexuality.

Hiob extensively deals with the discussion on the centrality of redemption through Jesus Christ, which has consequences for our entire psychophysical constitution. This is a fact, not an abstract teaching. Any such abstract teaching positioning Jesus at the center is inclined to change God's message according to human needs (i.e., the Enlightenment). The risk of setting the human being as a measure is high.[47] According to Hiob,[48] results of the historical-critical study of the Bible are subject to the same risk; the volatility of those results attests to the problem of the reduction and destruction of the biblical message.[49] He supports his claim with the example of the historical-critical decision regarding the authorship of the Pastoral Epistles, which has led to diminishing the reliability of the holy tradition.[50]

As mentioned above, Lahe and Nõmmik point out that there are different theological consequences depending on whether one addresses homosexual practice or homosexual orientation, whereby the latter issue was not perceived in the ancient world.[51] They emphatically affirm the need constantly to reevaluate our understanding of biblical texts in light

---

[46] *Eesti Kirikute Nõukogu seisukoht homoseksuaalsuse küsimuses,* op. cit. (note 5).

[47] Hiob, op. cit. (note 14).

[48] See works cited in note 15.

[49] Hiob calls the historical-critical study of the Bible a "naturalistic new religion" (*Piibel usu ja teaduse vahel* [op. cit., note 15], 95–100); his argumentation makes use of authors, such as Klaus Berger, Eta Linnemann, Timothy Keller, Thomas Söding, Gerhard Ulrichs, Risto Santala, etc.

[50] Hiob, "Jah, tõesti ajaloolis-kriitiline reduktsioon," op. cit. (note 15).

[51] Lahe and Nõmmik, op. cit. (note 6).

of changing sociocultural circumstances.[52] The ancient context of biblical texts has to be taken into account in order to discover the original theological ideas of the authors. Only then a bridge to current issues can be built. Additionally, the scriptural context of a given passage together with religious context of the authors should be considered.

In their article on the historical-critical method Lahe and Nõmmik refer to another example from the Pauline letters: the reflection on the silence of women in the congregation in 1 Corinthians 14:34–35 interrupts the context and is moved to another place in the same chapter in some manuscripts. In addition to the suspicion that the author is not Paul, the verses cannot be evaluated in the same way as the surrounding verses on church practice.[53]

Giving examples, Nõmmik attempts to illustrate a certain hierarchy of theological assumptions in the Bible. For instance, the radicalism of the Gospel of Jesus Christ should be taken seriously if one is willing fully to understand other New Testament ideas. This radicalism reaches the point where a believer abandons their family in order to follow the Lord. Or, the question of the institution of marriage is a secondary question compared to the question of the relationship between God and the believer. A confidential and loving relationship between neighbors is more important than sex, blood relationship, worldview or other characteristics of the neighbors.[54] The basic questions are the following:

• When should our sociocultural context impact our understanding of the Bible and when not?

• How do we methodologically distinguish between socioculturally determined prescriptions and eternal biblical truths? How do we avoid the corruption of biblical interpretation by some fashionable trend?

• Are love and marriage as such related to each other hierarchically according to the Bible, or are they equally important?

Conclusion

The survey of the arguments used in the Estonian discussion on (homo) sexuality and the Bible, with a focus on Pauline letters, reveals fundamental

---

[52] Ibid.; Lahe and Nõmmik, op. cit. (note 16); Nõmmik, op. cit. (notes 12 and 16).
[53] Lahe and Nõmmik, op. cit. (note 16).
[54] Nõmmik, op. cit. (note 12).

differences in the understanding and use of the Bible. The most significant of these are: (1) the order of creation (e.g., the question of equality of all human beings or the institution of marriage); (2) the relation of Christians to the Old Testament law (is it a code of conduct, or a code of conduct but with many exceptions for Christians, or is it bound to its time of origin and/or to Judaism); (3) the attitude toward sociocultural phenomena (presupposed by the Bible or prescribed by it). The situation becomes even more complex if we consider the notion of "sin." Depending on the interpretation of the context, sin is understood as a concrete deed that leads to condemnation, or as a sign and result of apostasy. Besides, the notion of sin frequently seems to be included too soon into the argument and lacks reflection on changing sociocultural phenomena.

The discussion among Christians must never end, since there will always be a need to reflect on our understanding of the Bible. This is the most important conclusion one can draw, since different ways of understanding should not stop Christians from coming together and dialoguing with one another. In Estonia, this is our hope and the questions formulated above will help us to move forward in our theological reflection.

In conclusion I would like to mention two issues which affect the hermeneutical discussion, e.g., on (homo)sexuality. First, Eastern European countries, as different as they are, share one common historical feature: over the last thirty years, many sociocultural changes have taken place and many of them considerably quicker than in Western societies. This has been challenging and it is no surprise that the reflection on many sociocultural and religious phenomena has not progressed at the same rate as in other places. Even in religiously illiterate and calm societies such as Estonia, having some traditional values to rely on provides some existential safety and it is here that a conservative interpretation of the Bible comes into play. New perspectives are regarded with suspicion and considered as bringing pressure to bear from outside. Secondly, in reviewing the extensive material for this article, I got the strong impression that people's personal experiences cannot be underestimated in the discussion. Whereas the experience of different sexes is a usual human experience, people are more eager to understand the relation between creation theology and social justice. The experience with many (also sexual) minorities is less common, and those participating in the discussions are not prepared to reflect on the circumstances that the minorities cannot escape.

But paradoxically, the turning toward a "traditional" interpretation of the Bible can be helpful for further discussions. At least in the case of Estonia, the reflection on Martin Luther's basic ideas and Lutheran hermeneutics is essential. Not only Luther's writings are largely unknown but confirmation classes lack sufficient introduction and reflection. There is still plenty of space to "turn back" to the novelty of the Reformation and to reconsider what the consequences are for today's Lutheran communities in light of the equality of all Christians, the priesthood of all believers, the estate of marriage and, of course, the relationship between Law and gospel.

CALLED AND COLD SAINTS: SOME THOUGHTS ON HOLINESS IN THE HEBREW BIBLE AND IN PAUL

Mercedes L. García Bachmann

I hope you will pardon the pun in my title; it came to me as I was pondering how best to translate the expression *klētois hagiois* used by Paul in Romans 1:7 and 1 Corinthians 1:2. In both letters, it is part of the salutation. In Romans 1:1, Paul introduces himself as a servant of Christ Jesus, "called to be an apostle, set apart for the gospel of God." In verse 7a he proceeds to identify his addressees, whom he calls "all God's beloved in Rome, who are called to be saints." Likewise, he starts his letter to the Corinthians,

> Paul, called to be an apostle of Christ Jesus (*klētos apostolos*) by the will of God, and the brother Sosthenes, to the church of God that is in Corinth, to those who are sanctified in Christ Jesus, called to be saints, together with all those who in every place call on the name of our Lord Jesus Christ, both their Lord and ours (1 Cor 1:1–2).[1]

The usual translation, "called to be saints," is misleading in that it would seem that it is a call to become a saint sometime at a later point in time (perhaps never realized). But this call has been realized already and,

---

[1] All Bible quotations are from the NRSV, but I have left the divine name untranslated. I also find attractive T. Drorah Setel's translation of the Tetragrammaton as "The-One-of-Being." "Roundtable Discussion: Feminist Reflections on Separation and Unity in Jewish Theology," in *Journal of Feminist Studies in Religion* 2 (1986), 113–30, here 114.

therefore, those called to be saints are in fact called saints (or, in the case of Paul himself, called apostles). The problem is when called saints become cold saints.

To speak of the communion of the Holy is to speak of the communion of saints, where it is obligatory to have been called upon to become part of that community. But, is it also necessary to have accepted or recognized that call? Does it depend on our response, or on the caller, or on both? Here the relationship to the cold saints resurfaces. Is it baptism that makes us saints, no matter whether we acknowledge that calling or not? Does community with the Holy require some degree of recognition by the self or by other witnesses (other believers, neighbors, or family saying "s/he is God's instrument"), or can someone be an unrecognized saint? Since Paul addresses a particular group in each of his letters, it is obvious that he focuses on called saints who have answered God's calling in a particular place at a particular time. They are not Jewish saints (not all of them, anyway) and they are not Gentiles, following their traditional Greek or Roman deities, but they are Gentile brothers and sisters to one another and to Jesus, the Christ, gathered regularly for *koinonia* at some location in Rome. They are a religious community, "those who by having in common a relationship to the holy God thereby have a relationship to one another which is quite different from ordinary human bonds such as class or race."[2] And even though to my knowledge there is no such word as "religion" in the Hebrew Bible, it offers enough examples of a people who have a mutual relationship based on their relationship to their God.

As I read both his greetings I wonder what "called saints" signified for Paul. No doubt, it was a crucial element for him, since he uses the expression in what many scholars consider some of his main writings. Since Paul was a learned and practicing Jew, we may surmise that he knew this concept from his Bible school, synagogue or temple attendance. Where does it come from, then, and what can we glean from the Hebrew Scriptures that would help us in our hermeneutics today? There are several experiences of holiness in the Bible that are very much bound to their contexts.

What is holiness?

A study of any one Hebrew word would not suffice, since "[a]t the lexical level the Holiness Spectrum is principally represented by four Hebrew words: holy

---

[2] Thomas M. Raitt, "Holiness and Community in Leviticus 19:2ff.," in *Proceedings*, 6 (1986), 170–78, here 175.

[...], profane [...], clean [...], unclean [...]."[3] These are all important categories and should never be dismissed lightly or confused:

> And YHWH spoke to Aaron: Drink no wine or strong drink, neither you nor your sons, when you enter the tent of meeting, that you may not die; it is a statute forever throughout your generations. You are to distinguish between the holy and the common, and between the unclean and the clean; and you are to teach the people of Israel all the statutes that YHWH has spoken to them through Moses (Lev 10:8–11).

The most common translation of *qādōš* is "set aside," such as when the Sabbath was created and set aside from the weekdays (Gen 2:1). The text underscores the importance of this discernment by: (a) calling it a law for all time to come; (b) to teach people; and (c) by prohibiting the inebriation of priests while on duty. The holy and profane are not to be confused:

> [...] holiness (and its opposite, the profane) represents the divine relation to the ordered world, and the clean (with its opposite, the unclean) embraces the normal state of human existence in the earthly realm. The holy-profane represents (positively and negatively) the divine sphere, and this may be distinguished from the human sphere (which is marked by the opposition between clean and unclean). The presence of a holy God and a holy sanctuary in the midst of Israel ensures that these two points of view overlap in a complex way.[4]

Frankly, I am not entirely sure to what extent this disposition would have been explicitly present in Paul's mind as he moved from his pharisaic training to being the last of Jesus' apostles. Since symbolic language instills its truths in ways as powerful as or even more so than plain enunciation, I do not doubt that Paul would have been brought up in a system that clearly distinguishes between the holy and profane, the clean and unclean and he would always have been aware of these differences.

Let us now turn to a classic, *Holiness in Israel*, in which Gammie explores different biblical visions of holiness and cleanness after Rudolph Otto's categories for the Divine.[5] He looks at how particular groups represented in the Bible—priests, prophets, sages and the "schools" that followed them—understood the relationship between the cleanness or separation required of holiness and observance of certain ritual or ethical actions. He suggests,

---

[3] Philip Peter Jenson, *Graded Holiness: A Key to the Priestly Conception of the World* (Sheffield: Sheffield Academic Press, 1992), 39.

[4] Ibid., 47–48.

[5] John G. Gammie, *Holiness in Israel* (Minneapolis: Fortress, 1989), 5–8.

> In response to the divine holiness the priests perceived that God required an
> ethical and ritual purity as well as the ingestion only of foods that the priestly
> logic of separation and appropriateness would allow them to declare as clean.[6]

That ritual dimension (as understood in the Priestly material) is despised or
misunderstood by most Christians, even though many are fond of ritual and
share a keen sense of the holy as the Other. Gerburgis Feld reasons that rather
than taking this book's strangeness as a hermeneutical refuge, we should deal
with its main question, namely, the compatibility of the human and the divine.[7]

Gammie also alerts us that the classical preexilic prophets worked around
the three notions of righteousness (Amos), loving-kindness (Hosea) and holiness
(Isaiah of Jerusalem). Gammie notes that for Isaiah, "[s]ocial and legal justice
is the primary means by which the cleanness required of holiness can be attained but even this, the prophet taught, was not to be viewed solely as human
accomplishment."[8] God's holiness cannot be separated from human holiness
and human holiness may not be assessed without its divine component. This
sociopolitical dimension of the holy is closer to my preference than the one by
the Priestly school, even though not mutually exclusive.

Gammie develops seven theses about Isaiah's concept of the holy, the last
one of which reads, "Holiness calls," where he affirms that the "[e]ncounter
with holiness is not an end in itself. Rather, holiness summons, invites, directs,
and commands."[9] This is language particularly reminiscent of Lady Wisdom:

> Wisdom has built her house, she has hewn her seven pillars. She has slaughtered
> her animals, she has mixed her wine, she has also set her table. She has sent out
> her servant-girls, she calls from the highest places in the town, "You that are
> simple, turn in here!" To those without sense she says, "Come, eat of my bread
> and drink of the wine I have mixed. Lay aside immaturity, and live, and walk in
> the way of insight (Prov 9:1–6).

Lady Wisdom prepares her banquet of bread and wine and invites those who
want to acquire life. Acquiring life is not a solitary enterprise but a life-long
process of words and actions involving one's family, neighbors and society.
Lady Wisdom's invitation is a call to salvation; salvation that is different

---

[6] Ibid., 12.
[7] Gerburgis Feld, "Leviticus: Das ABC der Schöpfung," in Luise Schottroff & Marie-
Theres Wacker [with the collaboration of Claudia Janssen and Beate Wehn] (eds),
Kompendium feministische Bibelauslegung, second revised edition (Gütersloh: Chr.
Kaiser, 1999), 40–53, here 40.
[8] Gammie, op. cit. (note 5), 83.
[9] Ibid., 96.

from that offered by the priests or the prophets, but salvation, wholeness, deliverance, life all the same. Also Jesus prepares his banquet of bread and wine and summons, invites, directs and commands, reaching out to "the world." The Holy reaches out to those "without sense" (Prov 9:1–5); to those who "labor and are heavy laden" (Mt 11:28); to those who hear the call and become saints, according to Paul. The Holy communicates.[10] The Holy does not withdraw from human contact, does not remain isolated, enclosed among four walls, on a mountain top, or in heaven. The Holy chooses people, objects, time and space to interact with the Holy's own creatures. The Holy invites and commands on the streets, in the market, among children, whenever a large multitude or just two or three are gathered. YHWH draws people together.

> If one assumes that temple life, the cultus, worship, and other aspects of Priestly concern generate community no less than the Sinai covenant generates community, then some tantalizing puzzles lie before us. The holy has a many sided potential for drawing people together.[11]

Isaiah is not the only superb example of this combination of ritual and justice (at his calling he witnesses heavenly beings shouting "Holy, holy, holy"). Another example is an unlikely book such as Leviticus, since Leviticus is the book where we most frequently find the expression *miqrā' qōdeš*, "a convocation/gathering of the holy," perhaps the closest we can get to the "communion of the holy" in the Hebrew Bible.[12]

Before I turn briefly to Leviticus 19, let me summarize. Holiness may be defined as that which "represents the divine relation to the ordered world" (thus Jenson), lived out in different rituals and ethical behavior by diverse biblical groups (priest, prophet, sage, laity). Holiness, like religion or faith, always involves the person's relationship to other human fellows; it is never an individual relation with their Deity.

---

[10] Oda Wischmeyer, "Principles of Paul's Hermeneutics," 40 in this publication. "Since our interest lies in Paul's general concept of understanding God and God's way of communicating with humankind *en Christō*, our overarching question concerns not only his interpretation of Scripture, but his understanding of God's communication with humankind. In other words: we do not limit ourselves to asking how Paul uses and interprets Scripture, which he knows and refers to in the form of the Septuagint canon, what kind of authority he claims for his interpretation, and to which extent he understands Scripture as God's revelation and as given by the Spirit but, primarily, at what point he leaves Scripture behind and dares to argue beyond Scripture."

[11] Raitt, op. cit. (note 2), 170.

[12] The expression appears in Exodus 12:16 (x2); Leviticus 23 (x8); Numbers 28 (x2); and Numbers 29 (x3), all in legislation concerning one of the main feasts.

Leviticus 19: Being holy by living justly with the neighbor

Several scholars have sung their praises for this chapter. For instance, Erhard Gerstenberger calls it a catechism and notes that "God's 'formula of self-introduction,' 'I am Yahweh (your God),' is used more frequently than elsewhere in the Old Testament as an organizational device."[13] While the internal logic with which different laws have been arranged within each of these sections escapes us today, it is worth noting that "Be holy for I am holy" (v. 2b) opens the whole chapter, immediately followed by the injunction to honor both mother and father and keep the Sabbath (v. 3)—themes that reappear at the end of the chapter (vv. 30, 32).

According to Jonathan Magonet, Leviticus 19 is comprised of a short introduction and five units, arranged in an A-B-C-A'-B' model (vv. 3-8; 9-18; 19-29; 30-31; 32-36). "A/A' deal with man's [sic] relationship to God; B/B' with his relationship to his fellowman [sic]; C with his relationship to 'himself [sic]'."[14] A closer look also shows that Leviticus is arranged in response to the account in Genesis 1, where chapters 17-24 mirror the fifth and sixth days of creation, when living creatures were brought to life, each according to their species. Within chapters 17-24, chapter 19 stands out as a little Torah, with all the Ten Commandments alluded to or quoted.

> In Leviticus Rabba 24, we read as follows: "Speak to the entire Israelite people and say to them: "You shall be holy ..." Rabbi Hiyya taught: These words inform us that this section is to be read before the people in an assembly. And why is it to be read before the people in an assembly? Because most of the essential laws of the Torah can be derived from it. Rabbi Levy said: Because the Ten Commandments are embodied in it.[15]

This embodiment of the Decalogue offers good examples of the "divine relation to the ordered world" that holiness represents according to Jenson. "If the 'holy' is defined as that which belongs to the sphere of God's being or activity, then this might correspond to a claim of ownership, a statement

---

[13] Erhard S. Gerstenberger, *Leviticus: A Commentary* (Louisville: John Knox, 1996), 261. The phrase appears in vv. 2, 3, 4, 10, 16, 18, 25, 28, 30, 31, 34 and 37.

[14] Jonathan Magonet, "The Structure and Meaning of Leviticus 19," in *Hebrew Annual Review* 7 (1983), 151-67, here 166. Mark F. Rooker, *Leviticus*, New American Commentary (Nashville: Broadman & Holman Publishers, 2000), 251, prefers "two major sections, 19:3-18 and 19:19-36 [...]."

[15] Baruch A. Levine, *Leviticus*, JPS Torah Commentary (New York: Jewish Publication Society, 1989), 124.

of close association, or proximity to his cultic presence," further reasons this author.[16] To me, there is no better example than verses 2b–3:

> You [plural] shall be holy, for I YHWH your God am holy. You shall each revere your mother and father, and you shall keep my sabbaths: I am YHWH your God.

This relationship of ritual and ethical action permeates the whole chapter. For instance, to the command about the peace offering follows the prohibition wholly to reap the corners of the field. One might think it obeys rules of literary artistry, but there is more to it. "In the Priestly perspective, ethical behavior is not merely the necessary consequence of love for God; it is the fundamental prerequisite that establishes the authenticity of that love."[17] Because God is Israel's Only-One and has separated Israel from other nations for a purpose, Israel is to be a community where people deal with justice and righteousness with their neighbor. Who is my neighbor?, we might wonder, were it not for the fear of receiving a "parabolic scolding," like the rich man received (Lk 10:29). Whether we choose a broad or a narrow definition of "neighbor," we are to remember that the command to love speaks not of a feeling we ascribe somewhat obscurely to "the heart," but it is ethical decisions within the community of brothers and sisters.[18] Paul was well aware of this relationship of the person toward God and neighbor, as is evident in his letters on ethical issues such as slavery, gender, scriptures, food communion and others.[19]

HOLINESS AS SEPARATION

There is a darker side to the identity of God's people as called saints, that of identity by the annihilation of the other. Such annihilation may be literal, it may take the form of mockery, or it may persecute those who are or want to be different. If one is to believe stories such as those in Joshua and Judges, several people were expelled from their land, were killed (starting with the "Canaanites") or were forbidden to worship their own

---

[16] Jenson, op. cit. (note 3), 48.

[17] Samuel E. Balentine, *Leviticus* (Louisville: John Knox, 2002), 161.

[18] Feld, op. cit. (note 7), 47, aptly remarks that for women the question is not who is the neighbor, but "who truly lives this commandment of love for the neighbor/person." Women have been brought up to be everyone's caring neighbor, with the result that women have more difficulty caring for themselves than for others.

[19] Many contributions in this volume attest to this awareness. See, e.g., those by Magnus Zetterholm and Lubomir Batka.

Deities in the land that now was Israel's. There is a consensus today that most of the Hebrew Bible received its final edition during the late Persian period. This means that texts calling for the Canaanites' destruction, (e.g., Deut 7:1), are from a time when there were no longer any "Canaanites" and exterminating them was therefore out of the question.

On the other hand, several products of these times evidence mistrust of women if not downright misogyny. Portrayals of women as alluring, adulterous, scheming and responsible for men's unfaithfulness to YHWH appear in the books of Kings (particularly, Solomon's wives and Jezebel), Proverbs (particularly, Prov 7:6–23; 31:3) and in Ezra's decree of repudiation of foreign wives and children of mixed origin (Ezra 9–10; Neh 13:23–27). This mistrust is even introduced at the time of Israel's wandering in the desert, in Miriam's questioning of Moses' only authority in Numbers 12, in the Moabite women's invitation to the Israelites (Num 25:1-3) and in the story of Cozbi, the daughter of the Midianite prince Zur, whom Zimri brought unto his tent. Both Zimri and Cozbi were killed by Eleazar, the priest, to avert a plague (Num 25:6–16).[20] In response, God praises Eleazar for his action and grants him a covenant of peace. He is not the only priest to be praised for killing worshippers of other Deities, whether Israelites or foreign; and she is not the only woman sacrificed for Israel's *shalom*. At the bottom of Mount Sinai, after worshipping the golden calf, the Levites came to be ordained because they each killed their brother, friend and neighbor (Ex 32:26–29). Moses states then, "Today you have ordained yourselves for the service of YHWH, each one at the cost of a son or a brother, and so have brought a blessing on yourselves this day" (v. 29). Not only are we in the presence of holiness at the cost of killings, we witness how the agents of holiness, the priests (Levites and Aaronites) are ordained and/or praised by YHWH for their violent actions, allegedly averting more deaths by death. Much later we also find Paul approving Stephen's execution by stoning in the name of religion if not God (Acts 8:1).

These and other stories are disgusting to many modern (and perhaps ancient) readers, but they have much to teach us. Israel came into existence as a group of liberated slaves not only helped to flee but also protected in the wilderness (Exodus), but it also recognizes in its origins groups of "Canaanites" who turned to a new God and a new sociopolitical model (e.g., Rahab and the Gibeonites, Joshua chapters 2, 6, 9). The tension between remembering one stream and forgetting another, between expelling and embracing its darkest experiences, between uniformity and dissonance, is

---

[20] Max Sicherman, "The Political Side of the Zimri-Cozbi Affair," in *Jewish Bible Quarterly* 36,1 (2008), 22–24, blames not Cozbi but Zimri, whose actions were dangerous for the whole people and especially for the tribes at the border with Midian.

always there. And it witnesses to tensions regarding differing understandings of the holy as well.

THE HOLY AND WOMEN

We have gone through several biblical texts where different experiences of the holy took shape. On the one hand, there are the positive experiences evident in the priests' combination of law and ritual to answer to God's "Be holy for I am holy." On the other, we have focused on Isaiah's combination of these same aspects—law and ritual—with a more critical view: holiness is realized in social justice. Holiness, like Personified Wisdom in Proverbs, calls out, invites to "hands-on" actions in the market, on the streets, in the household, where bread is broken and wine is poured. Yet, another aspect of holiness was perceived—the need to protect it (its holders) from unwanted company. And in that case, anything goes: war against "harlotry" and against neighbors, separation of certain people or groups for the sake of purity (including *kashrut* but also leprosy, bodily discharges and bodily anomalies) and the increasing hierarchization and specialization of those authorized to handle the holy; a hierarchization and patriarchalization that until today persist in several Christian traditions. As mentioned, Raitt noticed that "The holy has a many sided potential for drawing people together." But the holy is always in great danger of being coopted by religion and, when appropriated, be reported as not wanting certain people in its sanctuary. Thus, holiness (or at least claim to it) has also a great potential for excluding, destroying and separating people from others.

This is not new theology. It is no secret that what we call "the Bible" is the outcome of a long and complex process, in which different groups—including priests and lay, prophets and sages, men and women, poor and élite—negotiated their share of recognition, their particular vocation and the degree of closeness to the holy that they would be able to hold. And that degree of closeness to the holy involved (and involves) power struggles. Thus, it is hardly surprising that, even offering such a wonderful divine manifestation as "Be holy for I am holy," Leviticus barely considers women. Most hierarchical priesthoods (old and current) have appropriated the divine for themselves, barring others (whether women as a whole or certain women, lay men, people considered blemished because of gender, bodily conditions, ethnic origins, etc.) from service at the altar.

Is holiness a male thing? Is it a priestly thing? Perhaps only a few people would be as bold as David Clines, who claims that in the Hebrew Bible holiness is male, because it is never used of a woman in the Hebrew Bible and it is associated with a male God:

> And what belongs to the male deity is also holy; thus his name (e.g., Amos 2:7), his temple and its objects (Jer 51:51), his sabbaths (Isa 58:13) and his priests (Ex 19.22) are all holy. Among humans, it is only males that are holy (in Israel, unlike many cultures, there are no female priests).[21]

It is, however, not the only picture of the holy, as I hope to have shown. The injunction to be a holy people is expressly commanded by Israel's Only-One to the whole community: "Speak to *all the congregation* of the people of Israel and say to them: You shall be holy, for I YHWH your God am holy" (Lev 19:2, author's emphasis). Granted, terms such as "the people," "the congregation," "sons of Israel" or "brothers" are ambiguous as to the degree of inclusivity they intend and at times they mean only men. But it seems rather unusual that only men would be expected to keep the holy convocations and the feasts, to love their neighbors, not to steal or curse a deaf person, to honor father and mother (all expectations expressed in that chapter). Likewise, I would hesitate to consider that only men sinned in the desert, every time "the people committed harlotry" (to keep an old-fashioned, troublesome, but well-known expression) against their God. Rather, I would argue that, as there was a process of specialization and hierarchization of the holy in favor of the priestly guild, other manifestations were ignored at best or persecuted at worse. These ignored manifestations include the fact that feasts such as Passover and unleavened bread were transferred from the household to the sanctuary, becoming holy convocations that men were obliged to attend but were optional for women. Yet, Passover and getting rid of leaven were related to the family and the household. And it is the household, even the *bêt-'āb*, the patriarchal household, where women were actively involved in work, in decision making, and—not a moot point—also in their own experiences of the holy. Archaeological evidence and prophets like Jeremiah (Jer 44) attest to their involvement and refusal to be dismissed as non-agents of the holy. Thus, I concur with Elizabeth Johnson's perception of God's holiness in the Hebrew Scriptures:

> In the abstract, the notion of divine holiness stands for infinite otherness and separation—the Godness of God; but in the concrete, glory as well as other metaphors function as a hermeneutic of holiness that affirms the elusive Holy One is powerfully near in and through the wondrous processes of nature, the history of struggle for freedom and life, and communities where justice and peace prevail. When connected with the biblical narrative, the incomprehensible holy mystery

---

[21] David J. A. Clines, "The Most High Male: Divine Masculinity in the Bible," at www. academia.edu/14079928/The_Most_High_Male_Divine_Masculinity_in_the_Bible, 1–18, here 17.

of God indwells the natural and human world as source, sustaining power, and goal of the universe, enlivening and loving it into liberating communion. [...]

At once ontological and ethical, holiness is essentially God's unfathomable splendor drawing near and passing by to create and to beautify, to heal, redeem, and liberate the beloved world.[22]

I do not claim to know Paul's mind as he greeted the called saints gathered in Corinth and in Rome. I can gather from Romans 8 that he was aware of what Johnson calls "God's unfathomable splendor drawing near and passing by." I also gather from Galatians 3 that he could see the holy made manifest in a new community in which believing Gentiles and Jews, slaves and free, males and females were called saints, never cold saints. His own ministry, as we can glean from his recommendations in Romans 16 and other letters, witnesses to his conversion on this matter. For "God's unfathomable splendor drawing near and passing by to create and to beautify, to heal, redeem, and liberate the beloved world" was just too powerful, too moving to let it pass by lukewarm lives. How each person lives that call to be a called saint has always been subject to circumstances, vocation and imagination.

---

[22] Elizabeth A. Johnson, *Friends of God and Prophets: A Feminist Theological Reading of the Communion of Saints* (New York: Continuum, 1999), 55–56.

A New Life in Christ: Pauline Ethics and its Lutheran Reception

Bernd Oberdorfer

When speaking about Paul, Lutherans are likely to refer to the concept of justification by faith alone without works. Looking back on his life, Martin Luther emphasized that his reformatory thinking was based on Paul's word, i.e., that the term "God's justice" in Romans 1:16 does not mean "the justice God is and urges us to fulfill," but, rather, "the justice God gives us and shares with us for free (*gratis*)."[1] Moreover, in his "Sendbrief vom Dolmetschen," Luther defends his translation of Romans 3:28, where he inserted the famous "alone" (*allein aus Glauben*, "by faith alone") although it does not appear in the Greek original.[2] Because of this emphasis, even his catholic opponents saw him as a Paulinist. In the twentieth century, the well-known catholic Luther scholar Joseph Lortz, for example, respectfully acknowledged that Luther had a profound understanding of Paul, but critically added that he had overemphasized Paul. Thus, Lortz claimed, Luther was not a "Vollhörer der Schrift."[3] In other words, he was not a balanced reader of the Bible as a whole, but preferred parts of it in a selective, one-sided way, neglecting other parts of the Bible that focus on the relevance of works, such as the Letter of James.[4]

---

[1] Cf. Martin Luther, "Praefacio," Martin Luther, *Opera Omnia* I (1545), WA 54, 179–87.

[2] Cf. Martin Luther, "Ein Sendbrief D. M. Luthers. Vom Dolmetschen und Fürbitte der Heiligen (1530)," in *WA* 30II, 632–46.

[3] Joseph Lortz, *Die Reformation in Deutschland*, vol. 1 (Freiburg i.Br: Herder, 1939/40), 176.

[4] Cf. Otto-Hermann Pesch, *Hinführung zu Luther* (Mainz: Matthias Grünewald, 1982), 68–70.

Evidently, this implies that, first, Paul does not show a particular ethical interest in his letters and, second, that the Lutheran doctrine of justification by faith alone underestimates the relevance of works for a Christian's life.

Both assumptions, however, are open to doubt. An unbiased reading of Paul's letters clearly shows that Paul is very much engaged in ethical issues. Large parts of the first letter to the Corinthians, for example, deal with practical questions of Christian life. And, as we know, the Lutheran tradition was not unaware of ethics. It is no coincidence then that Luther's interpretation of the Ten Commandments in his "Small Catechism" has for centuries been one of the most prominent texts used in Christian education in the Lutheran churches. Insisting on "by faith alone" while, at the same time, emphasizing the importance of leading a Christian life did not constitute a contradiction for either Paul or Luther.

How did Paul's ethics impact Lutheran ethics? Did Lutherans read Paul when developing their ethics? In other words, were Lutherans Paulinists also in the field of ethics? How do Lutherans today deal with Paul's ethics? These are the questions I intend to tackle in this paper. First, I shall go into Pauline ethics: How does Paul describe Christian life? Which criteria does he apply to evaluate the behavior of Christians? How does he argue in concrete cases? Second, I shall examine whether or how Lutheran ethics is inspired by Paul and, third, I shall discuss the relevance of Pauline ethics for our moral discernment today.

PAULINE ETHICS: A NEW LIFE "IN CHRIST"

Paul deliberately contests the idea that for those who are already redeemed it makes no difference how they lead their lives. Some members of the Corinthian congregation seem to have thought that the earthly, bodily, outward dimensions of life no longer play a role for those who are in the state of eschatological salvation. Everything is permissible; not even keeping the company of prostitutes touches and qualifies the state of salvation. Paul strongly objects to this: "Do you not know that your body is a temple of the Holy Spirit within you, which you have from God, and that you are not your own?" (1 Cor 6:19) And, most significantly, he adds, "For you were bought with a price; therefore glorify God in your body" (1 Cor 6:20).

Here we have a first glimpse of Paul's concept of ethics. Christians do not stand alone; Christian behavior is to display or mirror the salvation that Christ has "bought" for our sake. Christian behavior is rooted in and a result of salvation and is supposed to witness to salvation. This happens in the social context of the church as the "body of Christ." Through the Spirit, the Christian is incorporated into that body. As members of the body of

Christ, Christians are responsible for "edifying" it, each one in their place, with their special "charisma," aiming at the welfare of the whole body.

Paul draws a clear line from justification by faith alone to ethics: Christians owe Christ their salvation; he has paid the "price" to free them from the slavery of sin and now, that they belong to him, they are called to bear witness to this in their behavior.

Paul describes this fundamental correlation in several different categories and metaphors, the most important of which are the term "in Christ" and the reference to the Holy Spirit.

Being "in Christ" means to be new. "So if anyone is in Christ, there is a new creation: everything old has passed away; see, everything has become new!" Paul writes in 2 Corinthians 5:17. In Romans 6 and Galatians 2, he explicitly links the Christian's new life to the death of their old identity through Christ's death. We live with Christ because we are tied to his death. In Romans 6, he interprets baptism as dying with Christ in order to live with him. He writes,

> Do you not know that all of us who have been baptized into Christ Jesus were baptized into his death? Therefore we have been buried with him by baptism into death, so that, just as Christ was raised from the dead by the glory of the Father, so we too might walk in newness of life (Rom 6:3–4).

In Galatians 2, we find a similar dialectics of death and life:

> For through the law I died to the law, so that I might live to God. I have been crucified with Christ; and it is no longer I who live, but it is Christ who lives in me. And the life I now live in the flesh I live by faith in the Son of God, who loved me and gave himself for me (Gal 2:19–20).

"Being in Christ" and "Christ being in me"—both mean that the "old life" of the "flesh" has been left behind at the cross, while the "new life" is present "in Christ," or "in the risen Christ."

This "in Christ" also has a spatial or even socio-spatial dimension. It marks a space where Christians live. This is evident in the use of the term "body of Christ." The risen Christ forms a social body of which Christians are members. The new life is "located" within this body. Thus, as individuals, Christians are called to live their lives within the social space that is identified as the body of Christ.[5]

---

[5] The relation between the "body of Christ" and the "visible church(es)" would have to be further discussed.

In 1 Corinthians 12, the "body of Christ" is based on baptism and formed by the Spirit. "For in the one Spirit we were all baptized into one body—Jews or Greeks, slaves or free—and we were all made to drink of one Spirit" (1 Cor 12:13). The Spirit does not erase all distinctions within the Christian community but guarantees the unity-in-diversity of the body. This reminds us of the famous injunction in Galatians 3:28 where, after mentioning that by baptism Christians have "clothed [them]selves with Christ" (3:27), Paul states that "there is no longer Jew or Greek, there is no longer slave or free, there is no longer male and female; for all of you are one in Christ Jesus" (without reference to the Spirit). The Spirit is the eschatological gift of new life that forms and transforms the church to an eschatological community.

Paul fully agrees with his Corinthian opponents that we live a new life in a new era. But, he objects to the idea that, in the new life, there is no need for ethics. While the norms and categories of the "old life" no longer have unquestioned authority, the new life is not an empty space, a *tabula rasa* for moral discernment; it requires its own categories of moral discernment. Christians are to live in accordance with their being "in Christ." In today's terminology: the "indicative" of salvation implies an "imperative" of how to live.

The difference between Paul and his opponents is illustrated in the following example. When writing "All things are lawful for me," Paul most likely quoted the slogan of his opponents, who believed that in the ultimate reality of the new life, the old rules and restrictions had lost their validity. Paul agrees that everything is allowed, but adds, "But not all things are beneficial" and "I will not be dominated by anything" (1 Cor 6:12). Or, even more clearly, in chapter 10, "All things are lawful, but not all things build up" the body of Christ (1 Cor 10:23) and, "Do not seek your own advantage, but that of the other" (1 Cor 10:24).

The idea that we are liberated from the norms of the "old life" but committed to the "new life in Christ," which requires its own norms, is explicitly elaborated in the letter to the Galatians. Paul bases his argument on freedom. "For freedom Christ has set us free," he writes, "stand firm, therefore, and do not submit again to a yoke of slavery" (Gal 5:1). We are not obliged to follow a specific law in order to be "in Christ." Yet, he warns, "do not use your freedom as an opportunity for self-indulgence [literally: for the flesh], but through love become slaves to one another." In chapter 6, he calls this "the law of Christ": "Bear one another's burdens, and in this way you will fulfill the law of Christ" (Gal 6:2). Interestingly enough, however, he points to the continuity from the "old" law to the "new" law saying, "the whole law is summed up in a single commandment, 'You shall love your neighbor as yourself'" (Gal 5:14).

What are the criteria of living the "new life"? Obviously, Paul has strong feelings about what is appropriate for the new life "in Christ" and what is not. Being "in Christ" means to orientate oneself to Christ. The *locus classicus* is Philippians 2:5 where Paul introduces the famous "hymn" with words that are difficult to translate: *Touto phroneite en hymin ho kai en Christo Jesou. The New Revised Standard Version* translates it as "Let the same mind be in you that was in Christ Jesus," adding a verb in the past tense. Luther put it in a similar way, whereas the revised *Luther Bible* of 2017 translates "Let the same mind be in you as it corresponds to the community in Christ Jesus."[6] The following "hymn" is supposed to explain that. It is remarkable, however, that the point of reference is not the life and deeds of Jesus of Nazareth but the self-humiliation of the pre-existent Christ who, "though he was in the form of God, did not regard equality with God as something to be exploited, but emptied himself, taking the form of a slave, being born in human likeness" (2:6–7). So it is the selflessness and self-restraint of the God-equal Christ, who left his "splendid isolation" for the sake of humankind, which marks the space for a behavior that is adequate for those who are "in Christ," who are members of the "body of Christ."

It is easy to find examples of how Paul concretely uses this criterion. He challenges the Corinthians who, on Sunday evenings, when the congregation comes together for agape and holy supper, start to eat without waiting for the poor and the slaves (1 Cor 11); he advises against bringing conflicts to the public court (1 Cor 6); he strongly supports donations for the congregation in Jerusalem. A further example is the way in which Paul deals with the problem of whether or not to eat meat that comes from pagan sacrifices. He does not use an abstract norm of what is lawful and what is not. Quite the contrary, he agrees that "everything is lawful," and admits that those who eat this meat are right, because the "gods," in the names of which it has been prepared, do not exist and it is therefore part of God's creation that we are entitled to use. But then he adds a second order question, What effect does this behavior have on the Christian community? Does it help to "build up" the body of Christ? Or, does it rather irritate or harm the conscience of other members of this body? If this is the case, one should abstain from this behavior although, in principle, it is lawful. Paul leaves no doubt that those who have no problems eating the meat are right and have the right to do so. He calls them "the strong ones." But, precisely because they are strong, they can restrain themselves and abstain from making use of this right for the sake of the "weak ones."

---

[6] "Seid so unter euch gesinnt, wie es der Gemeinschaft in Christus Jesus entspricht."

This self-restraint is not necessarily ascetic. The "new life" is different from the "old one" but does not demand a total renunciation of the structures and pleasures of the "old life." Paul speaks of this in 1 Corinthians 7 with reference to marriage. He insists: "the present form of this world is passing away" (7:31). However, he does not demand "leaving the world" but, rather, to qualify the world. That means to "deal with the world as though [one] had no dealings with it" (ibid.). This famous "as though" indicates an independence, a distance to the world while living in it. It reminds us of the need not to be "dominated by anything" (1 Cor 6:12). Thus, Paul warns that marriage might imply being concerned about the partner instead of about God and therefore losing independence. However, while he provocatively states the he wished everyone lived in celibacy as he himself did, he does not prohibit marriage. If a celibate person experiences permanent sexual desire, they have lost their independence and in that case it is better to marry. It is interesting to see, then, that with respect to the behavior within marriage, Paul again refers to the idea of self-restraint when he advises not to abstain from sexual intercourse for too long.

By using the metaphor of the "body of Christ," Paul emphasizes that every member has its own function and dignity. The "new life in Christ," thus, implies an ethos of respect and equality. Explicitly, Paul says that God reversed the social hierarchy of the "old world" by not choosing the rich and noble but the poor and less reputable (cf. 1 Cor 1). Actually, in late antiquity, Christian congregations were attractive precisely because they did not copy the social hierarchies and did not exclude anyone. "In Christ," the old privileges have lost their validity—Paul is very clear on this point. But how does he apply this principle to concrete moral issues?

A highly interesting example is slavery. Paul insists that, in Christ, the distinction between freedom and slavery is no longer relevant. "Whoever was called in the Lord as a slave is a freed person belonging to the Lord, just as whoever was free when called is a slave of Christ" (1 Cor 7:22). But Paul does not conclude that slavery as a social and cultural order should be abolished. Rather, since being slave in the "old life" does not affect being free in the "new life," a Christian slave should "not be concerned about it" (7:21) and he advises to "remain in the condition in which you were called" (7:20). Certainly, "equality in Christ" matters—but only "in Christ," i.e., in the inner life of the congregation where distinctions of status, gender or ethnicity are not supposed to play a decisive role. But Paul does not infer the need for social reforms from that.[7]

---

[7] This was one of the reasons why Christianity accepted slavery for so long as it was part of the social order. But sadly we must add that Christians not even treated

As to women, Paul does not comment on social order. What he writes in 1 Corinthians 11 refers to the life of the congregation, which makes it even more difficult to detect an ethos of equality. Certainly, Paul concedes that

> in the Lord woman is not independent of man or man independent of woman. For just as woman came from man, so man comes through woman; but all things come from God (1 Cor 11:11–12).

However, it seems as if he has to remind himself of that after a long paragraph in which he gives theological arguments for gender inequality. "I want you to understand," he writes, "that Christ is the head of every man, and the husband is the head of his wife, and God is the head of Christ" (1 Cor 11:3) and concludes that "any man who prays or prophesies with something on his head disgraces his head" (11:4), whereas "any woman who prays or prophesies with her head unveiled disgraces her head" (11:5). Later he justifies this with even stronger emphasis, "For a man ought not to have his head veiled, since he is the image and reflection of God; but woman is the reflection of man. Indeed, man was not made from woman, but woman from man" (11:7–8). That only man is created in God's image, not only contradicts Genesis 1, but is also incompatible with Galatians 3:28 where Paul is convinced that there is "neither male nor female [...] in Christ Jesus." The New Testament scholar Wolfgang Schrage therefore concluded that here Paul "undermines his usual level."[8] Paul himself does not seem comfortable with this. On the one hand, as already mentioned, he seems to qualify if not correct his statement by referring to the concept to the idea of gender equality and mutuality. On the other, he defends his position by referring to "nature." "Does not nature itself teach you that if a man wears long hair, it is degrading to him, but if a woman has long hair, it is her glory? For her hair is given to her for a covering" (11:14–15). He refers to a cultural tradition that he affirms as being "natural." For us the hermeneutical challenge is how to deal with this when we no longer have this cultural tradition nor find it "natural," i.e., corresponding to the "ontological nature" of man and woman.

Paul seldom argues with "nature" (*physis*) as a category for moral discernment. This, in itself, is remarkable because to live according to nature was a crucial norm for pagan, especially stoic, ethics. The most famous (and most controversial) example is his dealing with homosexuality (or same-

---

their Christian slaves as their brothers and sisters "in Christ." Most certainly, Paul would not have approved of that.

[8] Wolfgang Schrage, *Ethik des Neuen Testaments* (Göttingen: Vandenhoeck & Ruprecht, 1982), 186: Paulus "(bleibt) unter seinem sonstigen Niveau."

sex intercourse) in Romans 1. In Romans 1–3, Paul attempts to show that all human beings—pagans as well as Jews—are in need of being justified by faith in Christ "since all have sinned and fall short of the glory of God" (Rom 3:23). As to pagans, he accuses them of having fallen into idolatry, "exchang[ing] the glory of the immortal God for images resembling a mortal human being or birds or four-footed animals or reptiles" (Rom 1:23) or, in other words, "exchang[ing] the truth about God for a lie and worship[ping] and serv[ing] the creature rather than the Creator" (Rom 1:25). According to Paul, this becomes evident in the confusion of the "natural" order of sexual intercourse: "God gave them up to degrading passions. Their women exchanged natural intercourse for unnatural, and in the same way also the men, giving up natural intercourse with women, were consumed with passion for one another" (Rom 1:26-27a). His argument is not clear. Why would homosexuality indicate idolatry? Why would it follow from making a creature God? Paul's basic idea seems to be that confusing God with creature results in disrespecting the God-given, "natural" order of the created world. For Paul it is self-evident that homosexuality is an expression of this disrespect and he therefore does not see any need for any further argument to convince his readers: same-sex intercourse is not "natural." In other words, here he refers to a cultural tradition, which he is sure is shared by the reader. The hermeneutical challenge is how to deal with this argument if its cultural self-evidence has been lost, as it has at least in parts of the world today?

Paul does not speak of the "new life in Christ" here, but obviously presumes that there are some moral standards that are common to all humankind. Following the principle *nulla poena sine lege* (no punishment without a law), he states that while the Torah is given to the Jews, to the Gentiles the law is written into their hearts and speaks to their conscience (cf. Rom 2:11–16). So he does not conclude that the world lives in a moral vacuum. "In Christ," neither Torah nor "natural" law are valid unconditionally. As already mentioned, Paul contracts the whole Torah into the "single commandment, 'You shall love your neighbor as yourself'" (Gal 5:14). Thus, love is the criterion of all norms, also those of the pagan world. Paul is surprisingly unbiased when referring to the non-Christian culture.

> Whatever is true, whatever is honorable, whatever is just, whatever is pure, whatever is pleasing, whatever is commendable, if there is any excellence [Greek: areté, virtue] and if there is anything worthy of praise, think about these things (Phil 4:8).

He is unbiased but not uncritical. Only that which is true and honorable in pagan culture is worth complying with. Thus, Christians have to discern:

"test everything; hold fast to what is good," Paul writes to the Thessalonians (1 Thess 5:21) about the words of the prophets (5:20), but it also applies generally.

Before I end with some hermeneutical remarks on how to deal with Pauline ethics today, I would like briefly to look at Luther's ethics, in order to assess whether and to what extent they are influenced by Paul.

Was Luther a "Paulinist" in ethics, too?

It is evident that Luther based the concept of "justification through faith alone without works" on his reading of Paul. It helped him to overcome a deep religious crisis that had resulted from his desperate attempts to reconcile God by complying with all of God's commandments. It implied a sound critique of late medieval church doctrine, which he believed to be more or less subtly based on salvation by human merits. From the beginning, he was challenged by the critique that neglecting the relevance of works for salvation destroys the sense of moral responsibility and therefore comprehensively dealt with the question of "good works" in his early reformatory writings. He emphatically insisted that reformation does not weaken but rather fosters the motivation to do good works, arguing that good works are not condition for but result of salvation. [9]

Luther elaborated this clearly in his famous treatise "On the Freedom of a Christian": Because God has already given us everything we need for our eternal salvation through Christ and in Christ, we are freed from worrying about ourselves. We no longer need to work hard to secure our own lives and to grab hold of what we think we need to this end. Relieved of the fear for our own well-being, we can selflessly be there for others and look out for their well-being instead. Luther explained that it was precisely because we are free in Christ that we can act in service of others. And because we do this freely, we no longer understand the commandments as being an external compulsion; we obey them gladly and of our own accord. Justification is therefore the source of love for our neighbor. Essentially, we pass on the joy that we receive by being accepted by God in Christ to our neighbors. Luther was thus able to say that we ourselves become "Christ" to our neighbors.[10]

---

[9] For the following, cf. my article, "How Do I Find a Gracious God?," in Anne Burghardt (ed.), *Salvation—Not for Sale* (Leipzig: Evangelische Verlagsanstalt, 2015), 7–14, esp. 10–11.

[10] *WA* 7,66 (Latin version); *WA* 7,35 (German version).

Obviously, Luther is inspired here by Paul's concept of freedom in Galatians 5. But the emphasis on the joy of being saved as a source or motive of selfless love and the idea that by salvation the commandments have lost their character as commandments because the justified comply with them without coercion and gladly, seem to be genuinely Lutheran. Luther could even say that Christians are capable of creating "new decalogues." This was not meant to qualify the historical Decalogue but, rather, to show that for Christians, norms have an internally binding authority; they are no longer heteronomous orders but expressions of an intrinsic, gladly adopted self-determination.

This idea can also be traced back to Paul, such as when he requests the "strong" Corinthians to restrain themselves in favor of the "weak" in order to "build up" the "body of Christ." Yet, it seems to me that Luther rearranged Pauline ideas within a different framework. For Luther, Paul's concept of "being in Christ" and thus forming an eschatological community does not play a crucial role. Rather, he was interested in how Christians can practice selfless love within the world. His focus was not the Christian community in the context of a pagan society, but the life of Christians within a Christian society. Thus, in his treatise "On the Freedom of a Christian" he quasi redefined what loving self-restraint meant in his time and age. He insisted that we still have to struggle with our own earthly desires and temptations and do not yet live in a fully released world. So loving self-restraint means first to "govern our own body" (which even includes asceticism) and, second, to accept responsibilities in family and society. To be responsible for a family or to serve in a public function can be seen as a form of asceticism because it implies abstinence from individual self-fulfillment, even more than being a monk.

Luther does not see the Christian community as an island of the released in the sea of an unreleased society; rather, he sees Christians within society. This might be the reason for a marked difference to Paul.[11] In Romans 7, Paul describes the slavery of sin as an era of the past that has been overcome by Christ. Luther, however, reads it as a narrative of the present because to him, faith is and will be challenged (*angefochten*) as long as we live. While, when looking at Christ, we can certainly trust in our salvation, when looking at ourselves we must nonetheless acknowledge that we are still under the power of sin. *Peccator in re, iustus in spe* (sinner in fact, just in hope), was Luther's formula in his early lectures on the

---

[11] To the following, cf. my article, "Der suggestive Trug der Sünde. Römer 7 bei Paulus und Luther," in Sigrid Brandt, Marjorie H. Suchocki and Michael Welker (eds), *Sünde. Ein unverständlich gewordenes Thema* (Neukirchen-Vluyn: Neukirchener, 1997), 125–52.

letter to the Romans; or, later, *simul iustus et peccator* (at the same time just and sinner). Paul knew that we still have to struggle (cf. Phil 3:12ff.), and Luther emphasized the certainty of faith to be justified and released. But they differed in the way in which they related the "already" (*schon*) of salvation and the "not yet" (*noch nicht*) of fulfillment.

I do not think, however, that Luther misunderstood Paul. He had to interpret Paul in the context of his own time and age, and he did it by adopting, rearranging and rethinking Paul's ideas within his own intellectual and cultural framework. He was, in other words, a creative reader of Paul, but he remained, as can be clearly seen, a reader of Paul. What does this mean for us today when we read Paul's ethics?

The hermeneutical challenge of reading Paul's ethics today

Paul's ethics is not a list or a system of fixed commandments. Of course, he gives (sometimes very concrete) advice or even orders regarding how to behave. But they are embedded in something that I would like to call a process of ethical hermeneutics, a school of moral discernment. To be "Paulinist" today, in my opinion, means to attend this school rather than to follow all of his concrete orders. Let me explain that by summarizing my idea of Paul's ethics in five points:

- First, ethics matters. To be justified by faith alone does not mean that it makes no difference how we live. Salvation is supposed to be displayed in our acts. What we do is supposed to correspond to the fact that we are saved. To live a "new life in Christ" means to correspond to Christ.

- Second, this implies some basic criteria for an ethos of "living in Christ" of which I name four: self-restraint, mutuality, equality and solidarity. This ethos combines freedom and responsibility for the "body of Christ": "All things are lawful, but not all things build up."

- Third, these criteria allow and require a qualification of the traditional (Jewish as well as pagan) norms: "test everything; hold fast to what is good."

- Fourth, Paul nevertheless sometimes refers to "nature" and seems to be convinced that there is a common moral ground that presents itself in the human conscience.

- Fifth, in his letters, Paul gives wide-ranging concrete advice and sometimes rigid orders. Famous is the list in 1 Corinthians 6: "Do you not know that wrongdoers will not inherit the kingdom of God? Do not be deceived! Fornicators, idolaters, adulterers, male prostitutes, sodomites, thieves, the greedy, drunkards, revilers, robbers—none of these will inherit the kingdom of God" (1 Cor 6:9–10).

The hermeneutical challenge in reading Paul today arises from the question how to relate points 2 and 3 to points 4 and 5. Presumably, Paul did not notice any tension between his basic ethical criteria for living "in Christ" and his concrete advice. For him, this advice followed from the basic criteria, and he had no problem to refer to "nature" to underline that. To us, however, this is not self-evident. There are, at least, two options:

Either, we could, as Paul did, regard his advice as being the binding consequence of his basic criteria. In this case we would also have to follow him when he, for instance, legitimizes gender inequality with reference to the Bible and "nature" (1 Cor 11). Or, we could deal with Paul's normative advice in the same way in which he dealt with the traditional norms. In other words, assess whether they correspond to the basic criteria of living "in Christ" (self-restraint, mutuality, equality and solidarity) and thereby follow Paul's maxim "test everything; hold fast to what is good."

Testing means taking seriously; in other words, we have to investigate Paul's arguments carefully. We have to anticipate that today there is possibly a tension between Paul's basic criteria and his concrete advice, although he himself apparently did not feel such a tension. Therefore, we have to ask, What does it mean today to practice self-restraint, mutuality, equality and solidarity? Following Paul's methodology might therefore result in drawing different conclusions on topics such as slavery, gender justice and homosexuality.

Obviously this is seriously debated and in the churches, the "testing everything" leads to controversial answers regarding what to "hold fast" as "good." Moreover, even something that has been identified as "good" might not have the same effect of "building up" the body of Christ in every region, and we are challenged to deal with this.

While this might appear to complicate things, we must remember that Paul himself does not allow for simple answers. He shows us a way of practicing moral discernment. It is up to us to follow that way with courage, wisdom and love.

CHRISTIANS ENGAGING IN CULTURE AND SOCIETY AND HOPING FOR THE WORLD TO COME

Hans-Peter Grosshans

As we engage in the hermeneutical process of reading and interpreting biblical texts, one of the steps that we undertake could be referred to as "modeling" or "constructing." In other words, based on the results of our reading and interpretation of a biblical text, we develop certain models or concepts of a doctrine or practice of the Christian faith. This step is a crucial part of the hermeneutical process if we want to avoid reducing hermeneutics to exegesis and pure history. Our reading and interpretation of biblical texts is to a large extent influenced by and dependent on the models and concepts familiar to us.

The following reflections will focus on the Christian's relationship to society and culture. Nowadays, we cannot do this without taking into account the various models for and concepts of how Christians relate to society and culture. What interests us here is their relationship to culture and society in light of the Christian hope for a better world to come. We shall first look at various models, and then, in a second step, reconstruct Paul's understanding of the Christian's relationship to culture and society.

A VARIETY OF MODELS

The history of Christianity and theology offers a variety of models for the relationship of the Christian to culture and society. These vary between extremes: the affirmation of the present life with its creative cultural production on the one hand and a dialectical enmity toward culture, emphasizing a strict distance to the world, on the other. They range from the prophetic engagement with the world to a mystical fleeing from the world.[1] In his 1951 book, *Christ and Culture*, Richard Niebuhr reduced the various concepts of the relation of Christians to culture to five possible models.[2]

1. Christianity is strictly distinguished, even separated, from culture. While this world and its cultures will vanish, Christians are called out of this world and on their way to what they hope for: to a new heaven and a new earth. According to this model, culture orders the life of those who live under the curse of the law and may even be understood as destroying creation. Christian freedom is understood as freedom from the culture of this world in order to establish the kingdom of God. In respect to ethics, this includes the strict orientation of the Christian life toward Jesus Christ. Here the Sermon on the Mount stands for the new law of life. We are instructed to love the enemy and to reject violence and retaliation. In these practices, Christians articulate their opposition to and denial of the respective culture, because cultures are based on the law of self-assertion and survival.[3]

2. The second type, which can be referred to as cultural Christianity, is more or less the complete opposite of the previous model. It relativizes the difference between culture and Christianity in such a way, that they almost become the same. In this case, Christianity is a cultural force. In theological terms, Christianity reaches its fulfillment and realizes its (divine) purpose in culture. Christianity exists for the sake of culture, which is its foundation and purpose. Christianity itself is understood as the true culture of the heart and humanity.

3. Culture is elevated and ennobled through Christ and his supernatural empire. An example of this third model is the Roman church in the Middle Ages, where Christianity and culture are not conflated, but ordered according to a hierarchical structure. Christ is the head and

---

[1] Cf. Liselotte Richter, "Kultur. II. Kultur und Religion," in *RGG*, vol. 4 (Tübingen: Mohr Siebeck, ³1960), 95.

[2] Cf. Richard H. Niebuhr, *Christ and Culture* (New York: Harper & Row, 1951); cf. Götz Harbsmeier, "Kultur: IV. Kultur und Christentum. Grundsätzlich," in *RGG*, ibid., 105ff.

[3] This type of Christianity (like similar types in other religions) has a strong ascetic profile: with escapism, abstinence from all worldly, earthly matters (such as from military service) and concentration on a strictly ordered specific religious life.

culture the body; here people have their specific, individual lives. The church is the soul, the spirit and the will of this body. In principle, this model preserves the relative independence of both, culture and the church, which coexist in a strict order.[4]

4. The relationship between culture and Christ is a dialectical one. This model is articulated, for example, in the Pauline ὡς μή, which may be the attitude of Christians to earthly things, as it is expressed in 1 Corinthians 7:29ff:

> [F]rom now on, let even those who have wives be as though they had none, and those who mourn as though they were not mourning, and those who rejoice as though they were not rejoicing, and those who buy as though they had no possessions, and those who deal with the world as though they had no dealings with it.

This distance to earthly things implies freedom from culture in order critically to engage with culture. If culture claims to be relevant and to contribute to salvation, then, from a Christian perspective, it is has to be rejected. If culture has no religious ambitions, claims or significance, then Christianity has to use culture critically and contribute to it. In accordance with this model, culture can be conceived as something in which God's will can be realized. It is possible for Christianity to become critically and constructively involved with a plurality of cultures. This implies that Christianity does not bind itself only to one culture.

5. Culture will be converted to Christ, because Christ's dominion renews everything. When Christians contribute to and are active in culture, then they do this in order to witness to the power of Christ's resurrection. Every Christian is obliged to cooperate and work toward a form of culture that can be justified against the horizon of Christ's dominion. According to this model, paradise is presented as an area of culture because, in creation, human beings are given the duty to cultivate the earth as a whole, all creatures and also themselves according to God's will. Human beings correspond to their creator in engaging with culture. A fundamental critique of culture or a culture-critical romanticizing of a pre-cultural harmonious form of nature is impossible.[5]

---

[4] Nature and culture have their own laws. The church, being the salvific form of trans-nature respectively transcendence, tops and limits these laws.

[5] These models of possible relations between Christianity and culture are constructed from the perspective of Christianity. For a complete picture, we should also reconstruct the various possibilities of how cultures define their relations

The Christian's true citizenship is in heaven— the relationship of Christians to society and culture in Paul's letter to the Philippians

We are now prepared to go into a rich interpretation of Pauline texts on the relationship of Christians to culture and society, taking into account Niebuhr's five models. One of the relevant texts is Philippians 3:20. It is assumed that in Philippians 3:20 Paul refers to a political concept when he states, that "our citizenship is in heaven." However, Philippians 3:20 is in fact not about the relationship between church and state,[6] but rather about the relationship of Christians and churches to society and to culture.

At first sight, Paul's statement that our citizenship is in heaven is irritating for those who promote public theology. Most contemporary Christians are interested in deepening their awareness of being citizens here on earth in their respective societies and states. Lutheran theology and churches, like many programs and activities of the Lutheran World Federation (LWF), put a lot of effort into promoting the full participation of people in their societies and in political power and, in this sense, into enhancing active citizenship. Lutherans contribute to the empowerment of all people, especially the marginalized and voiceless. Activities include encouraging and supporting Protestant Christians to become involved in the cultural and political life of their respective societies and to take over responsibilities for the common good and public welfare. Indeed, the emphasis is on the message that the Christian's citizenship is here on earth rather than in heaven. In Protestant theology, stressing the citizenship in heaven has become ambivalent, since this has been understood as directing Christians away from the reality here on earth to a fictitious future in another reality. Long before Marxism, this was understood and criticized as consoling people with a future paradise and thus discouraging them from trying to change their miserable situations.[7]

---

to religions, respectively to Christianity. Then it would be possible to construct various types of culture on the basis of the perspective of culture to religions, respectively Christianity. One culture may understand itself in relation to religions as independent, neutral or even hostile, while another culture may define itself as being based on religion. And in still another culture, religious practices may be privatized or a religion may be used as cultural ideology. Still another culture may reactivate its Christian or religious roots rather than cutting them.

[6] Romans 13 is a more adequate text than Philippians 3:20 for Paul's idea of politics.

[7] Within Marxism and since Karl Marx this has been expressed in the metaphorical formula of religion being the opium of the people. Cf. Karl Marx, "Zur Kritik der Hegelschen Rechtsphilosophie. Einleitung," in *Deutsch-Französische Jahrbücher 1844*, MEW, vol. 1 (Berlin: Dietz Verlag, [16]2007), 378–91, here 378 (English text at

Rudolf Bultmann and others have called Paul's perspectives the mythical worldview of the New Testament.[8] If we situate Paul's statement within its cultural-historical context, then we might interpret it in light of the mythical cosmology of its time and its cultural setting. Then Paul would locate himself and his fellow Christians in respect to their citizenship in heaven, as being a cosmological space, different from the earth. Hence Christians would consider themselves as foreigners on earth, as migrants, who are not really part of the cultures and societies they live in. Where they actually live, they do not really feel at home, being part of the culture and included in society—not because these cultures and societies do not want to include them, but because they do not want to be full citizens there, as they know about their citizenship in a much better place, which is in heaven.

---

www.marxists.org/archive/marx/works/1843/critique-hpr/intro.htm). Especially well known and effective was Lenin's formulation: Religion is the opium of the people; cf. W. I. Lenin, "Sozialismus und Religion," in *Nowaja Shisn 28* (1905), *Werke*, vol. 10 (Berlin: Dietz Verlag, 1970), 70–75, here 71. In this tradition religion was understood to console those suffering under economic exploitation and the social underdogs with the promise of a heavenly reward. But then, with the progress in society in mastering nature, and in respect to economic justice, social participation and comprehensive education, all religion becomes dispensable and unnecessary. The illusion of happiness, which religions generate, will be substituted by true happiness, when societies have made such progress, that people no longer need illusions. In the introduction to the "Critique of Hegel's Philosophy of Right" Marx states, "The abolition of religion as the illusory happiness of the people is the demand for their real happiness. To call on them to give up their illusions about their condition is to call on them to give up a condition that requires illusions. The criticism of religion is, therefore, in embryo, the criticism of that vale of tears of which religion is the halo" (ibid., 379). But Karl Marx was not the first who operated with the contrast between earthly happiness and religious hope for heavenly happiness. And the formula of religion being opium of the people relates to a similar expression by Immanuel Kant, who called certain comforting services of religion opium for the conscience; cf. Immanuel Kant, *Religion Within the Limits of Reason Alone* (San Francisco: HarperOne, 2008), 105. Reflection on the narcotic effects of religion seems to have been a motive already in the eighteenth century.
[8] Rudolf Bultmann, "New Testament and Mythology [1942]," in Rudolf Bultmann, *New Testament and Mythology and other Basic Writings*, selected, ed. and transl. by Schubert Ogden (Minneapolis: Fortress Press 1984), 1–44, here 1. "The world picture of the New Testament is a mythical world picture. The world is a three-story structure, with earth in the middle, heaven above it, and hell below it. Heaven is the dwelling place of God and of heavenly figures, the angels. The world below is hell, the place of torment." Between heaven and hell is the earth with nature, in which human beings live with all other creatures, but which is also a place of supernatural activities of God and God's angels on the one hand, and of Satan and his demons on the other.

In terms of hermeneutics, this conceptualization of Paul's statement in Philippians 3:20 not only reflects its cultural-historical context, but also the context of the interpreter. The reading interest of the interpreter is part of the hermeneutical process. I formulated my reading interest, when I related this biblical statement to contemporary public theology and to the discourse on the role of the Lutheran churches in contributing to politics, society, public welfare and culture. In the following, I will reflect on four aspects of Philippians 3:20 within its context and against the horizon of the interpreter's interest. In order to relate this interpretation to the Lutheran tradition, quotations from Luther's sermons on Philippians will be added.[9]

1. The Greek word πολίτευμα in Philippians 3:20 is used only once in the New Testament. In Philippians 3:17–21, Paul distinguishes between a true and a false Christian life. For Paul himself it is the distinction of his old and his new (religious) life. With the orientation of his life toward Jesus Christ he has broken with the past in at least a twofold sense: first, in the sense of breaking with his past religious life, and second, in the sense of breaking with the orientation of his life toward the past. In his past religious life he regarded himself as righteous because he lived according to the laws of his religion and his people. In his new religious life he regarded himself as righteous because of his faith in Christ, in the righteousness of God (Phil 3:9). Breaking with his past religious life went along with breaking with the past and reorienting his life toward the future. In his new religious life, Paul oriented himself toward the future, which he expected and hoped for in faith. In general, the main modes of orienting oneself to the future are fear and hope. As Paul oriented his new life to Christ, it is clear that his orientation to the future was based on hope. He looked toward the future with positive expectations and hope. In a sermon on Philippians 3:5–21, on 19 November 1536, Martin Luther emphasized this orientation of Christians to the future based on hope:

---

[9] For further interpretation of Philippians 3:20, cf. Eva Ebel, "'Unser *politeuma* aber ist in den Himmeln' (Phil 3,20): ein attraktives Angebot für viele Bewohnerinnen und Bewohner der römischen Kolonie Philippi," in Jörg Frey and Benjamin Schliesser (eds), *Der Philipperbrief des Paulus in der hellenistisch-römischen Welt* (Tübingen: Mohr Siebeck, 2015), 153–68; Gennadi A. Sergienko, *Our Politeuma is in Heaven!: Paul's Polemical Engagement with the "Enemies of the Cross of Christ" in Philippians 3:18–20* (Carlisle: Langham Literature, 2013); Joseph A. Marchal, *The Politics of Heaven: Women, Gender, and Empire in the Study of Paul* (Minneapolis: Fortress Press, 2008).

Therefore we are no longer citizens of earth. The baptized Christian is born a citizen of heaven through baptism. We should be mindful of this fact and walk here as if native there. We are to console ourselves with the fact that God thus accepts us and will transplant us there. Meantime we must await the coming again of the Savior, who is to bring from heaven to us eternal righteousness, life, honor and glory.[10]

2. In Philippians 3:12-16, Paul is in a process of better understanding his own experience of the fundamental reorientation of his religious life and his life in general. Paul is doing hermeneutics in light of his life.

Not that I have already obtained this or have already reached the goal; but I press on to make it my own, because Christ Jesus has made me his own. Beloved, I do not consider that I have made it my own; but this one thing I do: forgetting what lies behind and straining forward to what lies ahead, I press on toward the goal for the prize of the heavenly call of God in Christ Jesus. Let those of us then who are mature be of the same mind; and if you think differently about anything, this too God will reveal to you. Only let us hold fast to what we have attained (Phil 3:12-16).

This shows Paul's new religious orientation: looking forward to the future. Being faithful to the traditions of his religion and his people is of secondary interest. Still, Paul was aware that he was struggling to understand what this change in religious orientation means and what its implications are. Despite this, Paul insisted on this new way and therefore encouraged his fellow Christians in Philippi to live out the consequences of this new understanding of God and the corresponding religious life. As Paul was aware that he and his fellow Christians were not only undergoing a transformation in their lives, but that they were also in the middle of a process of understanding this transformation

---

[10] John Nicholas Lenker (ed.), *Sermons by Martin Luther,* Vol. 8 (Grand Rapids: Baker Publishing Group), 301. Cf. Eduard Ellwein (ed.), *D. Martin Luthers Epistel-Auslegung, 3. Band: Die Briefe an die Epheser, Philipper und Kolosser* (Göttingen: Vandenhoeck & Ruprecht, 1973), 224: "'Aber unser Leben ist im Himmel.' Ein Bürger ist im Himmel, wer getauft ist; da bist du (im Himmel) angeschrieben. Was angeschrieben ist im Himmel, muß die Bürgerschaft droben erlangen durch die Taufe. Wir tun nichts andres, als daß wir das Heil erwarten. Nicht dazu sind wir Christen, daß wir große Ehre haben; und wenn sie einer hat, ist er nicht dazu getauft; sondern das ist unser einziges Werk, daß wir warten und seufzen. Der Herr wird kommen, und wir sollen immer darauf sehen, wann er kommt. Wir sollen uns nicht erschrecken lassen, sondern warten und wünschen, daß wir bald (in das Himmelreich) kommen. Wir haben etwas andres als die weltliche Gerechtigkeit."

better and more deeply, he then—in Philippians 3:17—encouraged the
Christians in Philippi to imitate him and follow the example of the core
group around Paul. In a sermon on 20 November 1530, Martin Luther
raised the question whether Paul was not too arrogant and too proud
when he recommended himself as an example to the Philippians: as
if "you alone have the Holy Spirit."[11] But, in fact, Luther testified to
Paul's "great humbleness [...] because he does not claim this honor
only for himself"[12]—as Luther believed the Pope of his time was doing.
For Luther it was important, in what respect Paul and others claimed
to serve as an example. Luther found the answer in Philippians 4:8f.:

> Finally, beloved, whatever is true, whatever is honorable, whatever is just, whatever
> is pure, whatever is pleasing, whatever is commendable, if there is any excel-
> lence and if there is anything worthy of praise, think about these things. Keep
> on doing the things that you have learned and received and heard and seen in
> me, and the God of peace will be with you.

To these two Bible verses Luther adds, "Here you have the example.
Who wants to understand what the example of Paul is, can read it
there."[13] It would be too simple to say that Luther was not interested
in an ambitious Christian formation of the Christian's life. On the
contrary, Luther took the ethical advice in the Bible very seriously as
we can see here; Luther saw in Paul not an example in spiritual, but
also in ethical matters.[14]

3. Reference to his own example (and that of others) seems to be important
   to Paul, as the new religious life with its orientation toward Christ can

---

[11] Lenker, ibid., 291; cf. Ellwein, ibid., 215: "Gleich als wäre der Heilige Geist bei
keinem andern als bei mir!"
[12] Ellwein, ibid., 215: "Und doch bringt er eine große Demut mit sich, weil nicht er
allein diese Ehre haben will, sondern auch andre hinzugesellt, die so lehren wie
er" (author's own translation).
[13] Ibid., 216 (author's own translation).
[14] In reference to Luther's interpretation of the Sermon on the Mount I have shown
that Luther is not giving up the interest in an ethical perfection of a Christian's life,
but rather renews and strengthens this interest, although his ideas of a perfect
Christian life were going in a direction different from the Roman tradition of his
time; cf. Hans-Peter Grosshans, "Perfection of Christian Life in the Face of Anger
and Retaliation: Martin Luther's Interpretation of the Sermon on the Mount," in
Kenneth Mtata and Craig Koester (eds), *To All the Nations: Lutheran Hermeneutics
and the Gospel of Matthew*, LWF Studies 2015/2 (Leipzig/Geneva: Evangelische
Verlagsanstalt/The Lutheran World Federation, 2015), 99-114.

immediately be corrupted when Christ is wrongly understood and with that also the relationship between a Christian life and a respectable civil life. When he writes, "For many live as enemies of the cross of Christ" (Phil 3:18), Paul does not refer to Jews or heathens, but to Christians. For Paul, a Christian has to have a critical mind and needs critically to evaluate the various modes and concepts of religious life, including the Christian one. Not everything that is lived out in religion is good, and not everything that is called Christian is true. So Paul describes these Christian enemies of the cross of Christ: "Their god is the belly; and their glory is in their shame; their minds are set on earthly things" (Phil 3:19). New Testament scholars debate whether these people were libertines or rather ascetics (like those following strict Jewish food regulations)—both laying too much emphasis on the bodily respectively material aspects of Christian life.[15] We do not have to enter into this discussion but rather concentrate on Paul's remark that the minds of these people have been set on earthly things. In the semantic net of Pauline theology this expression is equivalent to the sphere of flesh and sin. In my opinion, we cannot reduce this to bodily, carnal desires of people, but need to include social desires, such as the desire to be established and respected and honored in one's society. Consequently, the enemies of the cross of Christ—as Paul calls them—are those who understand their faith in Christ and their orientation toward Christ as part of their overall attempt to settle in life and to become established and honored in society. For Paul, we misunderstand Christ if we use him to gain honor in society. A career in society is to be made by ourselves, based on our natural talents, skills, knowledge and work. This may be fine in itself, but it has no higher spiritual meaning and cannot be deified with Christ. For Paul, Christ is always and inseparably connected to the cross. Therefore, those who use Christianity as part of their own success story are, according to Paul, enemies of the cross of Christ. God, who is revealed at the cross, is in the depth of life, not in its high points; God can be experienced in misery and despair, but not in pride. The God, who is revealed at the cross, can be experienced,

---

[15] Cf. for example: Hans Dieter Betz, *Studies in Paul's Letter to the Philippians* (Tübingen: Mohr Siebeck, 2015); Peter-Ben Smit, *Paradigms of Being in Christ: A Study of the Epistle to the Philippians* (London: Bloomsbury, 2013); Ben Witherington, *Paul's Letter to the Philippians: A Socio-Rhetorical Commentary* (Grand Rapids: Eerdmanns, 2011); G. Walter Hansen, *The Letter to the Philippians* (Grand Rapids: Eerdmanns, 2009); Wilfried Eckey, *Die Briefe des Paulus an die Philipper und an Philemon. Ein Kommentar* (Neukirchen-Vluyn: Neukirchener Verlag, 2006); Ulrich B. Müller, *Der Brief des Paulus an die Philipper* (Leipzig: Evangelische Verlagsanstalt, [2]2009); Gerhard Barth, *Der Brief an die Philipper* (Zürich: Theologischer Verlag Zürich, 1979).

when people are expecting, longing and hoping, but not when they are saturated, proud and sure of what they have. In a sermon on 8 November 1545 on Philippians 3:17-19, Luther is very clear that,

> in this life those who rely on their own works are not Christians. They may be called a pious, upright and honest—and so it shall be—but because of that they should not be called Christians. Rather, you have to have the works of Christ, like the children pray in the creed: Christ is my Lord, who was born for me and has suffered for me; he is seated to the right hand of God, looks at me and governs me. These works do and make me a Christian. On these (his) works I am baptized; I shall receive and believe them.[16]

Luther distinguished between a Christian life and a respectable civil life. For Luther it is beyond doubt that people should strive to lead a respectable civil life, realizing the virtues and doing everything out of love and not selfishness. They should contribute with their talents, knowledge and skills to cultural and political life. But Luther was very clear that this could not be given any significance in terms of salvation. In spiritual terms, Luther followed Paul's terminology and called it rubbish (Phil 3:8). This understanding also becomes relevant for ecclesiology. The life of the church is not structured according to the civil, moral or even religious merits of its members.

> The true fellowship of Christ exists in the participation in the works of Christ, his blood and his wounds, his death and his resurrection. All who are baptized belong to this fellowship, whether they are men or women. [...] Here we are not asking for an "apostle" or "prince," but only whether we participate in the works of Christ, that we shall be resurrected because of his merit. If you come with another title, then you will be told to remain outside![17]

---

[16] Ellwein, op. cit. (note 10), 227, "In diesem Leben ist der kein Christ, der sich auf seine Werke verläßt. Er mag wohl ein frommer redlicher Mann heißen—und so soll es auch sein—,aber davon soll er nicht ein Christ heißen. Sondern du mußt die Werke Christi haben, wie die Kinder im Symbol beten: Christus ist mein Herr, für mich geboren und gelitten; er sitzt zur Rechten Gottes, sieht auf mich und regiert mich. Diese Werke tun's und machen mich zum Christen. Auf diese (seine) Werke bin ich getauft, ich soll sie annehmen und glauben" (author's own translation).

[17] Ibid., 226: "Die rechte Bruderschaft Christi besteht darin, daß wir teilhaftig sind der Werke Christi, seines Blutes und seiner Wunden, seines Sterbens und seiner Auferstehung. Zu dieser Bruderschaft gehören alle Getauften, ob sie Männer und Frauen sind. [...] Wir fragen hier nach keinem 'Apostel' oder Fürsten, sondern nur danach, ob wir der Werke Christi teilhaftig sind, daß wir durch sein Verdienst auferstehen. Kommst du mit einem andern Titel, so heißt's: Bleib draußen stehen!"

4. Paul then reminds the Philippians

> our citizenship is in heaven, and that it is from there that we are expecting a Savior, the Lord Jesus Christ. He will transform the body of our humiliation that it may be conformed to the body of his glory, by the power that also enables him to make all things subject to himself (Phil 3:20–21).

Christian life finds its appropriate orientation within the horizon of heaven, where Christ reigns with God, the father, over heaven and earth, and from where Christians expect him to come again as the Savior. So Paul understood himself and all his fellow Christians as being located within that horizon of heaven—which made them citizens of heaven—and not only as being located within the (limited) horizon of the empirical earthly world (with their minds set only on earthly things). For the believers who understand themselves as being located in the horizon of heaven, earthly things are neither attractive nor decisive—although they may be necessary. Therefore, Paul understood himself and his fellow Christians to be citizens of heaven. But what did Paul mean by this?

Paul was familiar with the civil model of living in a town or society while being a citizen of another town or society. At Paul's trial in Jerusalem, he referred to his Roman citizenship, with the consequence that his trial had to take place in Rome. Although Paul himself was fully part of Jewish society and shared Jewish culture, he nevertheless understood himself as a citizen of another community, located in heaven. Following Paul's considerations implies that even Christians, who are very familiar with a society, its culture and its politics, in the end regard themselves as foreigners there where they live.

We can further reflect on this motif in Peter's first letter, in which Christians are understood as a community of foreigners, aliens and exiles. In 1 Peter 2:11 they are addressed as πάροικοι and παρεπίδημοι: aliens and exiles.[18] They are not at home there where they live and do not feel like citizens. Peter's first letter is written later than Paul's letter to the Philippians, probably at the end of the first century. It reflects the situation of Christians who are no longer part of the Jewish community, which is one reason why they understood themselves as being foreigners and aliens in their society.[19] In 1 Peter, Christians are not only foreign in spiritual

---

[18] "Exiles" is also used in 1 Peter 1:1.

[19] In his letter Peter wanted to encourage them to live in correspondence to Christ, to give hope in a situation of being under pressure and to give advice regarding life as a foreigner in a hostile environment. As the elected, the kingly priesthood and

terms but they are also excluded from society. The terminology is also used in other texts, where Christians are described as foreigners without citizenship rights. The Christians' foreignness also implies a distance from the heavenly home. Both dimensions of the Christian's foreignness imply that the church is located in the diaspora—foreign in the world and a minority. The social exclusion, which these people experienced, was not only a result of the intolerance of the rest of society, but also a result of their new religious life. In transgressing the borders of the old religious, cultural and social world, Christians set new borders. Their overcoming of borders established a new border to which those who follow the old orders reacted with exclusion, denunciation and persecution. Christian faith and baptism result in a life that does not conform to the life of the surrounding society.[20] From a sociological perspective, at least two developments are possible in such a situation. Either such a social minority isolates itself in a kind of social ghetto or people try to reform and design culture and society according to their vision. The later one was not possible for the communities of 1 Peter. Later on this changed, and Christian communities contributed substantially to the renewal of cultures and societies.

A BRIEF CONCLUSION FROM A LUTHERAN PERSPECTIVE

What we gain from understanding the Christian's citizenship as being in heaven as proposed in Paul's letter to the Philippians is distance: distance to whatever immediate and pressing realities that we face in the societies and cultures we live in. With distance, new possibilities come to light, some of which might not have been visible before. To see new possibilities means that amidst the pressing realities of life we can imagine that life could be different and that there is more than one way to go on in life, despite the so-called necessities of reality.

It is not clear, whether Paul's reference to the Christians' citizenship in heaven is identical to the ὡς μὴ in 1 Corinthians. Yet, the ὡς μὴ-model does not satisfy a Lutheran concept of the relationship between faith and

---

the holy people of God, Christians (1 Pet 2:9) are called to live a truthful Christian life as foreigners. "Beloved, I urge you as aliens and exiles to abstain from the desires of the flesh that wage war against the soul. Conduct yourselves honourably among the Gentiles, so that, though they malign you as evildoers, they may see your honourable deeds and glorify God when he comes to judge" (1 Pet 2:11-12).

[20] In the case of 1 Peter the social exclusion was not strict, as in 1 Pet 3:1 a marriage of a female Christian with a heathen is mentioned, or in 1 Peter 2:18-25 a Christian slave who lives with a non-Christian master.

society. The ὡς μή-model also operates with distance. The question is, What form of distance is this? The ὡς μή-model goes along with an understanding of the Christian's citizenship in heaven as implying a kind of exile in the earthly societies that Christians live in. The Prophet Isaiah and some Psalms bear witness to what it means to live in exile, as do numerous writings in modern times, which are called exilic literature.

If we understand Paul's reference to citizenship in heaven not in the sense of exile, then we have to modify the model. Then Christians may define themselves in light of earthly matters on the one hand and heaven on the other. Against the horizon of earthly things, Christians have to face the realities of life, there is no "as if not." Against the horizon of heaven new possibilities come to light and many earthly things are seen in a new way. Therefore, to locate oneself in the horizon of heaven affects the understanding of earthly things within one's own horizon. Both horizons, earth and heaven, should not be confused.

Martin Luther differentiates Christianity and the various fields of society more clearly than Paul. From a Lutheran perspective, Christians live in their societies and responsibly contribute to culture and politics with all their competences and talents, in the full awareness that they are not living in heaven and do not contribute with their activities to a heavenly society. They know that it will be better still than in their respective societies and cultures, despite all the love, faith and hope that are present in them. Their expectation of and hope for a finally perfect, just and harmonious society are not grounded in their own works and efforts for such a society, but in their faith in Jesus Christ, from whom they expect fulfillment not only of their individual lives, but also of their societies. According to the Lutheran understanding, Christians do not attribute spiritual significance to their activities, although these activities may be motivated and inspired by their faith and express their Christian hopes and expectations. Consequently, the main purpose of these activities in society and culture is to contribute to the various fields of society and culture in the best possible way in order to serve fellow citizens, society and the common good. Such responsible contributions also include contributions to the field of religion, especially in serving society with Christian worship services, to which all people in society are invited and welcomed.

List of Contributors

Batka, Lubomir, Dr, Dean, Evangelical Theological Lutheran Faculty, Comenius University, Bratislava, Slovakia

Becker, Eve-Marie, Dr, Professor of New Testament Exegesis, Aarhus University, Denmark, currently Distinguished Visiting Professor at Candler School of Theology, Emory University, USA

Bjelland Kartzow, Marianne, Rev. Dr, Professor of New Testament Studies, Faculty of Theology, University of Oslo, Norway

García Bachmann, Mercedes, Dr, Director of Instituto de Pastoral Contextual, United Evangelical Lutheran Church, Argentina-Uruguay

Grosshans, Hans-Peter, Dr, Professor of Systematic and Ecumenical Theology, University of Münster, Germany

Junge, Martin, Rev. Dr, General Secretary, The Lutheran World Federation, Geneva, Switzerland

Mahali, Faustin, Dr, Senior Lecturer New Testament Exegesis and Hermeneutics, Tumaini University Makumira, Tanzania

Mtata, Kenneth, Rev. Dr, General Secretary, Zimbabwe Council of Churches, Harare, Zimbabwe (former Study Secretary for Lutheran Theology, Practice and Formation, The Lutheran World Federation, Geneva, Switzerland)

Nõmmik, Urmas, Dr, Associate Professor of Old Testament and Semitic Studies, Head of the School of Theology and Religious Studies, Tartu University, Estonia

Oberdorfer, Bernd, Dr, Professor of Systematic Theology, Augsburg University, Germany

Siahaan, Rospita, Rev. Dr, Lecturer, STT HKBP (Theological Seminary of the Batak Christian Protestant Church), Pematangsiantar, Indonesia

Wanke, Roger Marcel, Dr, Professor of Old Testament and Hebrew, Academic Dean, Faculdade Luterana de Teologia, São Bento do Sul, Brazil

Wischmeyer, Oda, Dr Dr h.c., Professor em. of New Testament, University of Erlangen-Nuremberg, Germany

Zetterholm, Magnus, Dr, Associate Professor of New Testament Studies, University of Lund, Sweden